Convergences: *Inventories of the Present*

EDWARD W. SAID, GENERAL EDITOR

Opera

The Art of Dying

Linda Hutcheon

Michael Hutcheon

HARVARD UNIVERSITY PRESS

Cambridge, Massachusetts
London, England
2004

Library of Congress Cataloging-in-Publication Data

Hutcheon, Linda, 1947–
    Opera : the art of dying / Linda Hutcheon, Michael Hutcheon.
      p. cm. — (Convergences)
    Includes bibliographical references and index.
    ISBN 0-674-01326-3 (alk. paper)
    1. Death in opera. I. Hutcheon, Michael, 1945– II. Title. III. Convergences
(Cambridge, Mass.)

ML1700.H88 2004
782.1—dc22   2003058737

In memory of Edward W. Said (1935–2003)

Contents

Illustrations

Opera

The Art of Dying

Introduction

Music and "Murky Death"

We tread with music as our shield,
Through murky death's darkest field!

Wir wandeln durch des Tones Macht,
Froh durch des Todes düstre Nacht!

Mozart, *The Magic Flute*

Death is both a likely and an unlikely theme for a book about opera. The four-hundred-year-old history of this art form has demonstrated that composers and librettists look for powerful subjects that speak to their audiences, and it would seem that few subjects speak as loudly or powerfully as love and death. Tackling the more final of these subjects, this book combines the different perspectives of a practicing physician and a literary theorist, looking together at a series of operas that raise fundamental issues about death and, indeed, offer lessons in what was once called the "art of dying."[1] We have two aims: to examine Western concepts of mortality, as manifested historically in opera, and to speculate on how modern audiences respond to witnessing these concepts on stage. *Opera: The Art of Dying* is therefore intended to be of interest to those audiences—in all their variety, from opera fans to physicians, from people with musical, literary, or general cultural interests to, say, medical historians. (This is also why the reference notes are placed at the end—to be consulted, if desired, or to be ignored, if not.)

Why Death?

The reader may ask: Why the interest in death? The short answer: We all die. Death is also of importance in our two personal "day jobs." It is not only a practical problem in medicine and the thematic staple of literature. It is also a central issue for all human beings individually, as well as for the human imagination throughout the ages. As such, mortality is of interest to everyone, in the abstract and general as much as in the concrete and particular. But death has not always meant the same thing: it depends on where and when you live—and die. Important, if controversial, work on these cultural differences was undertaken by French historian Philippe Ariès in his books *Western Attitudes towards Death: From the Middle Ages to the Present* (1974) and *The Hour of Our Death* (1981).[2] Because most subsequent thinking on this topic, including our own, begins with these works, a brief outline (and critique) of their central ideas is perhaps warranted before beginning in earnest.

Ariès argues that Western Europe has had changing cultural "attitudes" toward mortality: a series of different social practices and states of mind has evolved gradually, with long periods of overlap. The concept of death that he claims was present in Europe before the twelfth century is one he labels "tamed" or "tame death."[3] Here, death is seen as part of a collective fate for everyone. When people understand that they are about to die, they become the center of a ritual, which they themselves organize, involving expressions of grief, the pardoning of others, prayer, and absolution. The move to a new "attitude" came with the increasing concern for the fate of the individual over the collective. Ariès calls the resulting view of mortality "one's own death."[4] At this time, the actual moment of death becomes the issue: it becomes the site of a cosmic struggle over the dying person, the occasion for judgment (and temptation), and the separation of the just from the sinful. Great importance is now attached to exactly how one conducts oneself while dying, because this will determine one's fate. As we shall see, this is where the teachings and books known as the *ars moriendi,* the art of dying, assumed important roles in the fifteenth and sixteenth centuries. The Renaissance and Reformation "exaltation of the individual" clearly intensified both the moral introspection and the psychic anxiety provoked by mortality.[5]

For Ariès, the next shift comes with the concept that death is not our natural fate but, instead, marks a traumatic rupture. Beginning in the eighteenth century, he suggests, dying is seen as the plunging of the individual into an "irrational, violent and beautiful world, not desirable but admirable in its beauty."[6] The eroticization of death accompanies this return of an untamed force. Ariès calls this "remote and imminent death."[7] It is not hard to see how this could translate into a morbid fascination, even an aestheticization of death. From this view came the idea of the "romantic death" of the nineteenth century. He calls this attitude "thy death" (in contrast to "one's own death"). In other words, this is when, for those remaining, death becomes invested with "passionate sorrow."[8] The intense grief of mourning and its cultural trappings become constants, as exemplified publicly by Queen Victoria's many years of mourning her consort's death as the "Widow of Windsor."

Like many others, Ariès argues that a major shift occurred in the course of the twentieth century and, in particular, from 1930 on into the 1950s. Arguably, however, the poetry of World War I had already manifested a major change in the attitude to death: honorable death in war was recast as wasteful death. World War II and the horrors of the Holocaust completed the move of death and

Facsimile of page from *Ars Moriendi,* or *De tentationibus morientium,* showing a dying man in bed approached by demons. Wellcome Library, London.

dying from the natural realm to the realm of the unnatural and the arbitrary. Ariès is not alone, of course, in arguing that, for Western cultures, this is when the meaning of individual death changed, becoming shameful, in a sense. He calls this "forbidden" or "invisible" death.[9]

He notes the displacement that has occurred as the provision of care moved from the family to the medical team, from the home to the hospital. Add to this the continuing tendency to medicalize normal human states, and suddenly mourning too has come to be seen as a morbid condition that must be treated and shortened. This shift was associated with changes in funeral rites and other public manifestations of grief. As Sherwin B. Nuland writes in *How We Die: Reflections on Life's Final Chapter,* "Modern dying takes place in the modern hospital, where it can be hidden, cleansed of its organic blight, and finally packaged for modern burial. We can now deny the power not only of death but of nature itself."[10]

Nevertheless, in recent years, the AIDS epidemic has moved death and dying onto the front pages of the newspapers and into the forefront of the world's attention. It may have become a truism to say that modern Western culture denies death, but it is also worth noting a recent spate of books on death and dying—from all possible perspectives. Their very existence implies that this taboo may be lifting and that we are ready, even eager, to talk about our own mortality. In fact, some see this as the next development in the Western attitude to death.[11]

Indeed, the amount of scholarly and popular writing on the topic has increased exponentially in recent years, suggesting a renewed fascination with death.[12] A number of encyclopedias of death and dying now exist, not to mention an *Oxford Book of Death* and a *Fireside Book of Death.* Death is now a timely and significant topic. Not surprisingly, a collection of concepts and theories has grown up in recent years to form something actually called "death studies." Academically, this field has been strikingly separated along disciplinary lines. The biomedical and social sciences (sociology, psychology, anthropology, medicine) deal with real-world pragmatics. The humanities (philosophy, history, the study of literature, music, and art) traditionally work on historical and cultural manifestations. This book explores the concepts of death and dying in an attempt to bring together the perceptions of both worlds, for they have not often "spoken to" each other, despite the obvious need for dialogue on this, often the most difficult of topics.

One of the reasons for this silence has been a fundamental difference in their approaches to the incommensurability of death. Scientifically based perspectives are limited to investigating and describing real-world practices and entities. Where science stops, the arts begin—endowing death with meaning and value, which it is the task of the humanities to study. The sciences and humanities are also separated by different concepts of what constitutes "knowledge." Scientific knowledge has come to be understood as knowledge that is held to be true because of its ability to withstand refutation. But there is yet another concept of knowledge, one that has been called "narrative knowledge."[13] This involves an understanding, often unspoken, but widely shared among individuals within a culture, about the stories or the explanations that we use to make sense of our world. Narrative knowledge is a mixture of the cultural and the pragmatic that comes from and reinforces a set of social values and norms within a given group. In a sense, this knowledge is what tells us how to understand our world and how to behave in it. To a large extent, this knowledge depends on the stories we tell ourselves, as a society, over time. It is reflected through all parts of the network of communication—newspapers, television, films, novels, and (of course) operas. This is one of the reasons why we draw on concepts from many different disciplines in order to study those stories, as staged in opera, perhaps one of the most death-obsessed of all Western art forms.

Why Opera and Death?

Opera is our cultural vehicle of choice because it has both a limited canon and a historically clear thematic orientation toward death and dying. As the chapter epigraphs suggest, even Mozart's redemptive comic fantasy *The Magic Flute* betrays an obsession with this theme. Opera's stories are concise—forcibly so—since it takes longer to sing than to speak a line of text. Its themes must also be selected for their accessibility, to have the greatest possible impact on an audience. Opera is, after all, an expensive art form to produce, and an audience has to be lured into the theater. How? As we argued in *Opera: Desire, Disease, Death* and as we shall again try to convince you here, we think the answer lies in appealing to audiences' anxieties as well as their desires.[14] Opera's power also, of course, comes from its ability to bring together dramatic narrative, staged performance, a literary text, significant subject matter (in this case, death), and complex music in a particularly forceful way. Its impact likely derives from what might be called an excess of effect: the combination of the dramatic, the narrative, the thematic, along with the verbal, the visual, the auditory. Kent Neely's description of the impact of theatrical representations of death may fit operatic ones as well, in fact, best of all: "The immediacy of art, the poetry of literature, the action of film, and the lyricism of music can be united in theatre where there is the added and unique experiential dimension. Theatre's shared time and space of representation is different in kind and magnitude from the other arts and therefore can make scenes depicting dying, death, or merely the contemplation of such, palpable in a most distinct way."[15] Our guiding premise is simple: that art forms like opera explore imagined or imaginary experience in ways that both reflect and generate meaning within a culture. Their representations of death necessarily reveal much about the cultural values, beliefs, and customs of the societies that create and enjoy opera.

Opera is an art form that has proved to be obsessed with death from its birth. Jacopo Peri's early *Euridice* (1600) and Claudio Monteverdi's *La Favola d'Orfeo* (1607) establish a story pattern of love and loss that influences the staged representations of operatic death from the very start. Until recently, given the repertoire of most opera companies, "opera" has meant nineteenth- and early twentieth-century works, and those indeed are the major focus of this study. In most Italian and French operas of this period, especially those of the conventionally tragic variety, a preoccupation with death dominates—and is associated with love—but the deaths are most frequently what we might call simply "dramatic" ones, that is to say, violent plot devices: stabbings, shootings, drownings. To take Verdi's operas as examples, it is true that some characters are haunted by death from the start: for instance, Azucena in *Il Trovatore* (1853). Others learn to face death, like the poisoned Simone Boccanegra (in *Simone Boccanegra* [1857; revised 1881]). Still others are warned that salvation can come only in death: Don Carlos, for example (in *Don Carlos* [1867; revised 1884]). Most of these protagonists are given moving arias either meditating on death or lamenting the loss of life (such as Aida's "O terra addio, addio valle di pianti" [1871]). But despite the important narrative and dramatic function that death clearly has in the Italian operas of this period, it took the German Romantic obsession with mortality to make death an open and constant theme in opera and therefore in this book. Richard Wagner's 1865 *Tristan und Isolde* is "about" death in a different way from *Il Trovatore,* for instance. In a very real sense, death is the only (musical and literary) subject matter of Wagner's music drama, its compulsively repeated theme, intertwined forever with love.

Pace Catherine Clément's (in)famous *Opera, or the Undoing of Women,* the operatic dead are not always women: a quick autopsy of the many bodies littering the operatic stage shows that male and female deaths occur with equal frequency, however strange that may seem.[16] These "dramatic" deaths, however, are *not* the primary concern of this book. Instead, it focuses on notions of death and dying in the mostly non-Italian repertoire, as they play themselves out overtly, in terms of *thematic obsession* and plot action. These operas, we feel, yield the most interesting and complicated contributions to the history of human responses to mortality—both past and present. The exceptions, of course, are the operas that center around illness—such as Verdi's *La Traviata* (1853) and Puccini's *La Bohème* (1896). These, however, are works we have treated in detail in our first book, *Opera: Desire, Disease, Death.*[17]

Presenting the act of dying on stage, however, has been a fraught enterprise historically. Deaths in classical drama, for instance, were always off-stage, and early Renaissance playwrights risked the laughter or indifference of their audience if they dared to represent dying characters. Christopher Marlowe is said to have been the first English writer to use death dramatically, making the manner of speaking and acting at the moment of death relevant to the character's personality. This gave death a new and shocking intensity.[18] In short, responses to artistic representations of death are cultural, not natural; they are learned. In opera too, it was not always socially or aesthetically acceptable to represent death on the stage. The seventeenth- and eighteenth-century operatic convention of the *lieto fine,* or happy ending, put the emphasis on the joyful reunion of the lovers, even in tragedies. Villains were allowed to die; reunited lovers were not, even when this necessitated plot alterations to well-known story lines (from myth, for instance). The longevity of this convention has been attributed to audience taste —either aristocratic (since many of these operas were court entertainments) or more plebeian (after the opening of public opera

houses in seventeenth-century Venice).[19] Only at the beginning of
the nineteenth century did the traditional tragic ending take over
the operatic stage. It is not accidental, we argue, that this shift
coincides with what Ariès presents as a change in the public attitude to death itself. No longer considered in terms of familiar-
ity, death was now seen as rupture and transgression, "admirable
in its beauty," and thus attractive in its operatic (aestheticized)
form.[20] The relationship between operatic conventions and notions of death (and therefore its acceptability as both a topic of
conversation and a theme that could be presented onstage) is an
important part of this study, especially as those meanings and acceptable representations of death change over time.

Of utmost importance, however, is the fact that the operas that
do seriously deal with death as a theme are, curiously, not negative
or pessimistic, despite their obsession with mortality. In the works
examined here, death can become the occasion for redemption, reunion, or transcendence. Sometimes, it is seen as a part of the natural order. Elsewhere it makes possible a restoration of peace,
honor, justice, or a vision of a better society. Death may well be a
human universal, but, as we must never forget, it is also given different cultural meanings in different times and places. Its univer-
sality gives it an inevitable power when used in art, but its different
cultural meanings complicate its reception and interpretation.

Audiences, Then and Now

Opera: The Art of Dying might be described as a speculative study
of the emotional force of these positive stories about death and dying (our shared fate) on audiences today and in the past. We explore why, in Oscar Wilde's terms (which echo Sigmund Freud's):
"We weep, but we are not wounded. We grieve, but our grief is not
bitter."[21] Our working hypothesis is that when people go to the
theater, at times and in part, they find themselves participating in a

ritual of grieving or experiencing their own mortality by proxy through an operatic narrative. As the next chapter explains in more detail, they can feel both identification and distance as they—safely—rehearse their own (or a loved one's) demise through the highly artificial, conventionalized form of opera. Michael Neill has argued that Elizabethan and Jacobean tragedy (after Marlowe) allowed contemporary audiences a safe way to confront the implications of their mortality: the staged tragic narratives made them rehearse and "re-rehearse" their encounter with death.[22] Opera, we argue, can do the same thing, but we will not invoke the classical notion of tragedy—because the portrayal of death in the operas we will be looking at is not, in fact, conventionally tragic at all. As Chapter 1 will explain, we argue that the relevant model for experiencing this distanced, yet still powerful, "rehearsing" of death is not tragedy, but rather the *contemplatio mortis*—a form of the "art of dying" we mentioned earlier that dramatized and "performed" imaginatively the experience of dying.

The problem we foresee, however, is that, for a twenty-first-century audience, the idea that death and dying could be positively valued may seem counterintuitive. Today we have come to think of death rather differently from Renaissance playwrights or even nineteenth-century opera composers, in part because of major medical advances. Twentieth-century science and technology generated a sense that everything should be controllable—including disease and death. Add to this longer life spans and cultural shifts in attitudes to things like diet and exercise as modes of control, and you have the modern sense that death is or should be avoidable, optional, or at the very least postponable. When, as is inevitable, death has to be faced, it is seen as a failure, at once medical and personal. The decline of belief in an afterlife has been part of the secularizing of death, as have major changes in how we deal with the dead in our funerary rites.

Death has become both a taboo and an obsession (witness the

usual violent fare on television or at the movies). Contemporary audiences are not necessarily going to interpret representations of death on the operatic stage in the same way as their creators. Today we have a different "attitude" to death, to borrow Ariès's term. This difference likely explains why audiences today tend to normalize death and dying to the (learned and thus familiar) conventions of tragedy, why *Tristan und Isolde* becomes another version of *Romeo and Juliet*—a tragic tale of star-crossed lovers and their unnecessary deaths. To normalize Wagner's opera in this way is to misread its meaning: here death is not sad, bad, or unwanted. Nor is it so in any of the operas we discuss—operas that challenge our modern resistance to accepting death as natural and inevitable.

Ours is not the first age to deny death, of course, and one of the reasons may simply be that many people can see death only as the end of their life stories. Death may have little personal meaning except as finality, for we cannot experience our own death. In the operas treated here, however, the stories give death meaning and allow it to give meaning to life. Death is made to feel logical or somehow right—morally, psychologically, and aesthetically (that is, in terms of the story's structure). Even a modern spectator takes this message home, as we shall see in the next chapter. In short, these operas, with their open dramatization of the issues around death and dying, challenge some of our most basic contemporary assumptions about the end of life. This book deals with these challenges by directing attention to two areas: the texts that lay out the challenges and the cultural contexts that make them comprehensible. To that end, we have drawn on many different fields that tackle the topic of death and dying, allowing the operas themselves to suggest the most fruitful approach.

In an attempt to replicate the advances of surtitling—advances that now allow audiences to follow the verbal text of an opera—we have chosen to cite the English translation first, followed by the original, in order to aid comprehension. (The translations are our own and are deliberately literal.) To this same end, we have provided historical, cultural, and artistic background useful to expanding the imagination or what has been called the "horizon of expectations" of readers as potential audience members.[23] This will be most evident in chapters like the second one, where we explore the importance of German Romanticism in general and of Wagner in particular to our argument. Here lie the roots of Western culture's positive understanding and evaluation of death. That context may not be well known to modern audiences, however. In other chapters, less context will be required, in part because the operas discussed speak more directly to today's spectators.

A word is needed to explain what we mean by the "audience." Do we mean real people watching a particular production? The answer is: not really. The performing arts "unfold their signs in real space and time, and engage spectators who respond cognitively and emotionally on the spot."[24] In other words, each time even the same production is staged, the audience members will see something different, and, of course, they will respond individually in different ways. The variety of possible responses and interpretations is immense. For this reason, the "audience" here is, in a way, a virtual one.

Our guiding assumption has been that the audience of any period carries into the theater its culture's common understanding about mortality, an understanding that inevitably forms part of its intellectual and emotional reaction to a dramatic representation of the theme of death and dying. Our study fleshes out the historical, social, and cultural context of this viewing for readers who would be part of today's real audiences. At the same time, however, it also aims to increase their understanding of the messages about death in the operas and heighten the impact of those messages in relation to their own lives. In our previous book, *Bodily Charm: Living Opera,* we argued the difference between the experience of live opera and that of recorded audio or video versions.[25] Opera audiences today can have recourse to those recordings and videos as well as to librettos and scores. They have many points of access—not just one single audience experience. Audiences can reflect over time upon the themes of these operas.

Throughout our own discussion, however, we will be using what Kier Elam calls the "dramatic texts" of the operas, that is, the libretto and the score, and not the "performance texts" of particular productions.[26] We acknowledge that scores and librettos are only relatively fixed texts, for new scholarly work produces new editions with some frequency. Yet they are still the shared raw materials, if you like, with which a production team (a second group of artist-interpreters) then works: directors, conductors, designers, singers, musicians, and so on. A specific production is, therefore, the collective interpretation of a second group of artists, but it remains only one possible reading of the dramatic texts. And audience members will, in turn, interpret that reading in their own multiple ways. Because the score and libretto are the constants that all individual productions and all performances share, in their infinite variety, we focus on the close reading of both and on their interrelations, always in the context of a cultural understanding of the changes in the meaning of death through the ages. Our hunch is that the historical imagination of today's spectators is decidedly going to be challenged when we are asked to think of death not as tragic or negative, but as positive. Think of this book, then, as an aid to imagining the unimaginable—death.

The Contemplation of Death

And when he shall have conquered death's fear,
Then shall he rise from earth to heaven's sphere.

Wenn er des Todes Schrecken überwinden kann,
Schwingt er sich aus der Erde himmelan.

Mozart, *The Magic Flute*

Like most of us, Blanche de la Force is terrified of dying. Unlike most of us, she is unable to repress the knowledge of her mortality. Her solution may not be ours—but neither is her time.

Blanche is a fictional character inserted into the historical story of the death of sixteen Carmelite nuns during the Reign of Terror in Paris in 1794, a story powerfully dramatized in the 1957 opera *Dialogues des Carmélites (Dialogues of the Carmelites)* by Francis Poulenc. The opera tells the tale of this frightened young woman's entry into the Carmelite convent and her eventual coming to terms with her fear of death, as she too mounts the scaffold. Clearly, this is not the usual operatic story of love and passion, unless we think of passion in its other meaning—as suffering. Poulenc knew that fear of death might well not be an immediately appealing theme for an opera audience, but his attraction to the play of the same name by Georges Bernanos was intensely per-

sonal, involving his own religious faith and his anguish at watching
a close friend die. But he was also responding to the peculiar power
of this strange story of the obsessive fear of dying.[1]

The historical account of this tale is the one recorded by the
only surviving Carmelite, Marie de l'Incarnation (written between
1830 and 1832). Its first fictionalized version appears in a 1931
German novella by Gertrud von le Fort, entitled *Die Letzte am
Schafott,* in which the nuns' collective fate in revolutionary France
is read as an allegory of the dangers of totalitarianism. During the
subsequent war years, a Dominican priest, Raymond Bruckberger,
and the director Philippe Agostini turned the novella into a film
scenario, but this time the story became an allegory of the French
Resistance. They asked Bernanos to write the dialogues and dramatization, perhaps not expecting how intensely he would inter-
nalize the drama. This important French Catholic novelist and
polemicist transformed the story from a national allegory into a
tale of individual psychological and spiritual development. It became the story of Blanche's personal victory over mortal fear. They
also may not have expected that Bernanos would add a major
theme to the work—the transfer of grace in death—or that he
would project onto one particular scene, a deathbed scene, all of
his own anguish and terror, as he too faced his own end. Bernanos
would die of cancer right after completing the final revision of the
film's "dialogues." A posthumously edited version of his manuscript was later performed as a play, which moved Poulenc im-
mensely when he first saw it staged and later when he read it, this
time with the idea of setting it as an opera.

Since it simply takes so much longer to sing than to speak a
line of text, the formal demands of operatic concision meant that
Poulenc had to make major cuts in the play's text. He removed
much of the class politics and many of the religious debates, leaving a stark existential drama of choice in the face of death. Although Blanche appears to lose her personality and her will under

pressure, she does actively choose her destiny. This opera may be *about* eighteenth-century France, but it is written *in* twentieth-century existentialist Paris. The cultural responses to death in a society where religious authority once held sway over a community are not the same as those in a society where that authority has passed to the isolated individual. Arguably, as religious men but also men of their times, both Bernanos and Poulenc were caught between these two worlds, and their version of the Carmelites' story is one of both community and individual choice in facing mortality. In this, the work reflects both some sort of Christian consolation and the existentialist belief that existence is illuminated by confronting the extreme situations that define the human condition—conflict, guilt, suffering, and death—and that it is in this confrontation that we achieve our existential humanity.

As Poulenc pared down the plot, he tightened the focus on that powerful human theme of death and the terror of death. As her name suggests, Blanche de la Force is a French aristocrat—at the wrong time to be one. In the opera's first scene, her father and brother worry about her debilitating fearfulness, a part of her personality that is seemingly her inheritance from her mother, who died giving birth to her after the family carriage was caught up in a mob disturbance. The men sing of Blanche's morbid imagination ("imagination malade"), her too impressionable nature ("Blanche n'est que trop impressionable"). She herself laments what she calls the horrible weakness that is her life's misery ("le malheur de ma vie"). As the opera opens, then, it would appear that she is afraid of living life, of its noise and agitation; with time, it becomes clear that she really fears something else.

Indeed, her staged physical responses to her terror—visibly almost fainting, crying out in panic at the sight of the shadow of a servant—are precisely what the psychiatrist Avery Weisman, in *On Dying and Denying*, has associated with the outward signs of fear of dying, described as "a state of episodic alarm, panic, turmoil . . . associated with excessive autonomic symptoms."[2] When the fear of dying is intense, he observes, "reality testing abandons the hapless victim. Familiar cues that indicate a stable world are no longer there. Ordinary objects and events seem strange and threatening." So too for Blanche in the opera. The dying patients Weisman studied were part of an extensive research project carried out in the 1960s and 1970s, but his observations and insights here resonate with the opera, which was written in the years immediately preceding.

In her terror of dying, is Blanche so very different from the rest of us? We know we must die, for that is the fate of all humans, indeed of all nature. But why is this knowledge of our mortality not always in the forefront of our awareness, as it is in Blanche's? Although Sigmund Freud argued that we are simply unable to imagine our own death, later theorists (like Melanie Klein and Gregory Zilboorg) claimed that death anxiety is actually the root of *all* anxiety, but that suppression of this fear of dying is necessary in order to achieve a normal existence.[3] According to these later theories, death (rather than sex—Freud's choice) becomes the dominant cause of human neurosis. As Norman O. Brown succinctly put it: "the struggle with ideas about death and the emotional content they contain is a fundamental source of human anxiety."[4] This view was perhaps most influentially articulated in the 1973 Pulitzer Prize–winning book, *The Denial of Death,* by the cultural anthropologist Ernest Becker. There he argues that fear of death is universal in the human condition; in fact, it is necessary as an expression of the instinct of self-preservation, which functions as a constant drive to maintain life and monitor dangers. Yet, while constant, this fear cannot be conscious because it would be paralyzing. It must be repressed.[5]

This is what Blanche cannot manage to do. This is why she turns to the Carmelite convent as a kind of sanctuary, only to be told by the Prioress that the order is *not* a refuge and that great trials await her. In the Prioress's music sounds a motive first associated with Blanche's anguish and fear in the opening moments of the opera, a motive that will sound again when the young woman chooses her religious name, Sister Blanche of the Agony of Christ.[6] Blanche's father and brother also fear that her seeming vocation is actually a sign or symptom of her fear. In restricting her life to a small circle of contacts and in narrowing the spectrum of her action, she is seeking in vain to keep death—and life—at bay. Becker's analysis of this common, human "failure of courage" led him to assert that "one must pay with life and consent daily to die, to give oneself up to the risks and dangers of the world."[7] In a later scene in the opera, Blanche's brother says very much the same thing:

> You have to know how to risk fear
> Just as you risk death,
> Real courage lies in this risk.

> *Il faut savoir risquer la peur*
> *comme on risque la mort,*
> *le vrai courage est dans ce risque.*

Existentialist psychotherapist Irving Yalom put it even more forcefully: "insofar as it limits one's ability to live spontaneously and creatively, the defence against death is itself a partial death."[8]

In the middle years of the twentieth century, when existentialist theories held sway in Western thinking, death and the human response to it inevitably became objects of study. For example, a series of "fear of death" or "death anxiety" scales were developed by psychologists. Although these have been much analyzed and criticized in the years since, they offer an interesting insight into two elements that we have not yet considered in discussing Blanche's fear of dying: her religion and her sex. Studies that use these scales have examined (real) people's responses to questions about dying. It appears that women report a greater fear of death than men— although the fact that it is socially permitted for women to admit such fear is no doubt a factor in these self-reported findings. (Women are also more often placed in the situation of being the primary caregivers for the dying, of course.) According to these studies, religion can be both a buffer against death anxiety, promising salvation and spiritual immortality, and yet a source of anxiety as well. The "Dies irae, dies illa" (day of wrath, that day) probably says it all: the fear of judgment and the severity of God's wrath can contribute in a major way to the anxiety of dying.[9] But from a religious point of view, what is curious about Blanche as a Carmelite novice is that neither the fear of divine judgment nor the lures of spiritual immortality seem to be part of her thinking. Unlike the novella, the opera's drama is presented as strangely secular, despite her vocation. Her terror of death is so visceral and so powerful that there can be no easy Christian consolation, as she discovers. Likewise, no Christian warning about possible judgment provoked it. Hers is an individual and personal existential terror, but what she fears is something we all must face.

Although death is natural and universal, our twenty-first century's medicalization of death is very different from the nineteenth century's Romantic aestheticization of it, or even this 1950s' existential view of it. A contemporary audience watching and listening to Blanche's reaction to the human condition could well experience a tension between possible ways of interpreting and responding to this representation of both the fear and the reality of dying. And if we know the historical and cultural context of the setting of the opera and the very different context of its composition, that information cannot but affect our response. Yet we will also filter what we see and hear through our particular society's current notions of death as well as through our own feelings about our personal mortality—which will depend on such things as age, personality, religious and philosophical perspective, and personal experience with death and dying. As mentioned earlier, there is a dual focus to this book, for we are interested both in the powerful representations of death on the operatic stage and also in their possible impact on today's audiences, who necessarily have different cultural assumptions about death from those of the creators of the particular operas.

We would even argue that, in a way, some operas function like more formalized funeral rites, "expressing the way people transform the given facts of biological life into values and goals of humanity."[10] This means that we will also focus, more generally, on the beliefs and attitudes that Western cultures have held about death and dying and on how these are played out in opera. The stories a society tells itself about such important things as mortality are revealing, for stories are one of our human ways of both making sense and controlling it. It is not accidental that psychologists, medical anthropologists, and sociolinguists have joined literary critics in the study of "stories," acknowledging that narrative "constitutes a mode of thought and representation especially suited to considering life in time, shifting temporal shapes, and the human path of becoming where death is never far away."[11] Stories may well be our human way of articulating and reinforcing community through a kind of object lesson, as many people from Aristotle to Hannah Arendt have suggested.

The staged dramatization of stories adds another, more public dimension. It is now received wisdom in the theater that the interpreting audience is always part of the creative process of dramatic art forms, always part of the active making of meaning. But Aristotle's early theory of tragic catharsis, of the pity and fear said to be experienced by audiences, is a reminder that audiences *feel emotions* as well as *make meanings*. The implicit double pull, then, between emotional identification and intellectual distance, which has been theorized by so many people, likely also lies at the heart of audience responses to dramatized death. The fact that opera is sung, in other words that its artifice is manifest and audible, both complicates and simplifies any discussion of artistic distancing. This unavoidable artifice is most likely a factor in composers' choices of operatic subjects. As Herbert Lindenberger suggests, in their hunt for suitable subjects, composers will be more attracted to those that might bring about a "higher and more sustained level of intensity" in order to balance the distancing conventions of the art form itself.[12] Yet the moving power of operatic music also works effectively against distancing, bringing the audience squarely into the emotional domain of the work, but *not* through words or action.

The tension between emotional engagement and critical estrangement always comes to the fore in discussions of audience response to drama and opera. As we sit in the dark, watching and listening, are we empathizing participants or objectifying voyeurs? Does the artifice of the singing, the lighting, the stage makeup, or perhaps the verse language work to make us feel less close to the story and the characters on stage? In opera, does the artifice emphasize the artistic aspects at the expense of the emotional? Though in the twentieth century it was Bertolt Brecht's "alienation effect" that most influentially articulated the idea of critical distance as a dramatic necessity, the concept goes back at least to Aristotle and was further developed by eighteenth-century British and nineteenth-century German theorists of aesthetic "disinterestedness."[13] If we weep when Blanche dies at the end of *Dialogues des Carmélites,* have we somehow failed the artistic test of keeping a proper distance? Or, to put it another way, do we need distance as a kind of psychic protection—especially when the theme of what we are witnessing on stage is the inevitable fate of us all, death? And what role does the power of music play in aiding—or thwarting—distance?

As we shall see in the following chapter on Wagner's *Tristan und Isolde,* Friedrich Nietzsche most certainly felt that it was the (Apollonian) function of artistic form to keep the (Dionysian) forces of chaos and emotional energy under control. Only then could the audience actually bear the experience of seeing and hearing Wagner's opera about the infinite yearning for death. Even if we think in somewhat less extreme terms, however, we might well feel there to be a certain common-sense truth to the notion that artistic artifice can act as a kind of protective buffer. Freud made the psychoanalytic case for the theory in these terms: the audience identifies with the suffering hero onstage, yet also knows perfectly well that the suffering is feigned and not real, that the person onstage is an actor in a play. This double distancing—through fiction and impersonation—allows the audience to identify, but to do so without danger, and indeed even to experience pleasure at the representation of suffering and death.[14] This would mean that when attending Poulenc's opera, we can become deeply involved in following the story and feeling sympathy for the characters; we can let the music's power work its magic on our emotions. But we will nevertheless not be able to forget that the characters are *singing* not *speaking,* that they are *enacting* not *living* a story about the fear of death.

To be frank, we would like to avoid those familiar but perhaps too easy explanations (such as voyeurism, sadism, and masochism) to account for the audience's pleasure in watching the suffering and death of others on stage. Instead, we prefer to test the hypothesis that the act of witnessing staged operatic narratives of death may well function in a different way. Audiences—of any period—are varied and diverse, but the one thing they share is that they are composed of mortal beings. But why should they enjoy (or even attend) a staged representation of mortality? Among the many possibilities is the fact that a performance might act as a commemoration or even as a form of therapeutic reassurance in the face of bereavement, making us ponder our social roles in and our emotional responses to the death of others. But is it possible to watch the death of someone on stage without at least for a moment considering one's own demise? We suspect not, even if each person will inevitably react differently. Elisabeth Bronfen has argued that representations of death force us to confront our own end in a kind of "death by proxy": we know we are mortal and must submit to our mortality, yet because (as safely distanced audience members) we do not actually die, but only witness staged death, we can feel as if we are asserting some mastery over the End: "Ultimately, the seminal ambivalence subtending all representations of death resides in the fact that, while they are morally educating and emotionally elevating, they also touch on the knowledge of our mortality, which for most is so disconcerting that we would prefer to disavow it. They fascinate with dangerous knowledge."[15] Would this ambivalence be at all different if the opera were openly and centrally about coming to terms with death?

As suggested in the introduction, we hypothesize that watching and contemplating a performed death in an opera could be seen as analogous to undertaking what the Early Modern period thought of as a pious devotional practice known as the *contemplatio mortis*, the contemplation of death. Essentially a formal meditation on mortality, this was a late addition to the medieval "art of dying" or the *ars moriendi* tradition that developed in the context of a generalized social anxiety caused by plagues, wars, and famines.[16] Interestingly and not irrelevantly, the flourishing of the *ars moriendi* in the late sixteenth and early seventeenth centuries coincides historically with the birth of opera as a distinct new art form in Italy. An inherently theatricalized and performative form, the *contemplatio mortis* specifically involved imagining one's *own* death in great (and personalized) detail by means of an extended sequential dramatic narrative. Its purpose was to prepare oneself, spiritually and emotionally, for one's end. Yet, when the performance of the meditation was over, one in a sense "awakened" and (like an audience member leaving the theater) reclaimed one's normal, active, healthy life.[17] The dramatized personalized narrative that was just imagined did, nonetheless, serve as a means both to practice the art of dying and, thereafter, to appreciate life more fully by contrast.

Shakespeare's *Measure for Measure* has been convincingly read as a kind of *contemplatio mortis* in which Claudio becomes "an emblem of mortality for Shakespeare's audience, a surrogate sufferer who is systematically fitted for death and then miraculously rescued from its fatal grasp." According to this interpretation, Claudio's victory becomes "the audience's victory and confers in the process moral and spiritual strength upon Shakespeare's viewers at a time of great anxiety in their lives"—a time of plague and social unrest.[18] Similarly, could attending an opera that stages death and dying not function as a kind of *contemplatio mortis?* At the conclusion of both of these imaginative exercises, we can walk away, alive and well, but having "rehearsed" our own demise. We can console ourselves, as Freud pointed out, with the knowledge that our psychic identification has been a safe one, that someone else (indeed, an actor) was "suffering" on stage. We might even persuade ourselves that death, at least given its portrayal in the operas we are about to examine, is not always something to be dreaded or evaded, but instead something natural and even acceptable.

In order to explore this hypothesis, we have had to think about opera not as a simple entertainment for a passive and appreciative audience. In Richard Schechner's terms, we have had to make theater "efficacious"; in this case, we have had to think of it in terms of ritual. Operas about human mortality are perhaps easier than others to cast in this way, for, like all rituals, they too deal with the basics and are potentially "interactive." They too hang on what Schechner calls "life's hinges where individual experience connects to society." Uniting music, dance, and theater, ritual performances, he argues, create an "overwhelming synaesthetic environment and experience" for their actively participating audience.[19] An analogy with the multisensory experience of opera is not hard to make. To continue for a moment in this anthropological line of reasoning, Victor Turner's theory of the close relationship between what he calls "social drama" ("where conflicts are worked out in social action") and stage drama (where they are mirrored in artistic forms and plots) also focuses on significant moments such as marriage and death, events he refers to as "life-crisis ceremonies." For audiences (or participating group members), these rituals are deemed "prophylactic" (rather than "therapeutic")—not a bad description of the function of the *contemplatio mortis* and, we would argue, of the act of witnessing representations of our mortality on the operatic stage.[20] Audience members feel, interpret, but also reflect upon what they experience, both at the time and after.

Witnessing Death

In *Dialogues des Carmélites,* many deaths are witnessed by the audience, but the first and in some ways the most disturbing is that of the Prioress, Madame de Croissy, at the end of Act 1. This woman once contemplated taking the same religious name as did Blanche, but was not sure she could live with it—or up to it: you recall that the novice's telling choice is Sister Blanche of the Agony of Christ, recalling the moment in the Garden of Gethsemane when Jesus felt a very mortal fear of death and abandonment. From her first interview with Blanche, the Prioress is presented as a wise, discerning, and pious leader. That she should be made to suffer a horrible death—in physical pain, psychological torment, and spiritual despair—is thus all the more striking. One of the most harrowing scenes in opera, the one portraying her dying is rare in that it is actually realistic. A deathbed scene on stage is traditionally a ritualistic arena for both personal and spiritual preparation, but here it is

anything but. This deathbed presents, in a sense, an ordinary, ba-
nal, although painful human end—that is, a death that is not in
any way an operatically aestheticized or a spiritually sanitized one.
In another sense, however, it is extraordinary in its intensity and
its unexpected difficulty for the Prioress. It is a death variously
described as violently rejected, denied, desperately repressed—a
death, in short, horrifically endured.[21] The dying woman's vocal
part is marked in the score as "très rude" ("very harsh"); the composer notes that we are meant to hear her death rattle.[22]

The scene for her horrific dying has been set, just before this, in
a conversation between the two novices, the fearful Blanche and
her happy young friend, Constance, in which the latter, though always rejoicing in life's pleasures, invites her friend to offer their
"two poor little lives" ("nos deux pauvres petites vies") for that of
the Prioress. Blanche finds this a childish response, but her manifest terror at the very notion of such sacrifice is unmistakable.
When Constance goes one step further and announces that when
she first met Blanche, she knew that her prayer not to die old and
alone had been heard by God. She senses that, somehow, she and
Blanche will die together. Rejecting both this presentiment and the
earlier "foolish and stupid idea" ("Quelle idée folle et stupide!")
that anyone's life could redeem the life of another, Blanche demands that she stop. Her panic and dismay over both Constance's
ideas and her easy acceptance of the notion of death are made explicit in the words, of course, but also in the suddenly high "hys-
terical" notes she sings, much more characteristic of Constance's
"chattery stratosphere."[23]

When the Prioress calls Blanche to her deathbed, the young girl
discovers that she cannot deal with the sight of her spiritual leader
begging forgiveness for her fear of death. As articulated by Régine
Crespin, who sang the Prioress at the Metropolitan Opera pre-
miere in 1977, this is a naked death, experienced in total fear, as the
character cries out her anguish at the spiritual void, her panic at

the physical reality of dying. It is a death that made the singer herself go through the process of fearing her own mortality.[24] Before
Blanche's arrival on stage in this scene, the Prioress, in the most severe distress, has scandalized the others by challenging God to
worry about her and not vice versa. She has also had a terrifying vision of the convent chapel being desecrated and interprets this as
God's abandoning of the order. In her agony, she feels only despair,
saying it clings to her skin like a wax mask. In short, she suffers
through a horrible death, a death presented as highly unsuited to
her religious status and her holy state, and accompanied by both
the musical motive of Blanche's fear and agony, and the one used
throughout this scene explicitly to signify the suffering and terror
of the Prioress. The convent bells ring as we hear her death cries,
thus identifying her inner anguish with the outer world and the
fate of the order. The curtain falls as the bells play a B-minor
triad—traditionally the key of suffering (in the music of Bach and
Couperin, for instance).[25]

Significantly, this death is not to be found in any accounts in the
history books (where Madame de Croissy dies on the scaffold) or
in the novella (where she simply passes away in a few lines). It appears first in the action-oriented film scenario, but it is the dialogue writer, Bernanos, and Poulenc, the later opera composer,
who give it its full power. Adding a line that makes the dying Prioress exactly his own age at the time (fifty-nine), Bernanos appears
to project onto this death all his own fears, for in these months, as
he is writing, he knows he is dying of cancer. Although the fear
of death is indeed a constant theme in all of his writings—from
his teenage letters to his last novels—when facing his own end,
Bernanos clearly felt its relevance and power all the more strongly
at this moment. For his entire life, he had identified his own fears
with those of Christ in his moment of human abandonment and
terror of dying while alone in the garden at Gethsemane.[26] In this
way, Bernanos joins Blanche and the Prioress in identifying per-

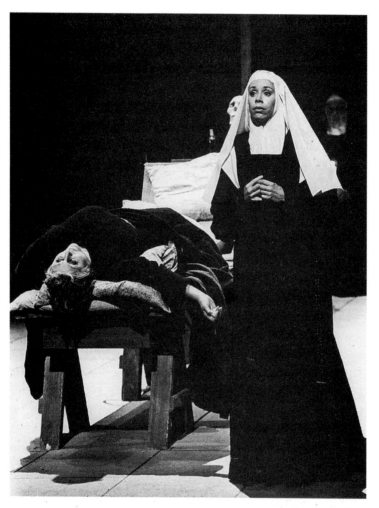

Régine Crespin as Madame de Croissy and Maria Ewing as Blanche de la Force in a scene from Poulenc's *Dialogues of the Carmelites*. Metropolitan Opera, New York.

sonal pain—mental, physical, spiritual—with the agony of Christ. But he also joins them, in the end, in his belief in the transmission of grace and the exchange of deaths, thanks this time to the model of Christ's death for all humanity. Poulenc's tormented music imbues the Prioress's final words and cries with "a passion that stresses its root meaning of suffering."[27]

Albert Béguin, Bernanos's literary executor, argued that the death of the Prioress is atrocious but not despairing because it is given meaning in the end.[28] Indeed, we later learn that Constance is right and that the Prioress's horrible death occurred in order to make someone else's—Blanche's—death easier. But, what is significant is that neither we in the audience nor the Prioress can know this *at this moment*.[29] In both the play and opera version, she dies in full despair. We witness only her staged (visible and audible) pain and torment. Like the agony of Christ, this pain will be redeemed and redemptive in the end, but *not now*.

What does it mean for the audience of Poulenc's opera to witness deathbed anguish and terror that are so strikingly realistic in their portrayal? And what happens if we know the circumstances of Bernanos's life at the time: his fatal illness, his fear of death? What does it mean for our response to the opera if we know that Poulenc himself had a breakdown (with a mortal fear of dying as its major symptom) and was also caring for his tubercular lover, Lucien Roubert, who died almost as the composer finished the last notes of the opera? Music theorist Jean-Jacques Nattiez would argue that this information in fact means a great deal to our interpreting and our responding. In his analysis of how we make meaning while experiencing a musical performance, he suggests that what we know of the creators' personalities, experience, and process of creation is indeed significant; once we know of it, we cannot stop from using this information in our interpretation of what we are seeing and hearing.[30] We construct meaning from the textual and performative givens, of course, but also from what we know of the context of creation. Our knowledge of the personal experience of death and dying of Poulenc and Bernanos has the added effect of endowing what we are witnessing with a certain authenticity and thus increased power.

To realize that this experience of "death by proxy" is not only our own but also that of the playwright and the composer may mean that we can accept what we are being offered on stage as that kind of imaginative knowledge of our own death that, in fact, is denied us in life. As surviving witnesses, we can face our mortality (and the repressed knowledge of it), while asserting mastery over it in a whole series of ways. We can "socialize" it into something familiar, transform it into something less fearful, poeticize it into something beautiful, or simply integrate it into our known world in order to overcome it.[31] But we can also resist identifying with this terrible end, and simply view it with horror. If we do, we may seek all the more intensely a way to redeem this death. As a complex form of *contemplatio mortis,* Poulenc's opera both prepares us for the inevitability of death and allows us an escape: we only *watch* someone else—here the Prioress—die. We experience her end with a great emotional charge, thanks to the music and the drama, but we do so vicariously. Our understandable resistance might well block *immediate* identification.[32]

Rewriting Hamlet's lines (the original words are in brackets), we might say:

> . . . I have heard
> That mortal [guilty] creatures sitting at a play
> Have, by the very cunning of the scene,
> Been struck so to the soul that presently
> They have accepted [proclaim'd] their mortality
>   [malefactions] . . . (2.2.584–588)

How, though, might we come to this kind of acceptance? Has the witnessing of staged death been cathartic, either in Aristotle's sense of purging the emotions of pity and fear or in Freud and Breuer's psychoanalytic sense of offering a means to transformation?[33] We argue that *at this point* the Prioress's particular death does *not* have this purifying or appeasing function at all. This failure of immediate catharsis therefore raises yet another issue: can we witness pain and mortal suffering and still feel aesthetic pleasure? Freud felt we could and that this was, indeed, the essence of artistic effect: the stage offers us at one and the same time masochistic satisfaction in struggle and defeat and also compensation for suffering.[34] But the witnessing Blanche cannot attain any such aesthetic or psychic balance. Nor can the dying Prioress. Nor can the audience—not yet, at least. Only at the end of the opera will this death change meaning—not only for the characters, but also for the rest of us.

Triumph over Death

Two full acts must pass, in fact, before any cathartic relief is allowed to anyone. Act 2 opens with Blanche's terrified flight from her watch over the corpse of the Prioress: the presence of the dead, like the dying, profoundly unsettles the young novice. A little later Constance and Blanche discuss the unlikelihood of the holy sister's terrible demise, asking themselves who would have thought she would have so much difficulty dying. Did God make an error? asks Constance. Did her death belong to another, because this one was clearly "too small" ("trop petite") for her? In the mouth of this happy and prescient girl, Bernanos placed his personal extension of the Catholic doctrine of the Communion of Saints, in which all members of the Church, living or dead, are bound together by grace into a community. The logical conclusion of this belief, as Father Owen Lee explains,[35] is Constance's notion that because of the Prioress's hard death, someone else will have an easy one:

> One doesn't die each for oneself,
> but for one another,

or even one in place
of another, who knows?

On ne meurt pas chacun pour soi,
mais les uns pour les autres,
ou même les uns à la place
des autres, qui sait?

As the young women consider this possibility behind the convent
walls, outside, revolutionary forces gather—both literally onstage
and politically. They attempt to suppress (or, in their terms, liber-
ate) the religious orders, "imprisoned" by superstition and the
Church's power, as symbolized by their dress and cloistered life. To
no one's surprise, in this climate of repression, Blanche's terror increases; yet she rejects her brother's request that she leave the convent for her own safety.

Act 3 opens with a scene that directly recalls the horrific vision
of the dying Prioress. The convent chapel is ransacked and desecrated. Inspired and provoked by Marie de l'Incarnation, the nuns
react by taking a vow of martyrdom for the preservation of their
order and the salvation of their nation. Much to everyone's surprise, this time, Blanche too votes to take the vow, indeed does
take it, but then flees the convent. The other nuns are soon turned
out into the street, forced to abandon their religious habits and
their communal life. Marie goes to Paris to find Blanche and recall
her to her vow, in the belief that the salvation of her immortal soul
depends upon it. She finds Blanche living as an abused servant in
the house that once belonged to her aristocrat father, who has just
met his end on the guillotine. Blanche confesses that she is still
consumed by fear: "I was born in fear. I have lived it, I live it still,
everyone scorns fear" ("Je suis née dans la peur. J'y ai vécu, j'y vis
encore, tout le monde méprise la peur"). The insightful Marie responds by calling her (for the first time in the opera) by her reli-

gious name, Sister Blanche of the Agony of Christ. By doing this, she places (for the audience and for Blanche herself) both the young woman's fear and her fate in the context of Christ's agony in the garden, reminding us all that He overcame His anguish through prayer and the assistance of the angel of God, and went on to die a death that redeemed humankind. Blanche, however, still refuses to accompany Marie back to Compiègne. Before Marie herself can return, her fellow Carmelites are arrested. One of the tremendous ironies of this version of the story is that the one who instigated the nuns' vow of martyrdom would survive their deaths to write about them for posterity. As the chaplain reminds Marie when she insists on surrendering to the authorities to keep her vow, it is God's choice who will sacrifice themselves for their faith, not hers. In the eyes of the Church, from Augustine onward, voluntary death, even in martyrdom, was potentially a mortal sin.

The opera's final scene takes place at the Place de la Révolution, as the nuns descend from the tumbrels to face their execution. In the bass, beneath the melody of the strident funeral march, we can hear the motive associated in Act 1 with the Prioress's horrible death. But then the nuns begin to sing the "Salve Regina," a hymn with separate but equally appropriate connotations: it was sung when the new Carmel was founded in 1604, and it is still sung when members of religious orders die.[36] The hymn's music eventually comes to dominate the Prioress's motive: as each Carmelite approaches the guillotine and dies, the number of voices singing is reduced, and when the second-to-last nun and Constance sing together, the motive is audibly suppressed. The scene is now set both musically and dramatically for the mystical exchange of deaths. At this moment, Blanche steps out of the crowd, "her face free from every vestige of fear," in the words of the stage directions. Constance beams and goes joyfully to her death. As the guillotine now silences forever the Prioress's death motive, we hear instead what Father Lee calls a "luminous theme" associated with intimations of the working of grace in the opera.[37] As Poulenc explained in a 1954 interview, this opera is both about fear and about the transfer of grace. That is why his Carmelites mount the scaffold with the calm and extraordinary confidence typical of all mystical experience.[38]

Blanche does not, as might be expected, finish singing the "Salve Regina" begun by her fellow nuns. As she approaches the scaffold in all her new and solitary strength, accompanied by joyously ringing bells, she slowly sings the last stanza of "Veni Creator"—a song of glory to God, affirming both life after death and the importance of the nuns' sacrifice within the Communion of Saints. Then the guillotine cuts off her voice as well; a bar of silence follows. The opera's music was deliberately thinly scored—to let the text shine through, said Poulenc. But in these final moments, large and lavish orchestral forces are used to bring home the cathartic message of Blanche's redemption in and through death: her own (accepted) death and the (despairing) one of the Prioress.[39] The sense of release, balance, and rightness missing from the end of Act 1, when the Prioress died, is now possible, despite the deaths of the Carmelites, martyrs for their faith and their nation.[40] Through the moving music and the powerful drama, we feel identification and emotional connection; but we also experience the aesthetic, moral, and intellectual harmony that allows for protective distancing.

In other words, the fact that, as audience members, we can experience catharsis at this moment (and not before) has something to do with the simple fact that we are at the end of the opera: narratives with probable or necessary endings are in themselves satisfying in offering a sense of completion. In emotional terms too, however sad we may be made by the nuns' deaths, we cannot help sharing some of their sense of spiritual fulfilment, as they die content in their faith or, in Blanche's case, having transcended the mortal fear that had cursed her life. As Marie had hoped, Blanche does attain her integrity as a person and as a nun by fulfilling the vow she accepted voluntarily as a Carmelite. In short, catharsis here cannot be explained simply as an intensification of emotions, a purging of pity or fear, or even as the result of a moving and transpersonal group experience felt by an entire audience.[41] Because of how this story ends, this catharsis also has something to do with the theme of death and dying: the end is about the End. The finality of death as our common human fate contributes to the power of the opera's finale.

Because we know we will die, that experiential certainty (or its denial) is inevitably going to be a touchstone for all our responses to staged representations of death. But our responses are also going to be conditioned by our satisfying sense that the chaos and confusion of living (and dying) have also been transformed into the safe order of art. Once made intelligible, the end feels probable, indeed inevitable. As Henry J. Schmidt puts it: "The ultimate anxiety addressed by an ending is the fear of death. Entering into a literary or theatrical experience means exposing oneself to the risk that the as-yet-unknown ending may turn out to be meaningless, or at least disappointing."[42] Even in opera, where (thanks to program notes and memory) we likely know the plot ending, the existential risk is still real, and not only because the ending might not "work" in this particular production, on this particular night. There is no guarantee of catharsis, argues Schmidt, but the gamble is part of the pleasure of the theater, even (or especially, we would add) when the theme of the work is death itself.

As Frank Kermode argues in his seminal study of narrative closure, *The Sense of an Ending*, "the End" is a figure for our own deaths and as such is feared; yet we have a deep need for "intelligible Ends." Although our own death is something we might not want to face, "the End is a fact of life and a fact of the imagination" for Kermode.[43] And, indeed, for Peter Brooks too, all narrative is "in essence obituary" in that its meaning comes after death: "The further we inquire into the problem of ends, the more it seems to compel a further inquiry into its relation to the human end."[44] We need to confer significance on experience (including the experience of dying), and stories offer what he calls "imaginative equivalents of closure," which accomplish this in ways we can never manage in our own lives. Calling on Walter Benjamin, Brooks suggests that representations of death give a story authority by giving us a knowledge of death denied us in reality.

Closure in opera, however, involves not only the formal act of bringing the story to a conclusion: Blanche's easier death is both redeemed by and (for the audience) redeems the horrific one of the Prioress. There is also another kind of closure, however, the one involved in the process by which we too as audience members complete the incomplete, making everything into ordered and satisfying wholes, creating a sense of significance and completion that is emotional as well as intellectual or formal. The Carmelites go to their death as martyrs; Blanche attains her full existential and spiritual personhood in her final moments. After an appropriate bar of silence, the music powerfully completes its formal resolution in our ears. But audience consent is needed for this to work. The end must feel right in cognitive and affective terms, for *we* must confer meaning on these deaths.[45] In *Dialogues des Carmélites,* as in many of the operas to be examined in this study, closure and catharsis are attained specifically by reinforcing the audience's sense of finality through the thematic content: death and dying.[46] Does this, then, make these operas "tragic," in the Aristotelian sense of the word?

Imagining Death and Dying

George Steiner has argued that in the last half of the nineteenth century, opera put forward "a serious claim to the legacy of tragic drama," but that, aside from Verdi and Wagner, this challenge was rarely sustained.[47] Although we have been using the Aristotelian term "catharsis" to talk about the audience response to operatic deaths, there is a very real sense in which operas such as *Dialogues des Carmélites* or Wagner's *Tristan und Isolde* (the topic of the next chapter) are not tragedies in the classical sense of the term as used in the Western tradition. They may well offer representations of personal suffering and heroism in the face of uncontrollable forces, as do tragedies. But their final moments are different, often revealing a move to moral, psychic, and spiritual transcendence. There is little of the terror and revelation that Steiner says are characteristic of tragedy. And the final focus is also not on the exhausted survivors. In Kermode's words, "In Tragedy the cry of woe does not end succession; the great crises and end of human life do not stop time."[48] In the operas we discuss in this book, death *is* the final message; time *does* stop, in a sense, with the curtain.

Although Steiner somewhat snidely suggests that melodrama's "frisson" of horror replaced "the abiding terror of tragedy" for nineteenth-century theater audiences, we should remind ourselves that some operas of this same period not only used specific melodramas as source texts but also structured themselves on the win-or-lose, moral black-and-white dualities that define this popular stage form. In the move to greater stage realism at this time, some have even argued, the ethos and structures of melodrama could actually reflect how audiences (and creators) felt they lived their lives—or wanted to—much better than could those grander ones of tragedy. The theory is that melodrama—in presenting honestly and without condescension its message of villainy outwitted and virtue rewarded—allowed its consoling message to help spectators face life's conflicts differently.[49] Such a theory offers analogies with our notion of opera as a form of *contemplatio mortis*. Melodrama, for instance, in which sympathetic innocents have done nothing to warrant the misery that afflicts them, seems as relevant a description of the fate of Poulenc's Carmelites as tragedy, with its divided and flawed heroes.

Were we to add the morbid fascination with death of European Romantic dramatists like Victor Hugo and Alexandre Dumas (so many of whose plays were used to create opera librettos), we can begin to see the traces of a complex stage legacy that perhaps should not be neglected in opera. After all, we suspect that opera has always been an art form characterized more by generic promiscuity than by purity.[50] Opera is inevitably related to many varieties of stage drama—and even film and television—at least from the point of view of today's audiences. For this reason, we have decided not to talk about opera in the rest of this study in the more conventional terms of tragedy or melodrama, but instead to draw on that analogy with the early imaginative but dramatic mode of the *contemplatio mortis*. Yet another reason for this less traditional choice is the need to accommodate the wide range of more positive responses to dying that figure in the admittedly death-obsessed operas that are the focus of this study. In a sense we did not choose these particular works; they chose to be included through their obsession with exploring philosophical, psychological, or ethical responses to death. Let us explain how this happened and provide an outline of the chapters to follow.

If Poulenc's opera stages the human terror of the idea of dying and its resolution, then Wagner's *Tristan und Isolde* is its opposite, for it dramatizes the lovers' intense yearning for the finality of death. To try to move beyond our sense that such a view is counterintuitive *for us today*, Chapter 2 offers material to supplement our modern historical imagination. It examines the intersection of the thinking of the German Romantic poet Novalis, of the philosophers Arthur Schopenhauer and Friedrich Nietzsche, of the father of psychoanalysis, Sigmund Freud, and of the composer Richard Wagner. In particular, it addresses their shared positive view of death. That chapter explores a view of life—seen as suffering and striving—that places death as its ardently desired and welcomed goal. From legend and one particular source text, Gottfried von Strassburg's thirteenth-century epic, Wagner crafted an idiosyncratic version of the Tristan story that resonates in important ways with earlier Romantic poetry and later psychoanalytic and philosophical concepts in its presentation of a positive view of death. This music drama enacts and prefigures the (Schopenhauerian) insights of Freud's later theory of the death drive in its musical and textual repetitions of trauma and obsession. Inverting the Orpheus legend, this lover returns to the world of light and life to find his beloved and take her to the world of night, death, and love. Adapting Schopenhauer's theories of ways of transcending the phenomenal world, we argue that the audience of this very Nietzschean—that is, positive—"tragedy" is offered a form of redemption through the *music* analogous to what Wagner's protagonists achieve through sexual love and through death.

It is appropriate that Chapter 3, "'All That Is, Ends': Living while Dying in Wagner's *Der Ring des Nibelungen*," builds on the German Romantic background of the previous chapter, because Wagner interrupted his composition of the four music dramas of the *Ring* (completed in 1876) to write *Tristan und Isolde* and to work out the implications of his developing theories—of both music and mortality. But this chapter's focus is not on the culture-specific nature of Wagner's representations of death and dying. Instead, it turns the tables to look at how the *Ring* still speaks to audiences today, despite its mythic subject matter and its decidedly nineteenth-century German preoccupations. After all, the *Ring* tells the story of the Nordic god Wotan and his struggle to come to terms with the earth-goddess Erda's early pronouncement that he and his world must end: "Alles was ist, endet." Annunciations of death and responses to them are in fact constants in the *Ring,* but except for Wootan no character has any extended time in which to come to terms with his or her end. Throughout this long and complex work, however, the moral mettle of gods and mortals alike is constantly being tested by these annunciations of death, for they shadow the act of living by creating an acute awareness that the end is imminent. In his reflective (and self-reflexive) moments during the long narrative, Wotan enacts a series of responses to both his personal and his "social" death, responses that mirror psychological theories of human adaptation to the knowledge of dying. In his final acceptance of death, however, Wotan performs perhaps the only act of redemption possible in a secular world: dying the "good" death. We will argue that, through observing this form of *contemplatio mortis,* audience members may come face to face with the disconcerting realization that Wotan's end is clearly also our own, while they are still protected by the artifice of opera—especially opera about mythic creatures and times.

From these works openly dealing with the theme of coming to terms with one's own death, Chapter 4, "Orphic Rituals of Bereavement," moves to consider responses to representations of the death of another, specifically of a loved one. Once again the method of investigation changes, as it will in each chapter, to respond to the breadth of suggestions these operas offer about ways to approach death and dying. Because of the importance of the Orpheus story to opera's origins, for instance, this chapter begins by focusing on some of the many early musical narratives of mourning, from Claudio Monteverdi's *La favola d'Orfeo* (1607) to Cristoph Willibald von Gluck's *Orfeo ed Euridice* (1762). It appears an historical oddity that new Orpheus operas almost ceased to be composed during the nineteenth century, because this was a time obsessed not only with representations of Orpheus in the visual arts but also, as Ariès argues, with the trappings of death and mourning on a social level. The Italian and French opera repertoire of the time provides proof of the accelerated operatic obsession with love and death in general. Yet Orpheus' particular story, one of extended grief and mourning, eventually gave way in these traditions to more violent and conventionally tragic depictions of the final separation of lovers through death. The Orphic theme of mourning reappeared in the twentieth century, however, but no longer offering a compensatory story of bereavement or even ritual consolation through art or love. In operas such as Ernst Krenek's *Orpheus und Eurydike* (1926), Philip Glass's *Orphée* (1992), and Erich Korngold's *Die tote Stadt (The Dead City)* (1920), the Orphic figure sings a modern song about the pathological witnessing of inconsolable death and of the inevitable end of human passions.

Chapter 5 brings the theme of the death of self together with that of the death of the other. "'Tis a Consummation Devoutly to Be Wished': Staging Suicide" uses Hamlet's famous positive image of voluntary death to explore the changes in the meaning of suicide at different moments in history. Monteverdi's *L'incoronazione di Poppea (The Coronation of Poppea)*(1642) portrays a positive image of suicide as a rational choice, modeled on ideas of the ancient world, but presents this image to a Renaissance audience for whom "self-murder" was irrational—either a crime or a sin. A very different and positive view of suicide emerged with the rise of Romanticism and Goethe's influential work, *The Sorrows of Young Werther (Die Leiden des jungen Werthers)*(1774), and its many operatic adaptations over the next century. National, cultural, religious, and gender considerations are all relevant to audience acceptance of suicide as somehow the appropriate end for characters like Cio-Cio-San in Puccini's *Madama Butterfly* and her Orientalist predecessors, Lakmé and Sélika (in *L'Africaine*). In this discussion, we adapt Avery Weisman's concept of "appropriate death" (what a dying person might choose, if the choice were possible) to suggest that some stage suicides function as what an *audience* might choose as appropriate: ones that expiate moral guilt or re-establish codes of honor (national or individual).

Of particular interest in the context of our secularized and medicalized understanding of suicide today are the representations of self-inflicted death in Alban Berg's *Wozzeck* (1925) and Benjamin Britten's *Peter Grimes* (1945). Here suicide is not a response to impossible love or political necessity. It is the end of men who have caused the deaths of others. However, in both cases, they have done so within an increasingly repressive society. Their deaths not only allow the characters to escape from social oppression but also indict society and its mores. Emile Durkheim's influential early theory of the social causes of suicide is a starting point for this chapter's investigation of the medical, legal, and religious meanings of voluntary death, in the past and in the present. Why else could suicide feel "appropriate" for audiences? Could this be in part because it functions aesthetically as an act of narrative closure, while at the same time reinforcing a sense of moral rightness?

The final chapter, "The Undead," asks the question: what happens if you imagine a life without death? The operatic stage has been the site of many a fairy-tale fantasy of immortality, but in all of them the fantasy proves inadequate, because love and happiness turn out to be predicated upon mortality itself. A related theme, the moving plight of damned creatures who are not allowed to die, also became popular in opera in the nineteenth century, from Marschner's *Der Vampyr (The Vampire)* (1828) to Wagner's *Der fliegende Holländer (The Flying Dutchman)* (1842). The clear message of both the immortality fantasies and the tales of being cursed to live is that death is what gives meaning to life. This is the lesson too of Leoš Janáček's *Věc Makropulos (The Makropulos Affair)* (1926). As its over three-hundred-year-old protagonist Emilia Marty seeks the potion to extend her life even further, she too finally decides to opt for death and give her long life meaning at last. But perhaps the most intriguing opera on this theme is one that portrays a world in which Death (this time, a staged character) refuses to do his appointed task. Viktor Ullmann's *Der Kaiser von Atlantis* was written in 1943 in the concentration camp of Theresienstadt, and its circumstances of composition and our knowledge of the fate of the librettist (Petr Kien) and composer—both died in Auschwitz—considerably complicates any audience reaction today to this opera's rejection of a life without death.

Clearly, human responses to mortality are varied and complex, and our different methods of approach have sought to reflect this richness by ranging widely across disciplines. The most striking feature of these operas is the positive valuing of death. In other words, death is shown to bring out the core of existential and spiritual personhood (for Blanche), to restore social order or moral honor (for Wotan in the *Ring* and in some operas that end in suicide), to bring about redemption and transcendence (for Tristan and Isolde), or even to offer some final peace (for the undead). As the message offered by these operatic forms of the *contemplatio mortis,* then, this positive sense of death is affirmative of life—that is, of *all* the processes of life, even the final one.

2

Eros and Thanatos

Richard Wagner's *Tristan und Isolde*

> No destiny doth sunder us
> Even if we be doomed to die!
>
> *Nun trennet uns kein Schicksal mehr,*
> *Wenn auch der Tod beschieden wär!*
>
> Mozart, *The Magic Flute*

The question this chapter tackles may seem especially counter-intuitive for a twenty-first-century audience: Can we conceive of a worldview in which death is not only welcomed but is passionately desired, even sought after as the final rest after a life of suffering and striving? Some have, in fact, taken exactly such a positive position on death, even outside a religious framework. They have seen death as the "end" of life in the sense of not only its termination but also specifically its aim and goal. In order to express this view in a convincing manner, as you might expect, they have had to reverse many of the expectations and assumptions of their age. In their different ways, a series of intellectually related German artists and thinkers all did precisely this: the poet Novalis, the philosophers Arthur Schopenhauer and Friedrich Nietzsche, the father of psychoanalysis, Sigmund Freud, and most powerfully, the composer Richard Wagner. Wagner's *Tristan und Isolde* (1865) offers a relevant focus for exploring this strangely positive view of death, in part because it is so often misinterpreted as a conventional tragic love story. But this music drama's obsession with death is not, in fact, at all pessimistic or tragic. For modern audiences to appreciate what feels like a challenge to common sense, we need to move back in time and look at how the German Romantics and their successors came to give this new kind of positive meaning to death. Unlike some of the other operas on the theme of human mortality that will be examined in this book, the message of this one is decidedly culture-specific.

Setting the Stage, Introducing the Players

Wagner is known to have read the philosophical works of Arthur Schopenhauer in 1854; what this meant was that when he was forty-one years old, he found in print both a confirmation and a validation of many of his own ideas. Because of this, his work would never be quite the same again. He wrote to Franz Liszt that year—with a characteristic lack of modesty—about his appreciation of Schopenhauer:

> His chief idea, the final negation of the Desire of life, is terribly serious, but it shows the only salvation possible. To me, of course, that thought was not new, and it can, indeed, be conceived by no-one in whom it did not pre-exist, but this philosopher was the first to place it clearly before me. If I think of the storm in my heart, the terrible tenacity with which, against my desire, it used to cling to the hope of life, and if even now I feel this hurricane within me, I have at last found a quietus which, in wakeful nights, helps me to sleep. This is the genuine, ardent longing for death, for absolute unconsciousness, total non-existence. Freedom from all dreams is our only final salvation.[1]

"The Death of Isolde" by Roger de Egusquiza, plate to "The Sphere" 12.8.1911, p. 187. Line block after the painting. Tristan and Isolde lying dead next to each other. Wellcome Library, London.

Soon after finding his own intuitions confirmed in Schopenhauer's systematic philosophy, Wagner began writing and composing *Tristan und Isolde*. As mentioned earlier, he had interrupted his work on *Der Ring des Nibelungen* in the last act of *Siegfried*, seemingly in order to solve certain aesthetic and moral issues, issues that the legendary story of the fated lovers named Tristan and Isolde also addressed, although in a different way.

The Tristan tale is an old and familiar one that had caught Wagner's attention when he read Karl Ritter's dramatized version. In Wagner's eyes, this version had concentrated only on the trivial elements of the famous thirteenth-century German epic by Gottfried von Strassburg. In contrast, Wagner's own version stripped the epic's story to its essentials, eliminating "superfluous" characters and action, and adding his own interpretation (and details)—all in order to tell in powerful, elemental terms the tale of the Irish princess brought to Cornwall as the unwilling bride of King Marke by Tristan, the man who is not only the King's nephew and messenger, but also the one with whom she has already fallen deeply in love—despite all odds. To avenge what she sees as Tristan's betrayal, Isolde prepares a death potion for them both; her servant Brangäne substitutes a love potion, and the mutual passion of the lovers is now fatefully acknowledged. In the feudal world of the court, their (courtly) love is clearly impossible: Isolde is to be the wife of Tristan's uncle. But even more significant for their chosen fate (and for their important position in this book) is their shared conviction that in death alone can their erotic passion be made eternal, for this is what leads them to pledge to die together in ecstatic bliss.

The operatic version of the legend focused, as Wagner himself said, on "inner motives." But these had to be represented *onstage*, of course. Wagner gave flesh, so to speak, to the theories of Schopenhauer in his portrayal of two conflicting worlds—that of day and that of night, or to use the philosopher's terms, that of the "phenomenal" world and that of the "noumenal" world. For Schopenhauer, in *The World as Will and Representation (Die Welt als Wille und Vorstellung)*, the phenomenal world of appearances is one in which the "will," the basic substance of all existence, can be perceived through individualized objects, according to what he called the *principio individuationis*. In the noumenal realm, on the other hand, an unindividuated oneness prevails. The phenomenal world of time and space is characterized by the endless striving of the will against itself, leading to a constant, insatiable state of yearning and desire. Suffering is therefore the norm. In contrast, the noumenal world is that oneness from which all life forms come and to which they return in death. Death, therefore, as Wagner sensed, is a pleasurable loss of individuation and an "awakening from the dream of life."[2]

Although it has become commonplace in Wagner scholarship to

read *Tristan und Isolde* through Schopenhauerian lenses, the music drama can also be fruitfully interpreted in the light of a more controversial and slightly later theorizing of that "genuine, ardent longing for death" and of the "quietus" death offers. That theorizing was to come in 1920 in Sigmund Freud's *Beyond the Pleasure Principle (Jenseits des Lustprinzips)*. The impact of Schopenhauer on Freud's thinking is clear, as it is on the early work of Friedrich Nietzsche. As we shall see, the very particular form of "tragedy" lived out in the ardently longed-for deaths of Wagner's Tristan and Isolde was provocatively articulated in Nietzsche's 1872 *The Birth of Tragedy from the Spirit of Music (Die Geburt der Tragödie aus dem Geiste der Musik)*, a book he dedicated to Wagner. The cultural web here is complex, but untangling its philosophical, psychological, literary, and musical threads will allow us to see how a positive and even erotic notion of death is possible in this music drama—although such a view might feel foreign today.

Repetition and the Narrating of Trauma

Wagner has sometimes been seen as anticipating Freud in his psychological insights into the nonrational in human behavior, and not a few critics have been tempted to interpret his works in generally Freudian terms.[3] However, it is specifically in relation to the theme of death and the death drive that the direct Wagnerian connections to Schopenhauer and the indirect ones to Freud are most evident—and, we believe, most mutually illuminating.[4] In the years immediately following World War I, influenced by the psychological trauma he had been witnessing and its clinical signs, which he could not explain, Freud tried for the first time to integrate the experience of death into his theory of psychic drives. Taking two concepts that were inseparable in earlier Greek thought —Eros (life/love) and Thanatos (death)—Freud added to his idea of a life instinct another primary drive in the human psyche that he called the death instinct. Although this was conceived as being in opposition to the life instinct, with its direct links to sexuality, it was this death drive that Freud came to consider the more primitive and basic. The postulation that "the aim of all life is death" was based on Freud's belief—in his terminology—that all life strove toward a reduction of tension to an inorganic zero point. In other words, he felt that the animate sought to revert to the inanimate.[5] But this drive was always countered by the energy of sexuality. Freud then rather ingenuously noted: "We have unwittingly steered our course into the harbour of Schopenhauer's philosophy. For him death is the 'true result and to that extent the purpose of life', while the sexual instinct is the embodiment of the will to live."[6] Although subsequent psychoanalytic theory has contested the validity of Freud's theories of the two drives, Eros and Thanatos,[7] their relevance to a reading of death in Wagner's work comes from their status as an important—if late—contribution to the German Romantic obsession with sexuality and death, or to what in later cultural shorthand terms came to be called the "Liebestod," or "love-death."

A significant part of this contribution lay in Freud's insight into the structure and possible meaning of repetitive behavior. One of the clinical findings that led Freud to conceive of a death instinct or drive in the first place was the curious tendency he noted on the part of those suffering from severe trauma to relive the traumatic moment and to do so in various forms: in analysis, in dreams, in unconscious habits. Given Freud's concept of the psyche before the positing of the death drive, such a tendency should not have been possible: the psyche was supposed to have defenses against such eruptions of "unpleasure." The pleasure principle, in its endeavors to keep tension and excitation to a minimum, was not supposed to be overridden in this way. But the evidence was clear: traumatized patients exhibited a "compulsion to repeat" that had a drivelike quality about it, giving the appearance of "some 'daemonic' force

at work."⁸ Freud saw this as a more primitive force than the pleasure principle, and thus it was evidence of a basic drive toward a return to the inanimate in death. Freud interpreted the act of repetition as an attempt to master the traumatic stimulus retrospectively.

The linking of death, memory, and this compulsion to repeat
is central to Freud's thinking here, and subsequent theorists of
trauma have stressed the intrusive, insistent quality of these repetitions—as if one were "possessed" by the belated re-experiencing
of the traumatic event. Out of this thinking about the power of
repeated associative memories and their attendant emotions has
come an emphasis upon the desperate need to *tell the story* of the
trauma-causing event and of one's reactions and suffering.⁹ Although psychoanalytic theorists such as Jacques Lacan have also
connected desire, repetition, and death, and have located the death
drive in language,¹⁰ it is Freud's original insight into the traumatic
compulsion to repeat and the need to narrate that is directly prefig-
ured in Wagner's presentation of Tristan and Isolde. The two fall in
love under the sign of death (literally, the death of Isolde's be-
trothed, Morold, and potentially, that of the wounded Tristan),
and they live their stage lives obsessed with death as much as with
love.¹¹

Most spectators have noticed that not a lot happens in *Tristan
und Isolde* in terms of dramatic action, but that, in true Wagnerian
fashion, a fair amount is narrated. But *what* is it that is narrated,
and indeed renarrated, so compulsively? It turns out to be the story
of Isolde's trauma—or more accurately, of the complex of traumatic experiences she undergoes after the death of Morold: her discovery that the wounded man named Tantris for whom she has
been caring is none other than Tristan, the killer of Morold; her
failure to act on her pledged revenge and her simultaneous falling
in love with Tristan; her subsequent sense of betrayal when the
healed Tristan then returns to claim her as his uncle's bride. It is as
if Isolde were "possessed" by this story—which she tells over and

over, often, as we shall see, at inappropriate times. Death is not only the sign under which Isolde comes to love. Death also determines how she continues to love and how she tells the audience about that love and about herself. The fact that she repeats her trauma narrative time and time again, often in the same or similar language (and sometimes even similar music), suggests not only the need to master the traumatic events, but also the centrality of those events and their narration to her sense of self.

Traumatic stories, however, are not the only things repeated in *Tristan und Isolde*. In fact, this is a most obsessively repetitive text—as befits, Freud might have said, a music drama about death. It has been called Wagner's most untheatrical work, the one in which he relies the least on action and words and the most on music. Yet, in fact, in this work he relies very much on words, although on fewer of them. He also repeats these words in ways related in aesthetic intent and psychological effect to his well-known repetition of musical motives. As his own librettist, Wagner was as careful and adept in constructing his structural and verbal repetitions as he was in composing his musical ones.[12] Wagner's lovers exult in repeating each other's and their own names. In the famous love duet in Act 2, they luxuriate in echoing each other's lines about love, night, and death. But in fact the entire opera is structured on what could be called the characters' compulsive repetitions.

A few instances may suffice to give a sense of Wagner's willed redundancy. Each act opens with examples of consciously staged music: the song of the unseen sailor, the hunting horns, the shepherd's piping. Plot details (such as the wounding of Tristan) are doubled. Scenes we have witnessed onstage are then repeated in that typically Wagnerian, narrated form. In Act 1, Brangäne narrates to Isolde her encounter with Tristan and Kurwenal. Both Tristan and Isolde later narrate the story of the potions. The same information is given repeatedly: four times in Act 1 we are told of the power of Isolde's mother's magic potions. Characters consistently repeat each other's words: Marke's grieving over Tristan's betrayal is echoed by Tristan's over Melot's. (Sometimes the repeating is done in an ironic manner, most frequently by Isolde.) The list could continue. So too could the even longer list of the verbal repetitions within individual sections of the text, as will appear shortly when we examine the libretto more closely. This drive to repeat in the text significantly exceeds even the normal conventions of repetition in romance narratives.

One way to think about such textual and structural echoings is simply as the verbal equivalent of the musical repetitions of motives about which so much has been written.[13] Theodor Adorno's attack on the compulsively repeated musical use of what he called "expression-laden gestures" in Wagner's compositions was based on his sense that the music "impotently" repeated itself, causing time and action to stand still "so as to accompany it down into the kingdom of death, the ideal of Wagnerian music."[14] And indeed, although intended as an insult, Adorno's insight is very much to the point in our reading of *Tristan und Isolde*'s "deathly" repetitions. (Of course, Wagner himself had musical reasons for his use of motivic iterations and developments.)[15] The effect of the musical repetitions on audiences is closely related to the effect of textual and structural ones: a similar sense of "possession" and compulsion. Far from being the static phenomenon Adorno claims it to be, Wagner's motivic technique is much more subtle, complicated, and dynamic. This complexity derives in part from the motives' dramatic and psychological associations, and in part from their purely musical interrelations. For instance, from the opening bars, two musical motives come to mirror the thematically linked concepts of suffering and desire that are part of Wagner's Schopenhauerian worldview that pervades the entire opera.[16]

Wagner claimed that he chose to open his drama of love and death with these musical themes of suffering and insatiable desire because, in this story, there was "no end to the yearning, longing, rapture, and misery of love: world, power, fame, honor, chivalry, loyalty, and friendship, scattered like an insubstantial dream; one thing alone left living: longing, longing unquenchable, desire forever renewing itself, craving and languishing; one sole redemption: death, surcease of being, the sleep that knows no waking!"[17] The two motives of desire and suffering are famously conjoined in bar 2 of the score in what is known as the "*Tristan* chord"—the symbolic musical bridge between suffering and yearning that will not be resolved until its transformation at the end of the opera.

In short, the musical and the textual repetitions function in parallel ways. Wagner had written to Mathilde Wesendonck in 1859 that the "secret" cornerposts of his musical form in Act 2 of *Tristan* were the turbulent emotions of life and love and the "most solemn, intensely felt longing for death."[18] This (not-so-secret) musical and thematic structure is unraveled, in a sense, in Isolde's final "Liebestod" or, as Wagner called it, her "Verklärung" ("transfiguration"). There, as many have pointed out, the music recapitulates the Act 2 love duet. But it does more than simply repeat. It abbreviates and simplifies the duet's more tortuous harmonics, its complex progressions. Isolde's music, although not simple harmonically, has a clear goal. In this, the music can be seen to repeat and echo the philosophical themes of the two passages: the Act 2 duet represents the yearning that characterizes desire in the Schopenhauerian view of life in the phenomenal world, whereas the goal of the final "Liebestod" marks the end of that yearning, the end of that struggle, and a return to the noumenal realm. The chord that has been denied musical fulfillment becomes a kind of aural enactment of the tension and striving of love's desire. Its resolution and transformation accompany the death that marks the triumphant end of such yearning. Isolde dies transfigured, in blissful and ecstatic reunion in death with Tristan.

That this is not the standard view of love, life, and death in

Western culture likely goes without saying. Schopenhauer went against conventional psychological wisdom in theorizing death as positive. Even more contentiously, Freud added to this theory the idea that there is, innate within us, a drive toward death. He then linked this drive to the compulsion to repeat that, we argue, would find its dramatic, musical, and verbal prefiguring in Wagner's opera. This Freudian and Schopenhauerian inversion of the meaning and value of death is also enacted in *Tristan und Isolde:* specifically, in the moment of the switching of the love potion for the death potion in Act 1; in the inversion of the usual cultural associations of night and death in Act 2; and in the portrayal of Tristan as a kind of Orpheus figure in reverse in Act 3, as he returns to the world of the living to bring Isolde to that transfigured state in death. These cultural inversions are Wagner's means of convincing his audience through his art that a new—and different—view of the end of life could indeed be held.

Love and Death in the World of Night

The idea of having Tristan and Isolde drink a death potion (which is switched for a love potion) is Wagner's innovative addition to the many other versions of the story. Wagner's stage-enacted introduction of what Carl Dahlhaus calls the "dialectics of the two potions, love and death" works dramatically to link from the start these two major themes of the work: Eros and Thanatos.[19] As if traumatized by the potion and by their now-acknowledged love, Tristan and Isolde compulsively repeat, in their ensuing duet, each other's name and each other's grammatical constructions, exclamations, and rhetorical questions. It is appropriate that here they first display the inversion of values that, from this point on, will make the behavior of the lovers incomprehensible to everyone else on stage. Isolde rids herself of the shame she had once felt, while Tristan sees the emptiness of honor, duty, and courtly glory. Their first major duet ends with their exalted affirmation of the supreme pleasure they feel in love ("höchste Liebeslust"), but Brangäne's revelation of the secret substitution of the potions soon makes clear that their joy, in Tristan's words, is one "consecrated by deceit": his "Trug-geweihtes Glücke" here deliberately echoes Isolde's earlier descrip-tion of Tristan's death-consecrated head ("Todgeweihtes Haupt") and is indeed sung to the music (slightly varied) that accompanied her earlier anguish. As the act ends, offstage trumpets and trom-bones sound in triumph as the lovers must confront the courtly world of King Marke. This is musically represented, as it will be in the next act, by the C-major chord of the motive linked to the world of day, the inverse of the lovers' world of night—the time of love and death.[20]

In the medieval source text, there is none of the opera's strong day/night opposition, so here again Wagner made significant changes. He was in the middle of writing *Siegfried,* the story of an extroverted day-world adventurer, when he began *Tristan,* the tale of an introverted night-world lover. With Schopenhauer's philo-sophical support and the German Romantics' literary example, Wagner inverted the traditional positive associations with light and day in pre-Romantic Western culture: enlightenment, reason, truth, consciousness.[21] In its Wagnerian version, day comes to rep-resent the superficial glitter of the life of the court and, more gen-erally, of Schopenhauer's phenomenal world. Here suffering reigns because of the ceaseless striving of the will, divided against itself. In contrast, night comes to represent not the fearful, mysterious dark-ness of unreason and unknowing, but rather restful death and unindividuated unconsciousness. Night is directly linked to the primary and permanent reality of the noumenal world, the time-less, undifferentiated oneness from which individuals are expelled at birth and to which they long to return.

Novalis was the German poet most eloquent (and influential) in his rejection of the Enlightenment ideals of progress and clarity characteristic of the day-world (in his 1799 *Christendom or Europe* [*Die Christenheit oder Europa*]). Instead, he espoused the night as that primal realm prior to individuation and the painful yearning that went with it. In his famous *Hymns to the Night (Hymnen an die Nacht)*, Novalis presented night as holy, mysterious, secretive ("der heiligen, unaussprechlichen, geheimnisvollen Nacht"), outside of time and space ("zeitlos und raumlos"), while light represented eternal unrest ("ewiger Unruh"). Wagner had clearly read Novalis and the other German Romantics and, like Schopenhauer, had more than likely been influenced by their frequent linking of love, death, and night in his own inversion of the standard cultural associations.[22] This is the inversion that structures Act 2 of *Tristan und Isolde,* but the fact that today's audiences may be unfamiliar with this cultural context may explain why the constant yearning for death by the characters can seem almost pathological or perverse to us.

Scene 2 of that act opens with the emphatic embrace of the lovers to the only *fff* in the entire score. They sing in alternating lines with Isolde's two top Cs occurring on "Mein Tristan!" echoed at once by Tristan's "Mein' Isolde!" Characteristic of any encounter between the lovers (after the potion) is this repetitive obsession with naming. According to Tristan, the "malicious" day is the "cruellest foe", the source of "hatred and complaint" ("Dem tückischen Tage, / Dem härtesten Feind / Hass und Klage!"). Like Schopenhauer's phenomenal world, it awakens only need ("Not") and pain ("Pein"). To Isolde, day is the time when Tristan betrayed her, claiming her for Marke and thereby consecrating her to death ("dem Tod die Treu zu weih'n"). Once again, then, here at a quite inappropriate moment—in a declaration of love—Isolde begins to tell her trauma narrative. The audience hears a narrated version of events that we have already witnessed onstage and, indeed, have already heard discussed once by the characters themselves.

Isolde laments that death and night were lost to them by the switching of the death and love potions, but Tristan sees the link between Eros and Thanatos as more direct and praises the effects of the love potion for opening the door of death for him, a door into the wondrous realm of night ("das Wunderreich der Nacht"). With the potion has come the realization that his love for Isolde is at the core of his being. So too has come a recognition of the lure of the noumenal night realm, compared to the superficiality, indeed, nullity of the day-world of phenomena. Tristan, once a warrior hero (correctly named by Isolde a "Tagesknecht," a "slave of day"), now claims to be "nightsighted" ("nachtsichtig"), foreseeing the promise of death. Echoing Isolde's repeated "Todgeweihte" (death-consecrated) he consecrates the lovers to night ("Nachtgeweihte!").

In the ensuing duet to this night of love ("Nacht der Liebe"), the debt to the imagery of Novalis (as well as to Schopenhauer) becomes even more evident and the connection to death even more openly articulated. Again, Tristan and Isolde echo each other's syntax, and rhyme their equal-length responses with one another. Although often singing alternate lines, their voices come together powerfully on significant words: for example, on their defiant and conscious wish never again to wake ("Nie-wieder-erwachens / wahnlos / hold bewusster Wunsch").

To Brangäne's offstage warnings to beware of treachery, Tristan simply repeats that he wants to be allowed to die: "Lass' mich sterben!" He cries out that he never wants to wake again ("Nie erwachen!"), that day must yield to death ("Lass' den Tag / dem Tode weichen"). Isolde's questioning response expresses her worries that, in the context of either day/life or night/death, their love would still be impossible. Tristan's strong and eloquent answer repeatedly allows for a continuation of love in death, of Eros in Thanatos. Isolde replies with a kind of meditation on the conjoining word "und" that unites the names of the lovers, "Tristan *und*

Isolde." If Tristan were to die, she asks, would not this sweet little word ("Dies süsse Wortlein"), symbolic of the binding agent of their love, die with him? Tristan's reply, once again with its frequent repetition of death ("stürbe"; "Tod") and love ("lieben"), does not calm Isolde's fears: her subsequent (briefer) trauma narrative centers again around the conjunction "und"—that is, this time, around the fears of separation in death. But Tristan explains that they will die together, inseparable and nameless, and he does so to music that will form the core of both the later part of the duet and Isolde's final transfiguration in death:

> So let us die,
> undivided,
> eternally one,
> without end,
> without awakening,
> without fearing,
> nameless
> embraced in love,
> given entirely to ourselves,
> to live only in love!

> *So stürben wir,*
> *um ungetrennt,*
> *ewig einig,*
> *ohne End',*
> *ohn' Erwachen,*
> *ohn' Erbangen,*
> *namenlos*
> *in Lieb' umfangen,*
> *ganz uns selbst gegeben,*
> *der Liebe nur zu leben!*

The clear tension between the self-absorption signaled by the lovers' compulsive repeating of each other's name and their professed desire to pass nameless into the unindividuated realm of death plays out in the text to the very end of the opera.

Sexual Love and Death

Another quality of both this death duet and the opera's finale requires some explanation today, perhaps: their explicitly sexual nature. Wagner had been influenced by Schopenhauer in his conception of the meaning of death, but the opera's relating of death to sexuality was also Schopenhauerian—up to a point, at least. To that philosopher, sexual love—a major theme in literature, as in life, he acknowledged—was the strongest and most active manifestation of will: it was disruptive, perplexing, destructive of "the most valuable relationships," capable of breaking the "strongest bonds": "it robs of all conscience those who were previously honourable and upright, and makes traitors of those who have hitherto been loyal and faithful."[23] Just as Freud was later to see sexuality at the core of the unconscious, so Schopenhauer before him saw sexuality as a manifestation of the will-to-live, the dark power that is central to the preservation of the human species. For him this alone is evidence that it is the species that matters, not the individual, even though this power of attraction is all the more mighty when individualized. It is in individuality, in what he calls the *principio individuationis,* however, that lie the longing and suffering of love—as of all life in the phenomenal world. With death the individual (who exists only as phenomenon) is joyfully dissolved back into the noumenal oneness. Because the difficulty of life lies specifically in individuation, death is the only release from the pain of individual existence.

For Wagner, however, sexual love came to share with death this ability to transcend individuation, to lose the self in a unity with a larger force. The use of the actual word "Liebestod" in the Act 2 duet in part presents this new view. Wagner may well have "gulped down, and metabolized into his own tissue" much of Schopenhauer's ontology, ethics, and aesthetics,[24] but he also contested the philosopher's views, specifically those on sexual love in relation to death. Schopenhauer had confessed to being unable to understand the suicide of lovers,[25] so Wagner wrote him a letter to explain the conjunction of death and sexual love (but evidently he never actually sent it). Perhaps the end of Act 2, scene 2 is another part of his reply, however. There, as in the letter he drafted, Wagner demonstrates his belief that the will-to-live could actually be pacified through erotic love.[26]

The state that Tristan and Isolde claim they will enter with death is not unlike the one they experience in their love. It is one of endless rapture, one in which they will be inseparable and therefore unindividualized, at least to the extent that their identities merge with each other. There is no longer any need of that little word "und." Tristan sings: "Tristan you, / I Isolde, / no longer Tristan!" ("Tristan du, / ich Isolde, / nicht mehr Tristan!"). And Isolde responds in kind. Together (appropriately) they sing: "Without naming, / without separating" ("Ohne Nennen, / ohne Trennen"). Proper names as markers of stable individual identity— and as obsessively repeated by the lovers—must be left behind if they are to enter the noumenal world of death together. The link between love and death is not one of obstacle, but one of fulfillment. Now they will have one consciousness ("ein-bewusst"); now they can enter into the space of death, the space of the "most supreme bliss of love" ("höchste Liebes-Lust").

Wagner's clearly climactic music here suggests that death and sexual love are both solutions to the suffering and pain of individuation. In Barry Millington's terms, on the music's second move to a climax, its "sequential repetitions and a sustained dominant pedal raise the tension to an unbearable level, which eventually reaches the point of no return."[27] He continues memorably: "The cadence, like the coitus, is *interruptus*" by a savage discord on the full orchestra and a "shrieking piccolo," as Brangäne cries out and Tristan's friend Kurwenal rushes in to warn him that King Marke and the traitor Melot have arrived, along with the dawn. The hunting call we hear in the orchestra makes it clear that the prey is the pair of illicit lovers.

Act 3 repeats the lovers' expulsion from the night realm. At the prompting of the "ancient melody" ("alte Weise") piped by the shepherd, the wounded Tristan regains consciousness in Kareol. His first question is not "Where am I?" but "Where have I been?" Kurwenal, for all his loyalty and faithfulness, is very much a day-world person, as his sunny, hearty, diatonic music has consistently revealed. He is not part of the chromatic night-world of the lovers, and so he does not understand that what he tells Tristan, intended as comforting, will in fact have the opposite effect. He announces that Tristan is now in the sunshine, where he will blissfully be healed from death and wounds ("im Schein der alten Sonne, / darin von Tod und Wunden / du selig sollst gesunden"). Tristan corrects him, trying to describe the place from which he has come —a place without sun, people, or land. He knows he cannot explain where he has been (and repeats this three times in ten lines) because he was literally in another realm, that of the world's night ("der Welten Nacht"). For Schopenhauer, as we have seen, the nonexistence after death was like that before birth, and being in either one was not to be mourned. This is also the noumenal space of eternal oblivion ("göttlich ew'ges / Ur-Vergessen!") of which the lovers had sung in their love duet in Act 2 (whose music Tristan here repeats and varies). For Wagner, as for Schopenhauer, unconsciousness, like sleep, meant a prefiguring, a presentiment of death's blissful loss of individuation. But Tristan has had to leave this realm to return to the day world because of what he calls a "yearning reminder" ("Sehnsücht'ge Mahnung"): Isolde, who had promised to follow, has not yet done so. She still lives in the kingdom of the sun ("im Reich der Sonne"). Mourning their continuing living state, Tristan explains that he has had to come for her and will take her back to death with him.

In a reversal of the Orpheus myth that is comparable in effect to the reversal of love and death potions in Act 1 and of traditional (pre-Romantic) light and night imagery in Act 2, Tristan grieves and mourns for his Eurydice because she is *not yet* dead. Orpheus's lyre is replaced by a shepherd's pipe (the *cor anglais*), whose melody Tristan has heard in the other realm.[28] But Tristan is an Orphic figure in reverse, one who returns from the world of death to fetch his beloved. He has heard the door of death ("des Todes Tor") slam behind him once again. So he has no choice but to forge onward into the light, as his desperately repetitive syntax suggests, "to seek her, / to see her, / to find her" ("sie zu suchen, / sie zu sehen, / sie zu finden"). It is only with her that he can be granted the peace of death, and so he must face the accursed day. It is she who has called him out of the night because she still lives ("Isolde lebt und wacht, / sie rief mich aus der Nacht").

Tristan recalls hearing that "alte Weise" when, as a child, he learned of how his parents had died. For him it is a song of yearning and mourning that tells him of his fate, a fate summed up in two verbs: "to yearn—and to die" ("sehnen—und sterben"). He must endure the eternal agony ("ew'ger Qual") of living again, tossed back by night into the cruel and merciless light of day. Tristan's pain mounts with every added moment in the day world, as the music increases in intensity and tempo. Yet when Isolde finally does arrive, a joyous Tristan appears to enter utterly (if temporarily) into the world of day. In fact, he praises the day; but we would do well to be suspicious of the extreme terms in which he does so ("most sunny day"—"sonnigster Tag"), extremes suggesting that he may do so only because it brings Isolde to him and allows him to move onward, in other words, actually backward to night / death. The music of night to which he sings this line makes the irony of the extreme formulation clear. Tearing off his bandages, he lets his wounds bleed, knowing that the healing which Isolde will now bring to him is eternal, rather than of this world. Now, in fact, this phenomenal world can pass away ("Vergeh' die Welt"). She enters; they embrace; he dies, after saying her name one final time. As the orchestra recapitulates the music of the opening of the prelude, it is as if the entire drama of yearning is now coming to fulfilment.

Isolde's famous "Verklärung" or "Liebestod" appropriately opens with the music from Act 2 that accompanied the desire of the lovers to die and be inseparable ("so stürben wir, um ungetrennt"), signaling perhaps the proximity of achieving that desire. Isolde fixes her eyes on Tristan's dead body and asks the others if they share her vision of him: serene, smiling, his eyes open—though viewing a different world, she implies. Foreseeing that those who inhabit the world of day will have difficulty believing her, she appeals four times to them as witnesses ("seht ihr's, Freunde?") to her vision of a radiant Tristan shining among the stars. But hers is a very physical Tristan, with a body whose heart swells and whose lips exhale sweet breath that she, if not her witnesses, can both feel and see. This is a sensuous hymn to the physical presence of the beloved. It is more sexual than Novalis's more spiritual (yet still corporeal) vision of his dead beloved in *Hymns to the Night*. But it functions equally powerfully in its luring of the one left living into the eternal night of death.[29] But, in the end, the opera's conclusion is not a true vision of the noumenal world in which all individuation is lost. In other words, Wagner was not a pure Schopenhauerian. As seen in Act 2, he believed sexual love was a way to transcend the phenomenal world that was equal in its power to

Schopenhauer's more ascetic solution of simply renouncing the will-to-live.

Liebestod and "Tragedy"

Wagner had at his disposal a strong aesthetic history that could be drawn upon to convey his belief in the redeeming nature of the erotic. German Romantic tradition allowed desire to find in death a heightened erotic ecstasy. This was a commonplace from Goethe's "Prometheus" (1773) to Schlegel's *Lucinde* (1799), from Novalis's *Hymns* to Clemens Brentano's *Godwi,* which first coined the term "Liebestod" early in the nineteenth century.[30] But there were, in fact, two warring traditions—one fully eroticized, the other a more spiritualized ecstasy—and these have influenced the interpretations of the ending of Wagner's music drama. Was the body a hindrance to spiritual union, part of the individuated phenomenal world that must be left behind in death? Or was sexual union more than a powerful metaphor for the union of souls in the refinement of passion? In other words, was erotic love itself a means of transcendence? Wagner conceived of *Tristan* as a twin to *Die Sieger,* his projected Buddhist opera of renunciation of carnal love, so it is not hard to see *Tristan* as a statement of love's fulfilment, not renunciation. After all, the music of the "Liebestod" repeats the "post-coital" passages from the love duet of the previous act. This orgasmic music arguably expresses eroticism as compulsive desire beyond simple enjoyment, desire that can only be fulfilled in death. As we shall see, in Wagnerian and Schopenhauerian terms, the audience too is offered through music a similar transcendence of the phenomenal world, a similar direct access to the noumenal realm that the lovers attain through erotic love and, ultimately, through death.

Wagner's insistence on the erotic as redemptive may help ex-

plain the much-commented-upon "synesthesia" in Isolde's final
lines, as the various physical senses are invoked and then mingled.
Tristan, in his dying moments, had responded similarly, as if he
could hear the light ("hör' ich das Licht"). But Isolde goes beyond
that single, simple mixing together of the senses. Following her
sensual vision of a transfigured Tristan, Isolde asks if she is the only
one to hear the melody that sounds from him, a lamenting, recon-
ciling, vibrating sound that physically penetrates her. Again in a
questioning mode, she asks if she is feeling waves of soft air that
sound around her, wondering if they are waves of perfume? Although such a mixing of the bodily senses does have parallels in de-
scriptions of the state of ecstasy, this is decidedly a sensual and
physical kind of transcendence.[31]

Her very last words, however, are not offered as a question. Nor
are they even offered in Isolde's own name, so to speak. The imper-
sonal infinitive verb form ("ertrinken"; "versinken") replaces the
usual first person, as Isolde seems to lose her individual identity
and to unite with the elements into which the transfigured Tristan
seems to have dissolved:

> in the surging flood,
> in the ringing sound,
> in the world-breath's
> blowing all—
> to drown—
> to sink—
> unconscious—
> most supreme bliss!

> *in dem wogenden Schwall,*
> *in dem tönenden Schall,*
> *in des Welt-Atems*
> *wehendem All—*

ertrinken—
versinken—
unbewusst—
höchste Lust!

This Schopenhauerian lapse into final unconsciousness ("unbe-wusst") follows the lovers' single consciousness ("ein-bewusst") of the end of the Act 2 duet and the consciousness of the beloved ("einzig bewusst") that results from the potion in Act 1.[32] For Schopenhauer, consciousness, like the body, is tied to our sense of individuality. The ecstatic word bliss ("Lust"), with which each of these states of consciousness is rhymed, is of utmost importance. In Acts 1 and 2, it was "the most supreme bliss of love" ("höchste Liebeslust"). Here it is simply "the most supreme bliss" ("höchste Lust"). The progression from consciousness of each other to a state of unconsciousness is the progression of love that seeks eternal du-ration in death. That Wagner should use water imagery to describe this final state is fitting, given the importance of the sea both sym-bolically and dramatically from the opening lines of the music drama onward, and given the cultural associations of water with both life-giving and death-dealing, that is, with both Eros and Thanatos. Images of drowning suggest becoming part of the nou-menal oneness and thus a loss of individuation that would accom-pany the Schopenhauerian loss of consciousness.[33]

In many ways, Isolde's final words—and the absence of the first-person pronoun—do indeed suggest a breakdown of the *prin-cipium individuationis,* and Schopenhauer had been clear that death offered "the great opportunity no longer to be I."[34] But this particular death is not a dissolution into an empty nothingness of nonbeing. Its eroticized ecstasy (of a particular woman for a partic-ular man) suggests that this death is a fulfilment of desire.[35] De-spite its ecstatic calm, there is little here of Schopenhauer's nega-tion or renunciation of desire, a willing end to insatiable longing and the life of the senses. Instead, erotic love is affirmed as itself transcendent, as a means to self-awareness and even self-denial. Wagner used his ecstatic, voluptuous music as much as his sensuous verbal imagery to stage his profound belief in the redemptive power of the erotic. The final, rising motive of yearning at last finds its long-awaited and "radiant"[36] resolution on a chord of B major played in the orchestra. The reduction of tension with which Freud identified the death instinct is embodied in the calmness of this musical resolution.

Radiant, ecstatic—these are hardly the usual words used to describe the mood attending the deaths of lovers. Not even Freud or Schopenhauer, in addressing death as the goal of life, managed to use quite as exuberant terms as have Wagner's critics—and Wagner himself. The related music of the prelude was what Wagner saw as catching "a glimmer of the attainment of highest rapture: it is the rapture of dying, of ceasing to be, of the final redemption into that wondrous realm from which we stray the furthest when we strive to enter it by force. Shall we call it Death?"[37] Given this, we would condemn ourselves as creatures utterly immersed in only the "day world" if we chose to see this work as tragic in the conventional sense of the word. Once again, despite their titular similarity, *Tristan und Isolde* is not *Romeo and Juliet:* Wagner's deaths are desired, willed, willing, triumphant. Had he wanted a conventionally tragic ending, Wagner would have kept the original close of the legendary story. There Tristan dies of grief, separated forever (by deceit) from his beloved Isolde. Instead the composer substituted an ending that he himself described in terms that suggest blissful fulfilment of ardent longing, eternal union in eternity.[38] Singers today who must perform these roles are often sensitive to the need to convey this sense of the joy of death—no doubt because such a response goes against the grain of so much of our current Western culture.[39] The response to death by Tristan (as a reverse Orpheus) and especially by Isolde is never grief, and it is their words and not only the music that tells us this.

The final words of the music drama—"most supreme bliss" ("höchste Lust")—are crucial to understanding the meaning of death in relation to erotic love in Wagner's work. The German word *Lust* is, however, ambiguous, for it can mean both "bliss" and the anticipation of that emotion (a longing for it). As such, it perfectly articulates the tension between fulfilment and desire that is at the heart of the entire work, a tension that has been seen as the analogue of the music's lack of harmonic resolution (or its redefinition of it).[40] When Freud later uses the term *Lust* in his writing, he too invokes a further tension inherent in the word and not irrelevant to Wagner's earlier usage: the tension between sexualized desire and the satisfaction of it (and thus a reduction in physical and psychic tension).[41] But it is Nietzsche's use of the very phrase "höchste Lust" in *The Birth of Tragedy* that echoes Wagner's most relevantly. In his typically extreme terms, Nietzsche argued that "it is through music that the tragic spectator is overcome by an assured premonition of a most supreme bliss [höchste Lust] attained through destruction and negation, so he feels as if the innermost abyss of things spoke to him perceptively."[42] Nietzsche offered the third act of *Tristan und Isolde* as his example of this supreme bliss—a bliss that paradoxically has the power to unleash great (Dionysian) powers of destruction within the audience.

This provocative view of the audience reaction to a now redefined idea of tragedy was clearly related in Nietzsche's mind to Isolde's supreme bliss in dying in an eroticized ecstasy. Why? While Wagner adapted or turned away from Schopenhauer on the redemptive possibilities of erotic love, Nietzsche moved away from the same mentor on the topic of tragedy. For Schopenhauer, the aim of the tragic was to represent "grievous suffering, the misery of existence . . . and the final outcome is here the vanity of all human striving."[43] But for Nietzsche, Greek tragedy—and its revival in Wagner's music dramas—did not involve any of Schopenhauer's will-negating resignation. Instead it meant a complex interplay of two forces: the energizing Dionysian powers (cruelty, sexuality, destruction of individuality) controlled by the "illusion" of the Apollonian powers (rationality, form, *principium individuationis*). Nietzsche explained how it is through the spirit of music that the audiences of his day (like the Greeks before them) could "understand the joy involved in the annihilation of the individual." The death of the tragic hero does not, therefore, provoke an Aristotelian catharsis of pity and fear in the audience, but rather creates joy.[44] It is the continued differentiation in life, not the destruction of the individual through death, that is "tragic" in the usual sense of the word. Therefore, to witness onstage the deaths of Tristan and Isolde is not to mourn them, but rather to experience "a higher, much more overpowering joy" (again, "Lust"), an aesthetic pleasure that is the very (re-)definition of the tragic—as exemplified, Nietzsche states, in Isolde's last lines. The "höchste Lust" of the audience, then, comes from the "destruction of the visible world of mere experience"—a world of suffering. For Nietzsche, the Dionysian, with its primordial joy experienced even in pain, is the common source of music and tragic myth. This is therefore, he claims, the source of that most supreme bliss, that "höchste Lust."[45]

The deaths in this opera can be called "tragic" only in a very different sense of the word, in short. Nietzsche's own reaction to a full performance of *Tristan und Isolde* in Munich in 1872 is on record: "This drama of death does not sadden me at all, on the contrary, I feel happy and redeemed."[46] Even after his break with Wagner, Nietzsche retained an ambiguous respect for this work that, he claimed, taught him so much about the Dionysian. The Apollonian power of language and the visual, staged drama must control (again, in his extreme terms) the "Dionysian flood and excess" of the music *for the audience:* without that control, we are likely to "break suddenly," to expire "in a spasmodic unharnessing of all the wings of the soul," as we put our ear "to the heart chamber of the world will" (that is, the music) and feel "the roaring desire for existence pouring from there into all the veins of the world."[47] Schopenhauer had argued that in opera the music is the main cause of audience pleasure, for music is what gives us access to the innermost soul of the events, "the mere cloak and body of which are presented on the stage."[48] It is music that works powerfully on the emotions of the audience, because it is music that both directly expresses the will and acts upon it. That this is not always a pleasurable experience in any traditional sense was accepted by Schopenhauer—and by both Wagner and Nietzsche.

Schopenhauer, however, had a second theory about the power of music upon audiences. He felt that aesthetic contemplation through spectatorship offered a temporary freedom for the disinterested audience, a way to rise above, even for a short while, the phenomenal world of suffering and pain. Tragedy and music offered the highest forms of art for this purpose, with music being supreme because of its immediate relation to will. In other words, to carry this logic a little further, music offers to the audience a temporary presentiment of what the fulfilment of death and erotic love would offer Tristan and Isolde—a state of supreme bliss.

When one critic asks, in passing, whether Wagner might have wanted to illustrate to his audience Isolde's final transformation by having the music dissolve the spectators' individuality too, our answer would be a resounding yes.[49] Just as the ear that has yearned for resolution in *Tristan*'s music is, in the end, satisfied, so the two lovers—through both erotic love and death—cease the restless striving of life and attain final satisfaction. The reduction of tension, which Freud identified with the death instinct, comes together with the reduction of musical tension, and both are made possible, paradoxically, in Wagner's Nietzschean "tragedy" by the power of the erotic. Eros and Thanatos work together and do not struggle against each other in *Tristan und Isolde.*

For the audience of 1865 or of today, this perhaps counter-intuitive, positive evaluation of death as the final consummation of love and the peaceful end to the struggle of living offers a new and different kind of *contemplatio mortis,* one experienced in the theater through the potent coming together of the hauntingly obsessive musical score, the disturbingly repetitive verbal text, and the provocative doublings of the dramatized action. Wagner had to go against the cultural grain to reverse the usual associations—then and now—with darkness and death, and he chose to do so through multiple redundancies that Freud would have understood only too well. These repetitions, however, augment both the meaning and the emotional power of a work in which (to appropriate to new ends the famous terms of John Keats's "Ode to a Nightingale") two lovers, more than "half in love with easeful Death" and each other, pour forth their "soul abroad / In such an ecstasy!"

3

"All That Is, Ends"

Living while Dying in Wagner's
Der Ring des Nibelungen

> . . . thou to death art doomed.
>
> *. . . dir ist Tod geschworen.*
>
> Mozart, *The Magic Flute*

Wagner's *Der Ring des Nibelungen* is famous for many reasons: its music, its Germanic mythic allegory, its sheer length. Called a stage-festival play meant to run three days and a preliminary evening, the *Ring* "cycle," as it is known, runs at least fifteen hours. But it is also an engrossing story of the struggle for a golden ring—and therefore for power—among giants, humans, Nibelung dwarfs, and the Teutonic gods. It contains several infamous love stories: that of the siblings Siegmund and Sieglinde, and also that of their son Siegfried and Brünnhilde the Valkyrie (who happens to be Siegfried's aunt). When people try to recount the story of the *Ring*, they inevitably have to focus their narrative on one of the work's dominant themes or else on a character.[1] Some, like Carolyn Abbate, have focussed on Brünnhilde, the Valkyrie who is reduced to being a mere mortal but who ends up as the engine of redemption.[2] Curiously, however, relatively few have been interested in

Wotan, the major god figure whose actions start the entire plot. Wagner himself, of course, changed his mind, over time, about whose story he wanted to tell: the *Ring* certainly began as the tale of Siegfried's death. (*Siegfrieds Tod* was, in fact, the name of his first sketch based on the medieval tale of the *Nibelungenlied*.) But we argue that it soon became the story less of Siegfried's death than of Wotan's dying, as Wagner not only drew upon other Nordic mythic materials as he wrote his own libretti, but also simply grew older himself.[3]

Watching Wotan's *Ring*

In this chapter, then, our particular focus is not on the strange and estranging drive to death that required so much background to understand in *Tristan und Isolde,* but rather on the much more common and, in a sense, ordinary concern with how we adapt psychologically and spiritually to the knowledge of our death. Changing our approach, we here explore this adaptation theme through Wagner's representation of the process of dying (that is, of living in the knowledge of death). We also speculate on the possible reception of the staging of this theme by modern audiences.

In the West, the general cultural knowledge on the topic of psychological adaptations to death was formed by the influential work of Dr. Elisabeth Kübler-Ross in her controversial 1969 book, *On Death and Dying.* In this she postulated, from clinical observation, a series of stages through which individuals progress in the face of death: shock, denial, bargaining, anger, depression, and acceptance, with hope continuing in all stages. Although each of these responses to the knowledge of the imminence of death has, in fact, been recognized and further theorized, the overall "stage theory," as it is known, has come under devastating criticism.[4] Nevertheless, it is clear that when the notion of mortality changes from being an abstract concept, and therefore a possibly avoidable event in the distant future, to becoming a concrete phenomenon to be confronted in a finite period of time, human behavior alters.

As the cogent critiques of Kübler-Ross's model suggest, a less rigid formulation of the process of adapting to death is preferable. One more flexible model is that of Avery Weisman, derived once again from clinical studies of dying individuals. In works like *On Dying and Denying,* Weisman agrees that death acts both as a "universal phobia" and as something that humans tend to believe can be avoided.[5] The outcome of this belief is that, faced with the certainty of mortality, we are all ill prepared. In Weisman's words, "we face impending extinction with bewilderment, anguish, and whatever denial can be mustered" (p. 13). Weisman notes that, in the process of dying, "the balance between denial and acceptance changes like a kaleidoscope . . . hope and despair are always balanced precariously" (p. 80). He proceeds to describe a kind of death (drawn from his clinical observations) that he calls a good or "appropriate death" (p. 37). In his terms, this is a death that people might choose for themselves—had they a choice. This would be a death that recognizes and resolves residual conflicts, and satisfies whatever wishes are consistent with one's personal plight and ego ideals (p. 41).[6]

Within this kind of medical conceptual framework, we examine the potential impact of the *Ring* story—as *we* shall tell it—on audiences today. Once again, the need to historicize audience response is important, even (or especially) when dealing with a human universal like death. For us, the *Ring* is a moving narrative about Wotan's process of adaptation to the concrete understanding of his imminent end. In other words, it is a kind of Wagnerian *ars moriendi,* a treatise on the art of dying. But it is one whose meaning has changed in the century since its creation. Yet, through Wotan, it still teaches analogically how to prepare for death and specifically for dying the "good" (or "appropriate") death. And such a death is one form that Wagner's famous (and very nine-teenth-century) concept of redemption *(Erlösung)* can take for au-diences in a twenty-first-century secular world.

Deryck Cooke may be only partially correct, then, when he notes that the actions of the Teutonic gods in Wagner's work may not be "immediately intelligible in ordinary human terms" to a contemporary audience.[7] That might well be the case (or so we would hope) for an action such as offering your sister-in-law in payment for building a home—as Wotan does when building Val-halla. But early on in the cycle, Wotan faces both a curse involving death and a prophecy worded in this way: "Alles was ist, endet" ("Everything that is, ends"). And most of the subsequent action of the *Ring* can be seen to center around Wotan's coming to terms with the knowledge of his own demise. And *that* is something we can all find "immediately intelligible in ordinary human terms," even if we (like Wotan) might prefer not to think about it. Freud was neither the first nor the last to remind us that the primary par-adox about death is that, although we recognize that it is our uni-versal fate, we cannot imagine our own death.[8] Once Wotan's end is announced—and his dying, his living in the awareness of death, begins—his attempt to deal with this paradox becomes the driving force of the *Ring* music dramas.

"Alles was ist, endet." This, the earth goddess Erda's other-worldly annunciation of death, prefigures and prestructures the many other announced deaths of the cycle: Siegmund's announced by Brünnhilde; Mime's and Fafner's, by the Wanderer; Siegfried's, by the Rhinedaughters. Each of these characters faces this knowl-edge differently, but as we noted earlier, none has the kind of ex-tended time to confront death that Wotan has—and that the *Ring* audience has. As a recent staging in Brussels and Frankfurt made materially clear by cumulatively amassing the bodies of the slain on stage over the four evenings, the number of people who die—di-rectly or indirectly—of the Nibelung's ring is large.[9] In fact, it in-

Scene from Herbert Wernicke's production of *Der Ring des Nibelungen* at the Théâtre de la Monnaie in Brussels. Archives of La Monnaie, Brussels (photograph).

cludes almost all the major characters. Just as death is at the core of the curse of the ring, so too can the confronting of death and dying be seen as being at the heart of the entire *Ring* cycle itself.

We suggest that this is one of the (usually unacknowledged) reasons for the fascination this work holds. As we argued in Chapter 1, this work too allows audiences to accommodate the painful realities of mortality through the distancing of art, while still experiencing all the emotional intensity that the subject of death inevitably evokes. In 1915 Freud wrote, in his "Thoughts for the Times on War and Death," that we repress consciousness of the inevitability of death and so cannot even deal with the deaths of those close to us, much less our own: we "seek in the world of fiction, in literature and in the theatre compensation for what has been lost in life. There we still find people who know how to die . . . There alone too the condition can be fulfilled which makes it possible for us to reconcile ourselves with death . . . We die with the hero with whom we have identified ourselves; yet we survive him and are ready to die again just as safely with another hero."[10]

The Annunciation of Death

The ancient Teutonic gods—those legendary models from which Wagner drew—were *not* immortal or omnipotent, and their universe was not eternal. These gods were driven by the power of Fate and necessity, and were at the mercy of forces they were powerless to control.[11] The Old Norse term "Ragnarök" refers to the future time of "judgment" of these gods, when giants and demons would attack them. The gods would fight bravely and face death like heroes.[12] This battle would bring about the end of the physical as well as social world. Such is the context for Wagner's gods. In fact, we actually see them withering and greying at one point, with the loss of the golden apples that bestow enduring youth, vigor, and life itself.[13] If Wagner's Wotan often seems more human than divine, he is not, of course, a real person. He is a mythic character operating in an elaborate dramatic plot. But that limitation may be one of the reasons why as spectators we can identify with him, can project onto him our own anxieties and fears, for we too are in the very same position. We know that, for us too, "everything that is, ends."

Yet, as Freud noted, we all show an "unmistakable tendency to put death on one side, to eliminate it from life . . . to hush it up."[14] Ernest Becker, in *The Denial of Death,* expanded on Freud's analysis of this resistance, arguing that our existential dilemma is precisely that we (like Wotan) know that death is our fate, however much we may want to deny it. When godlike reason confronts the fact that it is tied to a dying animal body, it may rebel. So, when Erda's prediction of Wotan's end upsets his complacent existence, the god behaves like the man Becker describes who "asserts himself out of defiance of his own weakness, who tries to be a god unto himself, the master of his fate."[15] But, adds Becker, "[o]nce you expose the basic weakness and emptiness of the person, his helplessness, then you are forced to re-examine the whole problem of power linkages." And to examine power linkages—especially in the *Ring*—you have to start right at the beginning.

However, to tell the beginning of the story of Wotan's *Ring*, we have to go back to actions that take place even before the curtain goes up on the prologue, *Das Rheingold*. (And from there we must move through the events and structure of the narrative of the entire *Ring* to make our argument clear: Wagner was nothing if not systematic.) In the prologue to the last of the music dramas, *Götterdämmerung*, the three Norns—the Nordic versions of the three Fates—not only summarize the action thus far, but also provide new information about things that occurred in the prehistory of the *Ring*. They tell that Wotan drank of the spring at the base of the world-ash-tree, and that he forfeited an eye for the knowledge he gained. He then broke off one of the tree's branches to fashion into his spear. Upon this, he carved the laws and treaties with which he proceeded to rule the world. As a result of Wotan's actions, the tree eventually died; the spring dried up. His act can be interpreted in many ways, but it can easily be seen as Wotan's primal sin against nature, a sin that will later be echoed in the act of the Nibelung dwarf, Alberich, when he steals the gold from the waters of the Rhine. Both are acts of violence against nature undertaken in order to gain power and control over others.[16] In order to expiate these two sins against nature, the Nibelung's ring (fashioned from that stolen Rhine gold) must be returned to the custodians, the Rhinedaughters, and Wotan's world—the world built on those laws, at nature's expense—must end. In Nordic mythology, after all, the ash tree had its roots deep in the kingdom of death. And Wagner drew his ideas for Nibelheim, the home of Alberich, from the old Norse "Niflheim," the place of the spirits of the dead. Indeed, his first prose summary of the *Ring* story on 8 October 1848 opens with macabre gloom: "From the womb of night and death, a race was begotten that lives in Nibelheim (Nebelheim), i.e. in gloomy subterranean clefts and caves; they are called *Nibelungs;* with restless agility they burrow through the bowels of the earth, like worms in a dead body . . ."[17]

In the final *Ring* text—our primary concern here—Alberich is able to fashion his stolen Rhine gold into a ring of power specifically because he is willing to renounce love. Wagner's irony here is most deliberate, for, in Western European culture, the golden ring is traditionally the symbol of love and marital commitment. In the *Ring* cycle, it will regain that conventional meaning only twice: when Siegfried gives the ring to Brünnhilde as a pledge of his love before heading off on his fateful adventures in *Götterdämmerung,* and again at the end, when she takes it from the dead Siegfried's hand and puts it on her own once again, so that it can be restored to the Rhine with her own ashes after her death. For Alberich and the others who covet the ring for other reasons, to be married to power is, in the end, also to be married to death. The golden ring belongs to the Rhine and the Rhinedaughters, as the fire spirit, Loge, keeps telling the gods throughout the first drama. Its very name *(Das Rheingold)* insists on this necessity.

When Wotan violently takes the ring from Alberich and exults in its power, Alberich lays a curse on it, a curse that is the first and the most generic annunciation of death in all the *Ring* dramas: "Now shall its spell bring / death—to whomever shall wear it!" ("nun zeug' sein Zauber / Tod dem—der ihn trägt!"). Even before such a death, the curse elaborates, care and worry will plague all who possess it; greed will devour those who do not ("wer ihn besitzt, / den sehre die Sorge, / und wer ihn nicht hat, / den nage der Neid!"). He continues to music that echoes the threat in his words:

> Forfeit to death,
>   may the coward be fettered by fear;
>   so long as he lives,
>   may he die there, pining away,
>   lord of the ring
>   as the slave of the ring (106).

> *Dem Tode verfallen,*
> *Fess'le den Feigen die Furcht;*
>   *so lang' er lebt,*
> *sterb' er lechzend dahin,*
>   *des Ringes Herr*
>   *als des Ringes Knecht.*

This curse of death, then, is directly connected to the ring and to ownership of it.

With the surprise entrance of the earth goddess Erda, this generic death becomes specifically the gods' end.[18] But she warns Wotan of two separate things: that the ring is deadly and that "everything that is, ends." Wagner added these words, "Alles was ist, endet," only when setting the text to music in January 1854, and a study of the various versions of the work involving this warning theme reveals a growing emphasis by Wagner on the idea of the gods' annihilation, indeed on their self-annihilation.[19] One of the reasons for the addition might well have been the influence of the thinking of the philosopher Ludwig Feuerbach, who felt that the major crisis in a person's life was not the point of death itself but the realization by the living person that he or she would really die: "The choice about what to do about death, then, is the choice about what life to live."[20]

Even with Erda's warnings, even with the gods' horrified witnessing of the giant Fafner's murder of his brother Fasolt in a conflict over the ring, Wotan still does not seem to believe in the power of the curse. He is already plotting how to get the ring for himself, despite having agreed to a treaty that forbids him to do so. The first drama ends with an intimation—spelled out in a new motive in the music—of his "great idea" of how to deny his mortality by assuring his own continuity. The music of what has been called the sword motive,[21] which accompanies the entrance of the gods into Valhalla, points forward to the story of that sword and of the Volsung twins, Siegmund and Sieglinde. This will be Wotan's first (and unsuccessful) plot to recapture the ring, a plot that signals his consistent denial of the inexorability of his world's end. The opening drama concludes with Loge's sardonic assertion that the gods are hurrying to their end, even though they think they will last forever ("Ihrem Ende eilen sie zu, / die so stark im Bestehen sich wähnen"). The very last words, uttered by the Rhinedaughters, condemn all that has occurred in this world. And their harsh words linger on into the next music drama: "False and cowardly / is that which rejoices there above!" ("falsch und feig / ist was dort oben sich freut!").

In a much cited letter to his friend August Röckel in 1854, Wagner wrote: "We must learn to die, and to die in the fullest sense of the word. The fear of the end is the source of all lovelessness; and this fear is generated only when love begins to wane. How came it that this love, the highest blessedness to all things living, was so far lost sight of by the human race that at last it came to this: all that mankind did, ordered, and established, was conceived only in fear of the end! My poem sets this forth."[22] That poem is the *Ring,* of course, and Wagner's obsession with death and dying in general has been well documented. But did death hold the same meaning for him and for his audience as it might today, for us?

In the nineteenth century, death was a major philosophical issue. As Feuerbach pointed out, it determined how you thought about life. The end was also a major concern of science, in the wake of Lyell's 1832 *Principles of Geology* and later Darwin's *Origin of Species* (1859), works that allowed for the extinction of entire species.[23] Although it is a vast generalization, we could say that, over the twentieth century, death became less a philosophical concern or a scientific worry and more a psychological and medical problem. According to Freud, writing earlier in that century, our evasion of death "has a powerful effect on our lives. Life is impoverished, it loses in interest, when the highest stake in the game of living, life itself, may not be risked."[24] What happens today, then, to a twenty-first-century audience watching the story of Wotan's dying?

An analogy may help set the dimensions of the issue here. In *Wagner and the Anti-Semitic Imagination,* Marc Weiner has shown how nineteenth-century audiences would have been especially receptive to certain signs of "otherness" encoded in Wagner's work.[25] But a voice or body type that would have signaled "Jewishness" to Wagner's audience could well have little or none of that meaning for audiences today. Can death—the human universal—also be seen to create specific associations in the minds of particular historical spectators? Yes and no. We argue that audiences today are still going to react to the *Ring*'s dramatization of Wotan's dying, however differently we have come to understand our inevitable end. And what all spectators will respond to is not just Wotan's story itself, but the text's insistent repetitions of the subject of mortality: its many annunciations of death, its frequent resurrection-like awakenings from sleep, its parallels between the (announced) deaths of Siegmund and Siegfried. These structural echoes are reinforced by the obsessive verbal repetitions of the word "Ende" (end)—not "Tod" (death), but "Ende"—a word whose reminder of finality is hammered home by its textual insistence. Instead of a nineteenth-century philosophical context in which to consider mortality, today's audiences, as we've suggested, are more likely to have a medicalized frame of reference. In either context, however,

spectators would be able to recognize that the Wotan of the conclusion of the first preliminary opera, *Das Rheingold*, is a Wotan
who has not yet learned "how to die."

Denial Strategies

Wotan's fear of the end, his denial, and his hope are all responses
that hold firm until he is confronted with his own self-deception
by his wife, the goddess Fricka, in the second music drama, *Die
Walküre*. Wotan explains to her what is in fact his denial mecha-
nism: that his son Siegmund (born of a human woman) is the free
hero who must, without his godly protection, recapture the ring.
But this plan—Wotan's way of denying his end and indeed trying to evade it—is revealed to be a delusion by Fricka. "Depressed"
is a word often used to describe Wotan in the next scene (Act
2, scene 2) in his despairing "monologue" to himself and to his
favorite daughter (born of Erda), the Valkyrie Brünnhilde.[26] According to one musicologist, Wotan's frustration here is "expressed
with a [musical] power which no words could achieve."[27] Arguably, however, words *do* help achieve that power. As Carolyn
Abbate has shown, there is a cumulative force to the repetitions
of the parallels Wotan draws in this monologue between himself and the Nibelung dwarf, Alberich.[28] But there is an equal
force to the obsessive repetitions of the very word—"Ende"—that
Erda had used and that had poisoned Wotan's peace of mind forever:

> . . . [Erda] warned of an everlasting *end.*
> About that *end* I wanted
> to know still more.

> . . . [*Erda*] *warnte vor ewigem* Ende.
> *Von dem* Ende *wollt' ich*
> *mehr noch wissen.* (our emphasis)

Arthur Rackham's illustration of Wotan and Brünnhilde in *Die Walküre*.

As Abbate further argues, Wotan's moment of self-revelation comes through his act of narrating, as if to himself, the story of the loss of "lightness of heart" that came with the knowledge of mortality. The music certainly reaches a despairing climax on the all-important, twice-repeated word "das Ende"—punctuated by a moment of dead silence between them:

> Get away, then,
> lordly splendour!
> Godly pomp's
> boastful disgrace!
> May what I have built
> all fall apart!
> I abandon my work;
> one thing only do I will:

the end—
the end!—
(He pauses in thought.)
And for that end
Alberich provides!

Fahre denn hin,
herrische Pracht,
göttlichen Prunkes
prahlende Schmach!
Zusammen breche
was ich gebaut!
Auf geb' ich mein Werk;
nur Eines will ich noch:
das Ende—
das Ende!—
(Er halt sinnend ein.)
Und für das Ende
sorgt Alberich!

Nevertheless, hope continues to surface throughout this long narrative of depression. Just as the engendering of Siegmund and Sieglinde was a sign of Wotan's denial of his end, so too was his creation of the Valkyries (Erda's offspring), whose task it is to collect the great human heroes fallen in battle and take them to guard Valhalla against Alberich. All these creatures have been part of Wotan's hope to evade the specifically *shameful* end of the gods that Alberich would bring about, were he to regain possession of the ring. Despite a treaty binding him to the contrary, Wotan still wants to obtain the ring for himself. Only thus, he believes, can he ensure the continuation of the gods' world. Brünnhilde's disobedience (as she tries to protect Siegmund, despite Wotan's decree that he must die) provokes a disproportionately powerful anger in

Wotan, an anger caused as much by displaced fury as by the combination of the failure of his own denial mechanisms (and the entire Siegmund plan) and the loss of his power and control—over even his own daughter. But when he learns that the sibling-lover Sieglinde has possession of the fragments of Siegmund's sword, which Wotan broke on his spear, and that she is pregnant, hope can return to combat despair, because another offspring, another agent of his denial, is on the way.

The Wotan we see in that next drama, *Siegfried,* retains this hope, even as he alters his strategy for dealing with his dying. It is as if he wants to make a deal with death, a deal that would go something like this: "I know that the laws of my world (and thus my integrity) prevent me from acting and breaking my original agreement, so I'll stay out of the action here, as long as my offspring can inherit my world." This can only come about if the planned destruction of that world by Alberich (were he to get hold of the ring) can be prevented. For this to happen, his grandson Siegfried (instead of Alberich) must gain possession of the ring from Fafner, the giant now transformed into a dragon.

In this music drama, Wotan has become the character known as the Wanderer, restlessly roaming the world and avoiding Valhalla, with its heroes and Valkyries—those products of his previous denial strategy. Part of his deal with fate, however, means that he must be an observer of, and not a player in, the action onstage. As Alberich reminds him, given his original contract, Wotan cannot take the ring from Fafner himself or the shaft of his spear would shatter. It is not until that spear actually does shatter that Wotan is forced to realize that, once again, he has deceived himself.

Before this realization can come about, Wotan must once more confront Erda, the figure whose announcement of his end caused his unease in the first place. In despair, the depressed god wants to know how to hold back the rolling wheel ("rollendes Rad")—of time, of fate, of mortality:

Primevally knowing
you once thrust
the thorn of anxiety
into Wotan's daring heart:
with fear of a shamefully
hostile end
did your knowledge fill him
so that worry bound his courage.
If you are the world's
wisest woman,
tell me now:
how does the god conquer his anxiety?

Urwissend
stachest du einst
der Sorge Stachel
in Wotans wagendes Herz:
mit Furcht vor schmachvoll
feindlichem Ende
füllt' ihn dein Wissen,
dass Bangen band seinen Muth.
Bist du der Welt
weisestes Weib,
sage mir nun:
wie besiegt die Sorge der Gott?

Despite Wotan's demand, Erda cannot tell him any more, in part because he has asked specifically for knowledge of the future of *his* world—and that world is about to end. It is at this point that Wotan very suddenly and defiantly announces that he is no longer consumed with fear for the end of the gods, but rather wills it. The music, with its rich and dense motivic echoes, reaches a climax of intensity on those words that "will" death:[29]

Fear of the gods' end
does not worry me
since my desire—wills it!
What in the savage pain of dissension,
I once desperately resolved,
    joyous and glad
I now freely perform . . .

Um der Götter Ende
grämt mich die Angst nicht,
seit mein Wunsch es—will!
Was in des Zwiespalts wildem Schmerze
verzweifelnd einst ich beschloss,
    froh und freudig
führe frei ich nun aus . . .

In this alternation between hoping to avoid perishing and believing that he can never in fact do so, Wotan in a sense enacts what Avery Weisman would call "middle knowledge"—that "uncertain certainty" of his own demise.[30] Many have read this as the Schopenhauerian moment of the *Ring*, although this may be a matter of "retrospective discovery."[31] Well before reading that philosopher's work, Wagner had already written both his *Ring* poem and this admittedly rather Schopenhauerian statement: "Wotan rises to the tragic height of *willing* his own destruction. This is the lesson that we have to learn from the history of mankind: to will what necessity imposes, and ourselves to bring it about."[32]

However, is this what Wotan has really done *at this point?*[33] Or will that moment come only later? Another way to put this question is to ask whether Wotan has really accepted his death when he sings the words cited above. Do we believe him? Or is this ostensible shift—and taking of control—really just another form of trying to make a deal with fate? Or is it perhaps a sign of despair, as he indulges in an immortality fantasy, that of bequeathing his world to Siegfried, his grandson, and Brünnhilde, his daughter? However, Erda had earlier implied that not only Wotan but *all his world* must end. He now scornfully commands her to descend again into the earth and behold his end ("erschau' mein Ende!"), not understanding that *his* end alone will not suffice to atone for those earlier violations of nature; the ring must be returned to the Rhinedaughters, and not kept by Wotan's offspring. Wotan does not yet see that his entire world of laws and treaties must end, and with it, Siegfried, for he too has been compromised by Wotan's desire to possess the ring.

There is no doubt that this moment when Wotan seemingly wills his own end is a crucial scene in the drama, one that Wagner added as an important revision from his early *Der junge Siegfried* version.[34] But this scene does not end the act—or the story. If it did, there would be no need for Wotan's humiliation, as his spear breaks on his grandson's sword and he leaves the stage in defeat. The dramatic and psychological function of Wotan's claim to will his personal death is that it underlines the difficulty of precisely the move to acceptance that he asserts he has made. Despite his bravado and his claim to have come to terms with the fear and worry that Erda induced, he has not yet really accepted the end of both himself and his world. He has simply projected his own immortality fantasy forward onto his offspring. He hopes that Siegfried and Brünnhilde will protect his world by keeping the ring away from Alberich. Most significantly, however, Wotan does not plan that they will return the ring to the Rhine. Yet when his spear shatters, the old order of laws and contracts that was engraved upon it shatters too.

Wotan is the character whose actions (in response to his approaching end) have influenced all of the characters—gods, giants, dwarfs, humans—thus far in the story. But Wotan here increasingly manifests what has been called a process of "social dying," a sequence of actions that betrays his declining social involvement.[35] This process is set in motion by his reactions to the advent of his end, and it is because of those very reactions that he starts to cease being an active agent in his own right. Essentially that is how he is now treated by his grandson, Siegfried: as an old man to be mocked or ignored.[36]

Secular Redemption

At this point Wotan disappears from the stage, although his story is continued by the Norns at the start of the final drama, *Götterdämmerung*. Although never again onstage, Wotan continues to be present both as the subject of narration and in the music. Carl Dahlhaus feels that the musical Wotan is even more "powerful and impressive than the indecisive and sometimes wretched god who appears onstage" earlier.[37] Coming immediately on the heels of Wotan's stage humiliation, this new increase in stature can be explained by the fact that the Wotan we now start to hear about—in words and music—is a being who *has,* finally, accepted the reality of his end and, in fact, is preparing the way for his death to be a "good" death. He has cut down the world-ash-tree, which had been killed by his original sin against nature, and has had its logs piled around Valhalla. There he sits, actually awaiting the fire that will bring about the end of the gods.

We learn these and other details of Wotan's story from the desperate Valkyrie, Waltraute, who has left Valhalla in order to beseech Brünnhilde to return the ring (which Siegfried has given her in love) to the Rhine waters. But arguably Waltraute has misunderstood Wotan's current mood: she believes that his self-isolation, his grave silence, and his refusal to eat the golden apples of youth are signs of depression and despair, when they may well be read by an audience as signs of acceptance of his end. The music, in fact, would underline this acceptance. As Carolyn Abbate has pointed

out, when Waltraute describes Wotan sitting in silence, "she does
so to music that resonates . . . from Brünnhilde's pivotal question
in the *Todesverkündigung* [her announcement of death to Sieg-
mund], 'does it mean so little to you, eternal glory?'"[38] Yes, it does
mean so little, to Wotan too—now. This is why he has sent out his
ravens and awaits their return with, as he states, "good tidings" in
order to smile again. Waltraute quotes Wotan saying just what
these good tidings might be:

> "if to the deep Rhine's daughters,
> she gave the ring back again,
>   from the burden of the curse
> god and world would be redeemed."

> *"des tiefen Rheines Töchtern*
> *gäbe den Ring sie wieder zurück,*
>   *von des Fluches Last*
> *erlös't wär' Gott und Welt!"*

To Waltraute (for whom the curse of the ring and the end of the
gods are inseparable—although Erda did indeed present them as
separate), this means that, were the ring restored, the end could be
averted. That is why she has come to beg Brünnhilde. To Wotan,
however, it may mean that, were the ring restored at last, the violations against nature (and his own integrity) would be expiated
and he could then die redeemed, that is (in secular terms) in peace
and with honor, avoiding the *shameful* end of which Erda had
warned.[39] In short, Wotan wishes to die an appropriate or a "good"
death, having put his life's accounts in order; he could then yield
control to Brünnhilde, in whom he trusts.[40]

Before the ring can be returned to the Rhine, however, Brünnhilde must suffer and learn. The ring, once again, must go from
being a token of love to being a token of power. And all this must

happen before the ring can be restored to its rightful place in the order of things: Brünnhilde must suffer and experience the evil power of the ring through Siegfried's betrayal and death.[41] Only then, and in pain, can she hear—and understand—what the Rhinedaughters will tell her. Only then can she prepare for the end that Wotan awaits. With Siegfried dead, Brünnhilde builds a funeral pyre on the banks of the Rhine for both Siegfried and herself—echoing Wotan's pyre constructed around Valhalla. She now understands why she has had to suffer Siegfried's betrayal. Only then would she have seen the ring for what it really was—a token of power, not of love. Only then would she have been willing to return it to its rightful place deep in the Rhine waters. She now knows it is Wotan who is guilty of condemning Siegfried to the ring's curse so that she might come to understand this. And understand she does, telling the ravens to take to Wotan the news he has been awaiting: the news of the ring's imminent restoration to the Rhine waters. At last he can rest; her words, "Rest! Rest, you god!" ("Ruhe! Ruhe, du Gott!"), mark the final and most gentle annunciation of death in the *Ring*. As Brünnhilde joins Siegfried in death, the stage directions announce that Valhalla comes into view with the gods and heroes assembled. As bright flames are said to flare up in the hall of the gods, we can believe, in Waltraute's words, that "then once again / —for the final time— / the god would smile eternally" ("dann noch einmal / —zum letzten Mal— / lächelte ewig der Gott").

The narrative drive of all four music dramas has been toward this final ending of endings. As Valhalla burns, the Rhine overflows its banks, Brünnhilde joins her beloved Siegfried in death, and Wotan can rest at last. The music's rich recapitulation of many of the cycle's motives likewise moves forward to this musical resolution. Indeed, through-composed music like this evades the usual interruptions of minor endings (of arias, and so on) to drive onward to the finale. Despite this death drive, despite all the dead characters onstage, however, these final moments of the *Ring*—like those of *Tristan und Isolde*—manage not to feel or sound tragic. One of the reasons for the strangely uplifting nature of the experiencing of the end of the *Ring* is that audiences (of any century) not only have vicariously experienced the overcoming of the terror of death and dying, but—in our modern terms—they have also come to see Wotan's death as "appropriate." They have watched and listened to Wotan's long process of reconciliation with the idea of "das Ende" and his preparation for a "good" death. This is clearly a secular, twenty-first-century way of reading Wagner's nineteenth-century notion of redemption *(Erlösung),* a word that resonates through the *Ring* as it does through Wagner's other works.[42] But such an interpretation may offer a clue to the continuing power of this narrative of death, even in our modern age, when the social meaning and context of death are so different from what they were in Wagner's time. Wotan—the dying Wotan—was the character with whom Wagner himself came to identify in the *Ring* and to whom he gave the central narrative perspective of the entire work.[43] Wagner's own private and public writings bear witness to an obsession with death and dying that goes beyond the romantically fashionable. "We must learn to die," he insisted.[44] As he once put it: "The last, completest renunciation [*Entäusserung*] of his personal egoism, the demonstration of his full ascension into universalism, a man can only show by his *Death;* and that not by his accidental, but by his *necessary* death, the logical sequel to his actions, the last fulfilment of his being. *The celebration of such a Death is the noblest thing that men can enter on.*"[45]

In Wotan's journey to the end in the *Ring,* Wagner probably came closest to living up to Thomas Mann's description of him as "a great explorer and interpreter of psychological nature."[46] Wotan is not a real person, of course, but the real people watching the *Ring* (either in 1876 or today) can identify—at a safe distance—with his struggle to come to terms with the knowledge of impending death. Freud felt that drama was the potent art form that could "explore emotional possibilities more deeply and . . . give an enjoyable shape even to forebodings of misfortune."[47] He wrote: "This relation to suffering and misfortune might be taken as characteristic of drama." It might be even more characteristic of music drama. What Wagner added to his many mythic sources is, of course, psychological motivation and a certain moral dimension.[48] Since we do not see or listen in a vacuum but in a culture, we are not necessarily going to respond to and interpret the psychological and moral parables of the *Ring* in the same way as Wagner's contemporaries did. But we are going to respond and interpret. And among the things that we are going to find it especially hard to ignore are those fifteen hours of obsessive verbal repetitions of "das Ende" and of echoing narratives of suffering and death that constitute Wagner's particular *ars moriendi*.

4

Orphic Rituals of Bereavement

Else for grief unto death I shall fade.

Sonst gräm ich mich wahrlich zu Tod.

Mozart, *The Magic Flute*

Orpheus accompanied the birth of opera into the world with his song. Jacopo Peri and Ottavio Rinuccini's *Euridice* (1600) is one of the first extant examples of this new art form, and thereafter the European stage of the seventeenth century frequently presented the classical story of the singer-poet whose love for his deceased Eurydice led him to the underworld to try to win her back.[1] This familiar mythic hero needed no excuse to sing, so any requirements of realism for this new dramatic musical form could easily be satisfied. Moreover, his story clearly involved using his musical talent to dramatic ends, that is, to try (even if unsuccessfully in the myth) to redeem his beloved from death. The story's theatrical history in the Italian Renaissance included its telling in the form of "intermedi," not to mention plays and recited poems, but with the seventeeth century came its incarnation in opera, the form that was intended to revolutionize the relationship between music and words. In the centuries since opera's founding moment, then, the story of Orpheus has been read as an allegory of the power of poetry and music, and thus of opera.[2] Although earlier polyphonic music had downplayed the words it accompanied, sixteenth-century madrigals had begun to make their music respond to the ideas expressed. Peri's opera was intended as the illustration of an even newer music that was to recreate the power of ancient Greek tragedy: the Camerata in Florence, of which he was a member, argued the need for monody, a more simplified accompaniment of solo song. Orpheus, the powerful solo singer, was an obvious model to embody this new musical form.

Origins, Lamentations, and Fantasy

The original, classical story of Orpheus is not only about the power of music or even the power of love. It is also a story about the inescapability of death, this time not of the self (as in Wotan's case), but of a beloved. Long before modern grief theory, people had always known that the death of a loved one brings about severe changes in life, self-image, and social role. We believe that the power of this particular plot over the four-hundred-year history of opera has something to do with audiences' recognition—and appreciation—of its enactment of what is essentially a ritual of mourning. As we shall see, even though some operas gave the story a happy ending—the conventional "lieto fine" demanded in the early centuries of opera's existence—the audience knew the original tale ended differently: that Eurydice died not once, but twice (after Orpheus turns to look at her on their way out of Hades, despite the injunction not to do so), and that Orpheus himself was torn apart either by the women of Thrace or the Dionysian maenads, depending on the version of the legend. No staged happy ending would be viewed without this knowledge in the background, that is, without the awareness that the "lieto

fine" was indeed a wish-fulfillment. Just as the poetic form of
the elegy shapes and orders grief, modeling mourners' emotional
course "from anger and despair to consolation,"[3] so we would suggest that Orpheus operas have offered their audiences a structural narrative of loss and bereavement that acts out a ritual of
mourning, often followed by a fantasy escape. Like the *contemplatio mortis* that allowed one to contemplate death for a time
but then cease, exit the imagination, and return to normal life—
changed and better prepared—the early operas about Orpheus
with their happy endings enact in their very form the final step of
cessation and exit through wish-fulfillment: the lovers are reunited,
despite death.

It is not surprising that both the forms and the interpretations
of the Orpheus story would change from the seventeenth to the
twenty-first centuries: the effects of bereavement are remarkably
constant throughout cultures and eras, but rituals of mourning—
the social expression of grief—vary widely and, we would suggest,
so do wish-fullfilling fantasies.[4] For instance, the transcendence of
death by divine intervention—as in Claudio Monteverdi's 1607
opera on this theme—might have been easily accepted by a seventeenth-century Italian audience steeped in the Neoplatonic tradition of Renaissance humanism, but it is not necessarily going to
elicit the same response today—from either audiences or from opera composers and librettists tackling the Orpheus theme. The loss
of faith in the transcendent, after two world wars and a century in
which death was privatized and grief made pathological, has made
for a different context for both the creation and the reception of
the Orphic theme. In twentieth-century operas, it is often the
unavoidability of physical mortality that is faced head on. Wish-
fulfilment will not work. Death is not so much *memorialized* (as in
Monteverdi), as its inevitability is simply *witnessed.*

Nevertheless, all versions of the Orpheus story—in the classical
sources as in the many operas with their different endings—choose

to focus on two things: the first death of Eurydice and the subsequent descent of Orpheus to the underworld to retrieve her. Therefore, his sung lament to the infernal powers is a constant in all the many variations. It is also the greatest challenge for the operatic composer: to write a song, as Julian Budden puts it, "so intensely moving and beautiful that even the laws which govern life and death are for once suspended."[5] It goes without saying that this is no mean trick. In fact, it may be impossible, as every composer facing the challenge has likely realized.[6] Ovid could describe in words the power of such a song and leave it to the fertile imagination of the reader of the *Metamorphoses*. Opera creators, however, must produce the song itself and not only show its power within the story but also ensure its actual, affective power on the audience. To accomplish that, they may have to turn to plot devices, characterization, argument, and so on to help out. Perhaps this problem of convincing the audience is one of the reasons why, in many of the operas, Orpheus's song alone is doomed, in the end, to failure. The underworld audience for the lament is variously moved, impressed, or put to sleep. But in most versions, Orpheus does not redeem Eurydice by his song alone. Nor does he do so forever: as in the myth, a condition is usually set for winning her back, which is, in the end, dependent upon Orpheus's ability to resist turning back to look at his beloved. Through understandable human frailty (in various operas, passion, curiosity, doubt, lack of faith, impatience, jealousy, or insecurity), Orpheus fails, and his final and solitary laments find no sympathetic ears—except those of the audience. In short, it is the more complex complete opera (with its words, drama, and music), and not Orpheus's simple lament, that works the requisite magic.

We know that, in more general social terms, this kind of lament for the dead has traditionally functioned as a link between the living and the dead, bridging despair and hope, and perhaps even bringing comfort and social reintegration through song. It is the sanctioned public manifestation of private grief, usually enacted by a collective of women. In the early operas on this theme, Orpheus's lamentations therefore inevitably stand out as being those of a solo male voice expressing intense personal grief, not communal consolation.[7] They are, at one and the same time, grieving responses to the loss of Eurydice and also seductive attempts to recover her by expressing his distress in such moving terms that the forces of the underworld will relent and restore her to him. In this, they are failures; yet Orpheus is still granted success—temporarily.

Is Eurydice's second dying an allegorical necessity, then, an illustration of the illusory nature of the belief that art can conquer even death? In the end, after all, mortals must die. Orpheus is not really what one commentator calls a "conquerer of death."[8] Is this why the happy ending must be inserted—layered, as it inevitably will be, on top of the audience's knowledge of the myth's familiar ending? Without the "lieto fine," all that art—both lament and opera—can do, in the end, is indeed memorialize (or witness) mortality and its pain, a pain made more acute by love. Anxiety is thus a human constant: we love that which is mortal and is therefore condemned to death. Without the spiritual consolations of transcendence allowed by the Platonic or Platonizing Christian traditions and without the consoling conventions of operatic closure, the mourning of human mortality is inevitable.[9] As we saw in Chapter 1, however, this does not mean that art—these operas, in particular—cannot offer, through their viewing, a transmutation of grief and death, a giving of meaning to these incommensurable realities of life.

In that chapter, we also linked the power of operas about death and dying to that of ritual, but in the Orphic operas, it is not only the *power* but the *structure* of ritual that is invoked. In all ritual, those partaking move out of their normal social setting and into a liminal space (here, the underworld) in which they are transformed, before returning to a new existence. In his well-known discussion of funerary rituals as "rites of passage," anthropologist Arnold van Gennep makes an aside on mourning that is helpful in understanding the continuing power of the Orpheus story in particular. During mourning, he writes, "the living mourners and the deceased constitute a special group, situated between the world of the living and the world of the dead."[10] For audiences, this literally describes the mythic world of Orpheus they know from legend. There, Eurydice is separated from the living, moves to the world of the dead, into which (after her second death) she is finally incorporated. Even in the operas with happy endings, it takes supernatural forces to bring Eurydice out of the world of Hades after Orpheus looks back.

Orpheus as mourner, however, also undergoes an initial phase of separation from the world of the living and a move to the underworld, home of the dead. The next phase of mourning requires a movement back from the world of the dead into that of the living—in the myth, without Eurydice. Even watching and listening to those versions of the story that insist upon the reunion of the lovers, audience members who know the basic elements of the Orpheus story know it as one of loss. They also know that, whatever the choice of ending, what they have witnessed in the central episodes of the opera is a voyage to the underworld and back, which is a ritualized, dramatized enactment of a process of coming to terms with death's finality. If mourning is a set of social rituals designed to help the living get on with life, then what is important here is not the story's actual conclusion but this dual process of the journey to the world of the dead and the articulation of the grief felt at the incommensurability of death.

The ritual process Orpheus undergoes is psychologically realistic as well. The many theories of the stages of grief developed in the last half-century all concur that mourners go from an immediate response—shock, numbness, a sense of disbelief—to experiencing intense feelings of separation, pain, and longing. The move to acceptance of loss and a reorganization of both identity and life is gradual. It is characterized by mood swings in which despair, anger, and guilt can all play a part.[11] Rituals of mourning may well have come into being to order the disruption of social roles created by this normal psychological process of dealing with bereavement. Orpheus' initial journey and lament enact the first phase of this process, but Eurydice's second death necessitates some wish-fulfilling intervention by a deus ex machina to ensure any social and personal reintegration.

Unlike the Ovidian myth, early operas on the Orpheus theme are not unconditionally about the triumph of art (or the poet) over death.[12] They are not even just about the triumph of love; they are about human death and, even more important, the pain of those left behind to mourn and the fantasies they turn to for consolation. The lament of Orpheus has power less through its artistry than through its expression of the profound human pain caused by the death of a loved one. It is this mourning that speaks across the years and miles to audiences even today, audiences with different philosophical sensibilities and operatic expectations. As Ross Chambers has argued, death today is still in some ways considered "ob-scene"—that is, literally "off-stage," peripheral to our conscious attention.[13] Hard to deal with culturally and personally, death and grief can both be, in a sense, unspeakable—except, that is, in ritualized forms that order their chaotic power. Grief in these early Orphic operas is not tamed. It is staged, for the audience to live through vicariously, displaced through the aesthetic form of dramatization. In this sense, the Orpheus story is about an education in pain and grief: Orpheus lives through his grief and "works through" it. For the audience too, the opera is an education in how to *witness* pain, how to live through it by proxy and learn to mourn successfully, even if with the aid of a wish-fulfillment. We go to the theater, where the spirits of the dead appear to us too. Separated from the world of the living, we descend into Hades with Orpheus and are moved by his grief. The rhetorical power of his lament and its expression of the deep knowledge of loss accomplish their magic for us, even if they do not for the infernal powers. This is because the entire opera as a ritual of mourning offers a broader context for the audience's understanding and safe, sympathetic identification.

Early Orpheus Operas: Mourning and Wish-Fulfillment

Of the dozens of works on the Orpheus theme in the early centuries of opera, three stand out for their historical significance as well as their philosophical interest: Jacopo Peri and Ottavio Rinuccini's *Euridice* (1600), Claudio Monteverdi and Alessandro Striggio's *Orfeo: Favola in musica* (1607), and Christoph Willibald Gluck and Ranieri de' Calzabigi's *Orfeo ed Euridice* (1762–1774). One of the founding texts of opera as an art form, *Euridice* was written for the wedding of Maria de' Medici, and this joyous occasion may well explain the choice of a happy ending. In this simplified version of the story, Orpheus wins back his Eurydice; there is no second death; the couple is reunited on earth; and art triumphs. But this description is misleading, for it downplays many of the darker aspects of the libretto. The prologue, sung by "Tragedy," explains the reasons for the changes to the myth, whose impact on theater audiences has usually come by presenting the power of death; but given the occasion of the day, says Tragedy, this stage version will offer instead sweeter pleasures and emotions ("più dolci affetti"). And indeed, the chorus of nymphs and shepherds that opens the opera does sing of love and joy, beauty and valor in the context of the preparations for the wedding of Orpheus and Eurydice. The news of his bride's sudden death, however, brings a stunned Orpheus to lament the loss of (as he lists them) his heart, his life, his hope, and his peace. The chorus protests against cruel death, and

its refrain calls on all nature to weep with Orpheus. Three times
the power of death is lamented, and along with it, the human inability to combat death's finality.

And indeed, humans operating alone in this world do seem to
be unable to overcome death. Orpheus has to be aided by the goddess of love, Venus, who leads him to the underworld, promising
him triumph over death and suggesting that he should pray, sigh,
and implore, for *maybe* ("fors'") then his sweet lament will affect
the powers of the underworld as much as they did her. He takes
her advice, calling on the infernal shades to weep at the sound of
his anguished words ("al suon dell'angosciose mie parole"). Hearing this, Pluto admits that such music would have power if mercy
and lamentations had any role in his realm, but they do not.
Against Orpheus's repeated musical attempts to persuade him
through his grief and art, Pluto remains firm, even though he admits to feeling some new tenderness and emotion. But laws are
laws. Orpheus is forced to acknowledge the failure of his art, and
tries another tack: sympathy, reminding Pluto of his love for Proserpina. And indeed, the human Proserpina will use that love for
her to intercede for Orpheus. Pluto nevertheless continues to invoke the laws of the realm, until Charon suggests that he actually
has the power to break them. It is arguments, in the end, and not
love or grief or song that win over Pluto to sympathy and pity—although, interestingly, he grants to Orpheus the right to claim the
victory for his tears and his beautiful singing ("delle lagrime tue,
del tuo bel canto").

Perhaps in an attempt to attain some degree of mastery or control over the situation, Orpheus is only too willing to accept this
offer and proceeds to praise his own sweet sighs and well-versed laments. The libretto, in short, undoes its own portrayal of an Orpheus, armed only with his lyre, descending to the underworld and
challenging death by his song. Art's triumph is considerably more
mediated and conditional in Rinuccini's libretto than has usually

been admitted—at the time and since. Venus, Proserpina, and Charon have more impact on Pluto's decision to overturn Eurydice's death than does Orpheus with his song. Even when the second death of the beloved is omitted from the plot outline, as here, the triumph of *song* over death is not at all clear—as audiences who knew the myth's tragic ending with its double deaths might well have realized. Even read as a triumph of *love* over death (after all, this was composed to be performed at a wedding), there is a clear wish-fulfillment here: death *is* overcome, but only in fantasy, only in opera.

Alessandro Striggio, the librettist for Claudio Monteverdi's *Orfeo: Favola in musica* a few years later (1607), restored the tragic ending to the tale of the two lovers.[14] Many have agreed with the view that the wedding scene opening Act 1 presents a world in which "we can *believe* that man is in his heaven and all is well with his world. Verse and music celebrate the harmonious union of Man, Society and Nature."[15] But this interpretation ignores, once again, the darker details of the text that seriously undermine that harmony: the pastoral celebrations are haunted by an awareness of the power of death and the ephemeral nature of earthly joy. In what turns out to be a foreshadowing of later action, the first and second shepherds sing of the power of grief and despair: "Let there be no one who in despair / gives himself up in prey to grief, though at times it may powerfully assail us / and darken our lives." ("Alcun non sia che disperato in preda / Si doni al duol, benché talor n'assaglia / Possente sì che nostra vita inforsa.") Orpheus himself can also only sing of his present joy in the context of previous sorrow. In short, it is not simply with the entry of the messenger announcing Eurydice's death that darkness comes into the stage world. Earthly happiness has been presented as illusory from the start because of the reality of human mortality.

Orpheus's brief but poignant acknowledgment of his beloved's death—"Tu se' morta"—employs all the musical devices to manifest grief developed in the madrigal and the lament forms as perfected by Monteverdi in other works.[16] Not surprisingly, the composer himself considered the lament the most essential part of the opera.[17] So too is it for the audience, who must here become convinced of the sincerity of the singer's grief and the power of his song. We cannot feel for Eurydice—for we did not know her. But we can and must feel for Orpheus in his grief at her loss. Orpheus decides he will journey to the underworld to reclaim his bride *if* his verses have any power ("*se* i versi alcuna cosa ponno"). The conditional here suggests his doubt in that power, as does his decision that, should he fail to soften the heart of the king of the shades, he will remain in death's kingdom with Eurydice. In saying farewell to the world of the living, Orpheus begins his ritual of mourning and enters the liminal realm, accompanied by a chorus sung by nymphs and shepherds, which underlines the fleeting quality of the joy of mortal man ("uom mortal").

It is a personified, if deified, human quality, Hope (rather than the more powerful goddess of love, Venus), that guides this Orpheus to the underworld, telling him that on this journey he will need both courage and artistry. Neither will appear to be immediately necessary in his confrontation with the guardian of the river Styx, even though Charon does forbid him entry, as a living human being, into the realm of the dead. Orpheus's arioso "Possente spirto" is a song of persuasion and professional bravura, as well as profound human grief.[18] Confident in the power of his lyre, he sings of his desire to have Eurydice restored to him, but in this version, he sings to this middleman and not to Pluto himself. In the first verses of the piece, as has been pointed out, Monteverdi has Orpheus use "all the sensual artifice of which Renaissance man was capable, rioting in vocal arabesques of fantastic virtuosity, doubled and echoed by voluptuous violins and cackling cornetti, reinforced by a luxuriance of parts for continuo instruments, including of course lyre-emulating lutes and harps."[19] By the last stanzas, however, Orpheus changes his tune, so to speak, and pleads in a more direct and simple, unembellished musical idiom, with a new bass line and chord pattern, as if he knows that he now has to rely on his sheer human grief to move Charon, since the virtuosic show of his art clearly has not worked.[20]

Neither tactic works. Charon admits to being somewhat charmed but refuses to pity Orpheus, a refusal that drives the singer to increased lamentation. Instead of giving in, Charon falls asleep. Here it is not at all the power of Orpheus's song that is emphasized. Orpheus himself, in fact, openly acknowledges his failure. Even if his lyre cannot arouse pity in Charon's stony heart, at least his singing can put him to sleep, he ruefully notes. Stealing Charon's boat, Orpheus crosses the river Styx and enters the realm of the dead. There, as Proserpina recounts, she (like Pluto, but unlike the audience) overhears Orpheus singing as he seeks Eurydice throughout the underworld. She *is* moved to pity by his grief and love, for she too is human and not divine. Interceding on Orpheus's behalf with Pluto, she uses the god's love for her as her most convincing argument. This time he actually does surrender to what he explicitly refers to as her beauty and pleading ("A tal beltà congiunta a tanti prieghi"). Proserpina thanks him specifically for listening to *her* pleas (not those of Orpheus), and the chorus of spirits following her words underlines the victory here, not of art, but of compassion and love.

Out of human failings (jealousy, doubt, impatience) blamed on love ("commanda Amore"), Orpheus loses Eurydice a second time, as he turns around; the chorus of spirits then claims that he conquered hell but was then conquered by his own affections.[21] But even that is not quite accurate: he was *helped* to conquer hell. Upon this second loss, he realizes the truth of his situation: that nothing—no amount of praying, weeping, and sighing—will bring the dead back. Such is the human condition. What his song can and will do is voice his pain and pining grief to himself, to nature, to the obliging, consoling Echo, and of course to the audience. This is what mourning rituals allow: a living through pain and a learning to grieve.

The mourner's father, the god Apollo, however, descends in a cloud to put a stop to these lamentations.[22] As we suggested earlier, this deus ex machina is one a modern audience might find illogical, overtheatrical, or even unnecessary, but seventeenth-century audiences would likely have accepted it as a conventional way to deal with Orpheus's suffering.[23] (And even a twenty-first-century spectator might find some consolation in its artifice and the insurance of satisfying closure.) Scolding his son for giving in to pain and being a slave to his affections—that is, for being human—the distant and coolly rational god tells him that he had delighted too much in transient human happiness earlier and so is disproportionately upset now in his grief. Human mortality is then contrasted with the immortal life Apollo offers Orpheus, a life separated from Eurydice, but experiencing her semblance in the stars. This Neoplatonic apotheosis (allegorically, the quest for heavenly beauty through the love of a beautiful woman)[24] is one way to transcend both the physicality of human death and the pain of human grief. Sorrow here explicitly brings grace. Undercut in its power throughout the opera, art arguably is left in the end with the single role of memorializing both the dead and the grief of the survivor. The form wish-fulfillment takes here is in fact closer to that of more modern times, as we shall see: an immortalization through memory and art, including the art of Monteverdi's opera, in particular.

Perhaps this specific role for art had been foreseen from the very start, however. Striggio's prologue is sung by "Music," not "Tragedy," as in Rinuccini's. But, like her predecessor, Music sings of her power to calm troubled hearts and to inflame frigid minds with anger and love. The ears it can charm are (specifically) *mortal* ears ("mortal orecchio"), but it can inspire souls with longing for the harmony of heaven's lyre. Of course, in one sense, the mortal ears that have been charmed are ours, in the audience. Monteverdi's music and Striggio's poetry ultimately have more success than Orpheus's own music can and does within the opera's story. His lyre and his verse cannot undo death, but the opera's music and words can and do express the pain of human loss. Given the necessity of divine intervention and cosmic transcendence at the end, this version of the Orpheus story enacts not the victory of art or love, but the very human suffering of bereavement. The popular success of this opera, since its rediscovery and reentry into the repertoire in 1904, suggests that the power of the mourning ritual is perhaps just as strong as any consolation offered by its very culturally specific, Neoplatonic allegorical ending.

Although Orpheus operas flourished on the European stage well into the eighteenth century,[25] they began to disappear from the French musical scene in the classical age, until Gluck brought his 1762 Italian version (originally done for Vienna) to Paris, and revised and translated it into French in 1774. Its effect on later French audiences was enormous. Both this version and the 1762 Italian original, to a libretto written by Ranieri de' Calzabigi, openly present a story about Orpheus's mourning. When the curtain goes up on *Orfeo ed Euridice,* the heroine is already dead, and we witness the moving funerary rites at her tomb.[26] To some ears, however, ache replaces agony, as Monteverdi's music of despair gives way to Gluck's representation of the "grief of an artist who turns his melancholy into song."[27] Some have argued that we are seeing here the control of Enlightenment man grieving musically with simplicity and directness.[28] (Others have explained the difference by pointing out that this is the first of Gluck's three "reform" operas, with their ideology of simple plots and purer musical lines to achieve "tragic credibility with the audience.")[29] This Orpheus, unlike that of Monteverdi and Striggio, has more confidence in the power of his lyre to soften sternness. But here too he must have the

aid of supernatural forces. Amore (Love) informs Orpheus that
Jove has allowed him to descend to the underworld to seek to restore his beloved. And, again, the conditionals dominate his gram-
mar and mood: *if* his lyre's sweet sounds work, *if* his divine song is
successful, he will be victorious ("*Se* col dolce suon di tuo lire, / *Se*
col tuo cantar divin")—that is, if he doesn't look back at Eurydice.
It is Amore, not Pluto, who gives the injunction not to look back
here. It is love who warns him to restrain his desire.

Orpheus descends into the underworld, playing his lyre, begging the scornful spectres to listen to his "barbaro dolor." It is this
"barbarous pain" that will move them, not simply his accompanying music, as Orpheus acknowledges when he sings that, if they
could see his pain, they'd have pity. After considerable (musically
exciting) resistance, the furies give way and open the gates of hell
in the face of this suffering. It is not the song alone, once again,
but the human pain of mourning expressed in it that moves them,
as it had moved Jove earlier. There is no confrontation with Pluto
in this version, but only with the spirits in the Elysian Fields.
Again, after Eurydice's second death, Orpheus blames love and
calls for death, for he believes this to be his final loss. In his famous aria, "Che farò senza Euridice" ("What will I do without
Euridice?"), his extreme emotion is presented in a simple lament
in C major. He is prevented from killing himself by the deus-ex-
machina return of Amore. Telling Orpheus that he has proved a
model of constancy and love and so deserves to be released from
suffering, it is Amore—love—not art that has control now. This
wish-fulfillment is closer in spirit to Ovid's "vincit Amor" for it is
love, not art, that finally defeats death and restores Eurydice to Orpheus. As Amore puts it: "No more deny / my power. / From that
painful reign, / I come to free you" ("Più non negar / La mia po-
tenza. / Dal doloroso imper, / Vi vengo a liberar"). Death does
seem to have been overcome. The lovers remain on earth, together.
The move here is not one of transcendence to a heavenly realm,

but instead, since these lovers are clearly mortal, they are offered what one critic calls a "temporary panacea well earned."[30]

We're told that audiences at the time liked the happy ending, not least because it saved them from going home "burdened with compassion."[31] Today's audiences may require (or at least desire) something else. The "lieto fine" convention in opera gave way, in the nineteenth century, to an increased sense of both the tragic and the realistic, and by the twentieth century there had been another change in sensibility. German director Harry Kupfer's radical and successful updating of Gluck's opera for Covent Garden in 1991 suggests the impact that the last two hundred years of operatic and cultural history have had on directors as well as audiences. Not only is the production set in our time—this Eurydice dies not of a snake bite but in an accident, attended by an ambulance—but it presents grief in ways a modern audience, accustomed to film and television representations, might recognize. This guitar-toting Orpheus is hurt and angry at his loss; he ends up in a hospital, where the voices of the furies are those he hears in his head. He carries with him the fetishized reminders of his beloved—her shoe and later her wig. This is Gluck's Orpheus effectively reenvisaged for an age in which grief is not only medicalized but made pathological, that is, not normal.

Modern Operas of Mourning: Pathological Grief

After Gluck, the Orpheus theme seemed to all but disappear as a subject for serious opera. Given the nineteenth century's clear obsession with death and its complex grieving rites, this may mean that the particular consolations of mourning rituals moved off the stage and into daily life and other forms of art. (This was the period Philippe Ariès called "Thy Death," when the focus of social practice changed from the dead to the bereaved.) It was not until the twentieth century that Orpheus reappeared in new opera nar-

ratives. Nineteenth-century Paris was certainly much taken with
Pauline Viardot singing Orpheus in Hector Berlioz's 1858 rework-
ing of Gluck's opera, but Jacques Offenbach's parodic *Orphée aux
enfers* of the same year and a spate of other operetta treatments suggest that this had become such a staple plot that it could at this
point actually be mocked. But the other arts—especially the visual—took up the Orphic obsession, concentrating with equal frequency on Orpheus as the suffering mourner and as the civilizing
poet.[32] And, of course, many instrumental music pieces of the time
(such as those of Berlioz and Liszt) commemorated Orpheus in
their titles. In its attraction to melodramatic and tragic source
texts, nineteenth-century opera moved away from staging Orphic
stories about mourning the death of *another* to presenting tales of
the violent and dramatic death of the *self*.

If it is true that, in the nineteenth century, talk of sexuality was
taboo but nevertheless generated massive interest and an enormous
amount of discourse (as Michel Foucault has influentially argued
in *The History of Sexuality*), we could say that, in the twentieth
century, it was talk of death that both was repressed (in general social contexts) and yet flourished (in artistic ones). Art forms—from
poetry to drama, from visual art to opera—were obsessed with
death and dying, despite the fact, as many have argued, that for a
long time there was little room in modern public space for talk
about this, the modern taboo.[33] With the loss of the consolations
of religion, it was said that death made no sense. Death threatened
with its absence of meaning, its existential isolation of the individual. As death became medicalized, Orpheus's mourning could seem
pathological, as a director like Kupfer knew. The reluctance of earlier periods to stage operatically the death of Orpheus himself was
overcome, in opera as in the plastic arts. Almost all the visual representations of his death date from the last 125 years.[34] In a world
that had seen mass destruction, that had journeyed into a wartime
hell, the death of a poet was horrible but all too familiar. It could

even be staged in all its mythic violence, as it was in Stravinsky's 1948 ballet and Alfredo Casella's 1932 chamber opera, *La Favola d'Orfeo*.[35]

Just at the moment when the nineteenth century's elaborate social rituals of mourning were being left behind, art works began to reclaim the mourning process for themselves. Likewise, just when modern urban life was ceasing to make time for death,[36] art tried to keep alive an awareness of it. The modern elegy was reborn at the time that Orpheus made his return to the operatic stage.[37] The decline in religious belief, the reality of longer life spans, the medicalizing of dying, the professionalizing of mourning rites, and the disappearance of the social symbols of grief (wearing black, hanging crepe) coincided with a moving of grief and mourning out of the public and into the private realm. There are no pastoral choruses of grieving nymphs and shepherds in modern Orphic operas to share bereavement in a social and communal context. There is no easy translation of tragedy into consolation through wish-fulfillment; there is no transfiguration of the dead through nature, the divinity, or even, at times, the memorialization of art. If anything, the usual consolations offered audiences watching an Orphic ritual of mourning are refused or at least made conditional. All the signs of what Jahan Ramazani has called the "vexed experience of grief" in our time are visible in these operas too: the "moral doubts, metaphysical skepticisms, and emotional tangles" are all there on stage.[38] But so too is the sense that grieving is still a necessary and human act that cannot be denied, no matter how extreme or how pathological. In Ramazani's words, "death and mourning help to deepen, enlarge, and intensify subjectivity in the face of an increasingly bureaucratic and de-humanizing economic life." Perhaps that is why audiences today still respond to operas about grief and why composers and librettists once again began presenting new ones on stage in the last century.

Symbolically, the twentieth-century Orpheus figure cannot *not* look back: his Eurydice has to die her second and final death in some form. This Orpheus only exists as the bereaved lover and poet, and so Eurydice must die.[39] He needs death and grief to create. The earlier Orphic operas had presented both the power of Orpheus's song (over the audience) and its limitations (over Eurydice's fate). The later ones portray a more complex and fraught relationship between art and bereavement, between creativity and loss. Philip Glass's 1992 *Orphée* (based on the scenario of Jean Cocteau's 1949 film) is a modern story of the poet's own Death (now a character) as the source of both love and inspiration in the face of loss. Death enters from a mirror, looking as beautiful as Orpheus always thought she would ("comme les gens veulent me voir"). The narcissism of the scene underlines the fact that this is more a tale of Orpheus's mortality than one of his mourning for Eurydice.

Ernst Krenek's earlier (1926) *Orpheus und Eurydike,* an operatic adaptation of an expressionist play by Oskar Kokoschka, uses the Orpheus myth to explore the fate of artistic creativity in the face of sexual passion and death, but does so in a considerably more anguished mode. Kokoschka's turbulent love affair (1912–1914) with Alma Mahler and his serious wounding in action in World War I had played significant roles in the strong (and often negative) views on love, death, and art presented in the play and opera.[40] The expressionistic ritual of mourning enacted on stage here is not easy to witness for either characters or audience. In this version of the story, despite the protection of Psyche, Eurydice is taken to the underworld by the Furies to live for seven years, to forget Orpheus. After the seven years have passed, Orpheus descends in order to offer his own life as ransom for one more summer with her. (This echoes the Proserpina myth, making explicit what was implicit in the earlier operas that also feature Proserpina: the link between death and rebirth within the tradition of fertility rites.) Psyche warns him not only to avoid looking at Eurydice, but also to avoid mentioning the time spent with the god Hades. He cannot resist asking, however, and learns that, with Psyche's help, she had in fact resisted Hades' advances for almost the full seven years. When her loyalty to Orpheus so impressed Hades that he agreed to let her return to him, she suddenly found Hades attractive and willingly gave in to his desire. Eurydice's increasing anger at Orpheus during this narration leads to her voluntary return to death and Hades: this is a different second death.

Different too is the end of Orpheus: he dies, strangled by Eurydice, who proclaims her final freedom. Unlike the other versions, this is a story about the impossibility of lasting love—or even compatibility—between the sexes.[41] But it is also a story of the ambivalence of mourning—of the inextricability of love and hate, as well as of sexual attraction and artistic creation. All Apollonian transcendence is denied. Characters die, not once but twice; a Dionysian Dance of Death is actually staged. In Freudian terms, this Orpheus cannot withdraw his passion from his lost object of desire; he must die first. Freud's description of the melancholic mourner—with his dejection, his loss of interest in the outside world, his loss of a capacity to love—describes this Orpheus. The physical desire he is supposed to be able to withdraw from the dead object cannot be extinguished.[42] Eros and Thanatos are not easily separable in this twentieth-century reconfiguring of the myth, which can easily make audiences uncomfortable with its frank enacting of a pathological kind of bereavement.[43]

Just as pathological an example would be the protagonist of Richard Strauss and Hugo von Hofmannsthal's *Elektra* (1909), who betrays many of the same symptoms and behavior associated with pathological grieving in her excessive and prolonged mourning for her dead father, Agamemnon. Until the end of the opera, there is no working through of Elektra's grief. The action opens with a representation of her repeated and, in a way, stereotypical laments: each evening, at the same time, she returns to the site of his murder to bewail her loss. It is made clear to the audience by Elektra and others that excess of grief has left her socially marginalized, physically altered, and psychically marred.[44] When *Elektra* premiered in 1909, Freud's theories of hysteria were used by reviewers to try to understand (and condemn) its protagonist. But by 1920, when Erich Wolfgang Korngold and "Paul Schott" (the pseudomym of Korngold's father) were creating *Die tote Stadt (The Dead City)*, it would have been Freud's theories about mourning and melancholia that would have been in the air (the essay of that name dates from 1917). This opera, therefore, remains "Orphic" in more ways than one. Based on, but radically altering, Georges Rodenbach's novel *Bruges la morte* (and the play adaptation, *Le mirage*), this opera offers audiences an extended meditation on (and staged confrontation with) mourning—initially pathological and, in the end, normalized. Since readers (like audiences) are less likely to be familiar with this work, our discussion is somewhat extended here.

Set in late-nineteenth-century Bruges, described as a dead city, the opera opens in late autumn in a memorial room, which the protagonist, Paul, calls a "church of what once was" ("Kirche des Gewesenen") dedicated to the memory of his dead wife, Marie. In it stands a life-size portrait of the deceased playing an Orphic lyre; a braid of her golden hair is preserved under glass. Paul worships the past—his dead wife, his dead city, as he puts it ("Die tote Frau, die tote Stadt"). The audience is told that suddenly his behavior has changed utterly: he wants the locked room opened because, in his words, the dead arise: "Die Toten stehen auf!" (This resurrection theme will recur throughout the opera as a signal of the stages of Paul's grieving process.) Paul has met a young woman who is his dead wife's exact physical double and has invited her to his house. Excited, he tells his friend Frank about this in terms that suggest pathology: "in her comes / my dead one, comes Marie" ("in ihr kommt / meine Tote, kommt Marie"). Frank warns Paul not to make himself the master of life and death, and not to force a living woman to stand in for a dead one. He accuses him of living too long alone with his grief and says he should simply enjoy a new love. Paul ignores this advice and repeats, compulsively: "In her who comes, comes Marie, / comes my dead one" ("In ihr die kommt, kommt Marie, / kommt meine Tote").

Left alone, Paul speaks to the portrait of his dead wife about the secret bond of their souls. Then Marie's double—named in the diminutive as Marietta—arrives. While the audience knows little of Marie other than what the still portrait and her husband's continuing reverence suggest, Paul's response to Marietta's entrance convinces us that, although she is certainly Marie's physical double (even in her dress), she will likely not fit Paul's image of his dead wife in other ways. This "serenely" uninhibited, erotic young dancer is an amiable but naive, spoiled theatrical beauty who finds both the city of Bruges and the memorial room too oppressive. Paul hands her his wife's lute and asks her to sing for him. What she sings is, for her, an uncharacteristically sad song about, as its opening lines put it, a true love that must die ("Das Lied vom treuen Lieb, / das sterben muss"); Paul joins in and sings with her a second verse in which the parted lovers will meet again, despite death. In what will not be the last echo of Wagner's *Tristan und Isolde* in the libretto text, they sing:

Death does not separate us.
If you once have to go from me,
believe, there is a resurrection.

Sterben trennt uns nicht.
Musst du einmal von mir gehn,
glaub, es gibt ein Auferstehn.

The audience is likely to be moved by this poignant and beautiful song (known as the Lute Song), which becomes a recurring motive in the opera.[45] Paul is certainly shaken and transformed by the mu-

sic and, no doubt, by the theme of resurrection. But Marietta de-
clares it a silly song. For her, in contrast, it is the physical joy of
dance that moves her, and she then describes and dances for him
"the last kiss of love" ("ich tanz den letzeten Kuss der Liebe!").
This is perhaps an echo of Strauss's 1905 *Salome,* with its seductive young princess dancing before Herod to win the head of
Jochanaan (John the Baptist) in order to kiss his lips, and serves to
construct Marietta as a classic operatic femme fatale. Appropriately, then, Paul is both attracted and repelled. He tries to embrace
her and in the ensuing scuffle, she accidently uncovers the portrait
and sees . . . herself. Although he has in fact been conflating the
two women in his mind, Paul now cannot reconcile the physical
similarity with the difference in character. He denies that it is an
image of her, telling Marietta that the woman pictured in it is
dead. An offstage song about love in the present is then heard in
counterpoint to Paul's pathological obsession with the past. Although the young woman must leave to go to an opera rehearsal,
she insists that her magic is as strong as the portrait's, and Paul is
left torn between his feelings of love for Marie and his desire for
Marietta.

At this point—diverging from the source text—a dream begins,
and will continue almost to the end of the opera, although even
reading the libretto, one senses that the audience may have as
much difficulty separating dream or illusion from reality here as it
does in Schoenberg's 1909 *Erwartung.* Marie steps out of her portrait to question Paul about his fidelity to her; he insists he has
been faithful, that she is always with him, everywhere in the dead
city. She says he'll forget her nonetheless because she does not live
and breathe beside him anymore. As if warning him to cease his
obsessive grieving, she says: "Go into life, another lures you—look,
look, and recognize." ("Gehe ins Leben, dich lockt die Andre— /
Schau, schau und erkenne"). To the music of the Lute Song, Paul
swears that their love is, was, and will always be ("Unsre Liebe ist,

war und wird sein"). As the illusion of Marie fades, Marietta's image replaces it, dancing seductively in the same costume. Act 2
continues the dream, with the voice of Marie repeating her injunction to go into life. The scene then changes. Shocked by his own
desire, Paul is pacing in front of Marietta's home, where he meets
Frank, who has also fallen in love with her. He tells Paul he is
wrong to divide Marietta between life and death and should leave
her sensuous youth and beauty to him instead and go home to his
dead wife.

A group of theater performers and their hangers-on arrive at the
same quai. They begin to sing in order to try to transform moody
Bruges into a more romantic Venice; the men all vie for the affections of Marietta, in particular. She agrees to perform for them the
role she has been rehearsing, a dancing part from Meyerbeer's opera, *Robert le diable,* in which she is to rise out of her shroud and,
once awakened from the dead, seduce Robert. On cue, the Director whistles the resurrection motive from the opera and Marietta
begins to dance. Paul cannot stand what he sees as a travesty and
stops the impromptu performance: "You, *resurrected from the dead?*
Never!" ("Du eine *auferstandne Tote? Nie!"*). Yet, what else has she
been in his own imagination? Berating her for besmirching his
dream of love, he says he was really kissing, touching, hearing his
dead wife, not her. Accusing her of being an unworthy double, a
mere shadow of his real beloved, he says he hates her for defiling
his grief. Marietta calls him ungrateful and reminds him of his
physical pleasure in her youth and sensuality, claiming instead to
have made his dream come alive. Twice Paul insists he has betrayed
both Bruges and Marie, while Marietta tries to seduce him, offering him the warmth and sweetness of the present and a chance to
forget the past.

She insists on returning to his house, in fact, to Marie's memorial room, to banish the ghost forever, and, Tristan-like, Paul
agrees, as he puts it, to drink the potion of forgetfulness. They

leave for his place. It is not accidental that the Tristan story, as told by Wagner, is, as we have seen, a reverse of Orpheus's journey. The next morning Marietta addresses the portrait in words that bring the Orphic associations to the fore:

> For the second time you died,
> you proud one, because of me,
> because of me, the living one,
> in a night of love!

> *Zum zweitenmal starbst du,*
> *du stolze Tote, an mir,*
> *an mir der Lebenden*
> *Liebesnacht!*

Paul, overcome with guilt and worried about what the neighbors might say if they saw her, shows himself to be not only bourgeois but religious, and is mocked for his superstition by Marietta. The young woman insists that she has fought her way from the gutter to enjoy life and that no dead woman can take that from her. Paul forbids her to compare herself to Marie, who was pure. Marietta fights back, woman against woman ("Weib gegen Weib"), the hot-blooded living pitted against the pale, painted dead. Taking Marie's golden braid from its shrine, she laughs and dances with it to music that suggests, in its rhythms and instrumentation, the infamous "dance of the seven veils" in *Salome*. She mockingly wears the braid as a necklace, until Paul can take the taunting no longer, and strangles her with the braid. In horror, he speaks (or rather, whispers) the telling words: "Now she looks just like her—*Marie!*" ("Jetzt gleicht sie ihr ganz—*Marie!*").

The dream ends. Paul awakens as Marietta returns for her umbrella, hinting that she'd be willing to stay. Paul does not take her up on this. In the play (and novella) on which the opera was based,

the murder is real, not dreamed, a macabre and violent finale of a
story about death, decay, and sexual obsession beyond the grave. In
Korngold's hands, this becomes instead a story of mourning and,
as we shall now see, healing. To his friend Frank, Paul admits that
his dream destroyed his fantasy of love, and put his entire prolonged and excessive grieving into question:

> The dead send such dreams
> when we too much with
> and in them live.
> How far should our sorrow go,
> how far *must* it [go]
> before it uproots us?

> *Die Toten schicken solche Träume*
> *wenn wir zu viel mit*
> *und in ihnen leben.*
> *Wie weit soll unsre Trauer gehn,*
> *wie weit* darf *sie es*
> *ohn' uns zu entwurzeln?*

Appropriately, he now decides to try to leave the dead city of
Bruges, the site of his pathological mourning, and accepts that, despite what the Lute Song had claimed earlier, life does separate one
from the dead: "Leben trennt von Tod." The resurrection theme,
mocked in Marietta's dance, but heralded from the opening, is here
recognized for the fantasy it was, as Paul asks Marie to wait for him
in heaven, for here on earth there is no resurrection: "hier gibt es
kein Auferstehn." The slow waltz music to which he sings these
words is, once again, that of the hauntingly beautiful Lute Song.
The new words he gives it this time signal the transformation of
his grieving into an acceptance of loss.[46] In pain, but determined,
he walks out of the memorial room.

Through his dream, Paul descended like Orpheus into the underworld, but this time it is an underworld of his own desires. This particular ritual of mourning is a pathological one, as he comes to realize. Only after it, however, can he return to the world of the truly living and follow the injunction of his wife at the start to "Go into life." Now he can mourn successfully, rather than remain what Freud would call a melancholic, with his passion still intact for his dead wife. Freud's insights into the consequences of failed mourning may not have been far from the minds of the opera's creators, but for the audience, both then and now, the generally pathological nature of Paul's extended and extreme response to his bereavement is hard to miss. This Orphic figure too goes through an education in grief, as does the audience, but this time it is an education in avoiding the excesses that poison life in the present.

In all these "Orphic" examples of *contemplatio mortis*—whether they be wish-fulfilling or pathological in their grieving—the death that is witnessed is that of another, indeed, of a loved one. Social reactions to such loss obviously change over the centuries, but Orpheus's story has lived on, in part because we can always count on its power: its staged—and therefore controllable—enactment of the ritual of bereavement that is the fate of every human who has ever cared for another.

5

"'Tis a Consummation Devoutly to Be Wish'd"

Staging Suicide

> Madness now doth cloud her brain;
> Thoughts of self-murder make that plain!
>
> *Wahnsinn tobt ihr im Gehirne:*
> *Selbstmord steht auf ihrer Stirne!*
>
> Mozart, *The Magic Flute*

Opera was born in the late Renaissance, a time we now see in retrospect as one in which the arts and new sciences flourished in the wake of the recovery of ancient learning. Of course, it was experienced at the time somewhat differently. As Georges Minois explains in his *History of Suicide,* it was a time of upheaval that reached a point of crisis in values—of which reflection on suicide was one sign:

> The pervasiveness of debate on suicide, a topic of conversation even in the courts of kings and the leading salons, reveals a crisis of conscience in the realm of culture. The shift from scholasticism to analytical reason, from a closed world to an infinite universe, from humanism to modern science, from a world described in terms of qualities to a mathematical language, from innate truth to methodical doubt, from certitude

to critical questioning, and from Christian unity to a division between rival confessions could not be made without weakening the entire value system. Fractures typical of times of crisis occurred in the years from 1580 to 1620, a time of transition when the modern mind was forming.[1]

These same years saw suicide become an important theme on the dramatic stage, as witnessed by Shakespeare's deft exploiting of its theatrical potential. It is no accident that his Hamlet's words form the title of this chapter. Opera too was not slow to explore the subject, and soon the self-inflicted deaths of historical figures like Seneca and literary ones like Dido were represented on stage. Contemporary audiences could see played out before their eyes and ears the intellectual concerns of the age. Self-murder, as suicide was then known, meant many things at this point in history: for some, it was sinful or criminal; for others, it was a sign of weakness or even madness. But now it could also be seen as a rational response to life, thanks to the example of the many ancient philosophers and public figures who had taken their own lives—examples that had recently been brought to people's attention by the rediscovery of that ancient learning.[2]

Self-Murder: Sin, Crime, Rational Choice

Twenty-first-century audiences carry much moral and psychological baggage about suicide: all these associations continue, layered through history, and new ones have been added. Besides the now familiar medicalization of suicide as a sign of mental illness, twentieth-century existentialist thought once again raised the question of suicide as a philosophical issue. As Albert Camus famously put it: "There is but one truly serious philosophical problem, and that is suicide. Judging whether life is or is not worth living amounts to

Seneca committing suicide in a bath. Engraving by Jean François Peyron, 1773.
Wellcome Library, London.

answering the fundamental question of philosophy."[3] Audiences
today watching operas on the topic of suicide inevitably have to
confront their own ethical position on the taking of one's own life.
After all, suicide is not the same as just any death; it is voluntary
death and as such, it poses a moral problem for audiences. As
Maurice Blanchot pointed out, "it accuses and it condemns; it
makes a final judgment."[4] As a form of narrative closure, suicide is
problematic in both emotional and ethical terms.

Suicide would appear to be a constant in human history, but its
meaning and thus its acceptability change with the time and the

culture. Despite being an individual's act, suicide is a social phenomenon too—or so we believe today, ever since sociologist Emile
Durkheim's influential *Le Suicide* in 1897.[5] Philosophical, religious,
moral, legal, and cultural issues, not to mention psychological and
medical ones, also enter in, but all are arguably at least rooted in
the general category of the social. As we shall see, on the operatic
stage it is often the individual's relation to society that frames and
conditions the decision to take one's own life. Audiences are sometimes presented with powerful indictments of an alienating and exploiting society that drives people to their deaths—as in Alban
Berg's *Wozzeck* (1925) or Benjamin Britten's *Peter Grimes* (1945). At
other times, suicide is presented as a sacrificial ritual in the context
of a society that looks positively upon such an act: strikingly, the
protagonists of these works are usually both women and non-Eu-
ropean. Cio-Cio-San from Giacomo Puccini's *Madama Butterfly*
(1904) is perhaps the best-known example. The individual and the
social are not separable in operatic representations of suicide.

   The question remains: will a twenty-first-century audience respond to this linking of suicide and the social order in the same
way as, say, a seventeenth-century one? As mentioned earlier, the
plurality of responses to self-murder in the Renaissance included,
through those many examples from the ancient classical world and
the philosophical tenets of the Stoics and Epicureans, the notion of
rational choice—that is, that suicide was both acceptable and ra-
tionally justifiable under certain circumstances. One of the most
famous suicides of antiquity had been that of Seneca, for whom
suicide was "the only genuinely free act."[6] When ordered by Nero
to kill himself, Seneca—modeling himself on Socrates—actively
and consciously chose to die. In his writings, Seneca had already
argued that the tyranny of a despot was one of the social circumstances under which suicide was justifiable.[7] In Nero's Rome, suicide authorized by the state was, in fact, legal. And, as Seneca insisted, not clinging to life was actually a virtue. In Durkheim's

terms, Roman society at the time was one in which "the man who renounces life on least provocation of circumstances . . . is praise-worthy."[8]

Seneca's death was one of the first suicides to be represented on the operatic stage. In Claudio Monteverdi and Gian Francesco Busenello's *L'Incoronazione di Poppea* (1643), Seneca expounds his teachings about reason over passion, but he concedes to the tyrant Nero that the poorest argument is bound to win when power contends with reason ("quando la forza alla ragion contrasta"). When Nero orders his suicide, Seneca accepts at once, telling the messenger: "You announce my death, ask not my pardon: / I laugh while you confer so great a gift" ("Se mi arrechi la morte, non mi chieder perdono: / rido mentre me rechi un sì bel dono"). As he prepares to die, he sings: "Friends, the hour has come to practice / the virtue that I have praised so greatly. / Death is a momentary anguish" ("Amici, è giunta l'hora di praticar infatti / quella virtù che tanto celebrai. / Breve angoscia è la morte"). The opera here lays out clearly the Renaissance understanding of suicide in the ancient world.

However, the stark severity of Seneca's death is softened for the audience (and for the operatic Seneca) by the narrative context in which it is presented. In the opera, after Pallas Athene had warned of impending disaster, Seneca immediately accepted the idea of his death, curiously stating that "death is the dawn of an infinite day" ("è di giorno infinito alba la morte"). We then learn from Mercury, sent by Pallas Athene, that Seneca is indeed to pass "into the eternal and infinite" ("all'eterna ed infinita"). This postulation of an afterlife is perhaps a subtle Christianizing of Senecan philosophy, likely making the scene more palatable (or simply understandable) to Monteverdi's audience.

Yet those same spectators would have watched this validation of rational suicide against a background of religious, legal, and what today we would call psychological injunctions *against* suicide. In the Middle Ages, the European view had been the opposite of the ancient classical one of suicide as rational; from this medieval perspective, to take one's life was always irrational, and the despair or madness that brought on the desperate act were instigated by the devil. From the Council of Braga (563 C.E.) onward, canon law decreed that suicide was a mortal sin, and the sinful deceased was refused religious rites. This influenced all continental European law thereafter: suicide and attempted suicide were criminalized—with resulting economic forfeitures and various prescribed indignities to the dead body.[9] The Church Fathers had debated suicide for centuries, but no one was more influential than Augustine (354–430 C.E.) in articulating the Christian position that "Thou shalt not kill" applied to the self as well as to others. In *The City of God,* he was responding in part to the various early religious groups (such as the Donatists and Circumcellions) who were given to mass suicide and thus, they believed, martyrdom in the state of grace.[10] Thomas Aquinas (1224 or 1225–1274 C.E.), in his *Summa Theologica,* later specified the particular reasons for the sinfulness of suicide: it was contrary to the "inclination of nature" and to charity; it was an injury to the community of which the individual was a part; and life was God's alone to give and take.[11]

Clearly, the (secular) world of the theater—here represented by Monteverdi's opera—both reflects and reflects critically upon this Christian context, in this case offering a classically inspired response to the dominant ideology. In so doing, it in a sense enacts in dramatic form the intellectual ferment of the Renaissance with its challenge to traditional values.

Suicide: Secular, Romantic, Medical

Modern Western audiences inevitably bring with them all or part of this history of suicide as criminal and sinful, as a sign of weakness or even insanity, or as rational choice, because our current perspectives have been informed by centuries of debate in which suicide was alternately defended and condemned.[12] The coining of the actual term "suicide" in English in the seventeenth century suggests "evolving opinion and an increasing amount of debate."[13] In the seventeenth and eighteenth centuries suicide did indeed become an important point of reference in ethical discussions among philosophers and poets as well as prelates.

Over the years, suicide gradually became secularized. Seen neither as a religious sin nor, especially after the French Revolution, as a criminal offense, it was at once rendered psychological, sociological, and medical. From the medieval idea that suicidal despair was prompted by the devil, there was a move to see it as a sign of what Robert Burton famously described as melancholia, as an emotional and mental disorder.[14] In the eighteenth century in many European countries, coroners' juries (or their equivalents) would bring down a verdict of insanity at a suicide trial in order to allow Christian burial and to avoid the forfeiting of goods and property.[15] Merian's 1763 "memoir" on suicide presented the act more as a disease than a sin or crime, and a disease with many possible causes, including delirium and despair.[16]

In parallel with the spread of medicalized ideas of suicide as related to mental anguish was the development of the Romantic notion of suicide as the fashionable fate of the "man of sensibility." As A. Alvarez puts it: "The ideal was 'to cease upon the midnight with no pain' whilst still young and beautiful and full of promise. Suicide added a dimension of drama and doom, a fine black orchid to the already tropical jungle of the period's emotional life."[17] When Goethe published *The Sorrows of Young Werther (Die Leiden des jungen Werthers)* in 1774, it was followed by a rash of actual suicides, presumably of sensitive young men suffering from unrequited love, who saw themselves, like the novel's hero, as unable to accept the social world of inauthenticity in which they were forced to live and (not) love:

> there was a *Werther* epidemic: *Werther* fever, a *Werther* fashion—young men dressed in blue tail coats and yellow waistcoats—*Werther* caricatures, *Werther* suicides. His memory was solemnly commemorated at the grave of the young Jerusalem, his original, while the clergy preached sermons against the shameful book. And all this continued, not for a year, but for decades, and not only in Germany but in England, France, Holland and Scandinavia as well.[18]

Throughout the next century, operas too would abound on this most dramatic of themes; of these, Jules Massenet and Edouard Blau's *Werther* (1892) is perhaps the best known today.[19] It aptly captures the despair of the hero and the Romantic attraction of the turn to suicide. As we saw in Chapter 2, the German Romantics conferred upon death positive associations that easily made their way onto the operatic stage.

The general secularizing of suicide prepared the way for the nineteenth-century scientific study of mental disease and of suicide as a symptom. Theories abounded at this time: suicide was caused by "brain lesions, excess phosphorus, heredity, liver disease, madness, and masturbation." It could be brought on by climate, food, or exercise; it might be the result of a thickening of the skull.[20] Secular and medicalized, these various theories form part of the background to our modern sense of suicide and its relation to "being of unsound mind." Our current psychiatric understanding, often developed from "psychological autopsies" of suicide victims, would suggest that the majority of suicides are seen to suffer from mental disorders, most prominently mood disorders and substance abuse.[21] For modern audiences the Christian anathema against suicide has been tempered at least somewhat by this current medical understanding about mental disease and perhaps also by sympathy for psychological anguish or social alienation.

"Sola e rinnegata": Women and Suicide

Giacomo Puccini and Giovacchino Forzano's *Suor Angelica* (1918) would seem set up precisely to invoke the standard Christian judgment, for it tells the story of a woman who has been placed in the convent out of familial shame at the birth of her illegitimate son and who takes her own life when she hears of the child's death. Superimposed on our responses to this death, sentimentally depicted in true Puccini fashion, is our sense of sympathy for her grief, loss, and distress as a mother. Sister Angelica addresses her dead son in moving terms: "Oh! sweet end to all my sorrows! / When can I join you in heaven? / When shall I die?" ("Ah! Dolce fine di ogni mio dolore! / Quando in cielo con te potrò salire? / Quando potrò morire?").

The opera foregrounds the obvious religious issue in a particularly provocative way, for she cannot join the child in heaven *and* take her own life. After swallowing the poison she has distilled from the flowers she tends, Sister Angelica is overcome by guilt, for she knows that suicide is a mortal sin and that she has damned herself: "son dannata!" she cries. But the libretto also plays on our awareness of the medicalized understanding of suicide, for she sings: "for the love of my son, / I have lost my reason!" ("per amor di mio figlio / smarita ho la ragione!"). Praying nonetheless for salvation despite her sin, she is rewarded by a vision of a host of angels surrounding the Virgin Mary, who leads the child toward his dying mother. How is the audience to interpret this ecstatic vision? Even while admitting that the director's decision about how to stage this scene will clearly condition our response, we would still have to decide if this was a sign from God of her salvation, despite her mortal sin, or whether it was a delusion or even an hallucination caused by the poison that merely allowed Angelica to die comforted by a wish-fulfilling fantasy.

Puccini said that he had hoped his Suor Angelica would become as well known to opera audiences as his Madama Butterfly. That she has not may in part be the result of religious qualms. Such qualms, however, seem to have little to do with the response to *Madama Butterfly* (1904), for although the Japanese protagonist converts to Christianity, there is never any overt question of sin raised in the text and never any mention of it in the critical responses to her suicide. Cio-Cio-San, as she is known to her own people, is another in a long (Romantic and late Romantic) line of Western representations of exotic "Oriental" women who die at their own hands for the love of an Occidental man. Her predecessors include Sélika, from Giacomo Meyerbeer's *L'Africaine* (1865) —a tale of Portuguese exploration and cultural encounter with Hindu Indians—and the title character of Léo Delibes's *Lakmé* (1883), a story of intercultural love between a Brahmin priestess and an occupying British soldier in nineteenth-century India. Both operas end with the suicide of the Indian woman, but both deaths are shown to be ecstatic ones, for they have been carefully framed in what the opera specifically presents as a culture and a religion in which suicide is both acceptable and understandable.[22] Cross-cultural love cannot work in either case, for the differences are too vast. In death, both women regain their cultural and personal integrity. Their suicides are self-sacrifices for a greater good—in two different senses: they die faithful to their own nations and religions, but also for the European cause, as the men are allowed to leave to go about their imperial duty. And because their religion condones suicide, there is no conventional European tragic ending here, as audiences might expect. Like the Parisian audiences of the nineteenth century when these operas premiered (and were immense hits), we too are allowed a consolatory fiction: their deaths are happy (if convenient) ones, poignant and moving but not tragic.

Not so with Cio-Cio-San's suicide. The social situation of the protagonist of *Madama Butterfly* is much more complex, and so too are the circumstances of her death. Separated by choice from her Japanese family and religion, Cio-Cio-San has turned her back on her heritage and become a Christian in order to "marry" Benjamin Franklin Pinkerton, a self-confessed sexual adventurer and "Yankee vagabondo" who doesn't understand or care to understand Japanese customs or people, but who is enchanted by this delicate fifteen-year-old. For this decision, she is cursed by her uncle, the Bonze, and renounced by her family, as horns and trumpets blare out a curse motive in the music. Alone and renounced ("Sola e rinnegata"), she finds solace in Pinkerton's love. His betrayal—foreshadowed from the first scene when he says he plans one day to have a real American wedding—is ostensibly the cause of her suicide. The libretto text has set up its inevitability and cause from the start, through repeated use of butterfly imagery for Cio-Cio-San, always in the context of Pinkerton as the one to pin her down, like a scientific specimen, or to damage her wings. The flute and clarinet music that accompanies the graceful young woman's first entrance reinforces the sense of a butterfly's fluttering. The gongs and trombones that signal her death at the end sound the brutal reality of her social alienation and personal destruction.

In the background of what Durkheim would see as a suicide caused by individual isolation and lack of social integration is the notion of a culture in which suicide is condoned. One of the personal things Cio-Cio-San brings to her marriage is the knife that the Mikado gave her father to use to commit seppuku, a form of self-execution permitted some Japanese to escape the shame of public execution at the hands of others.[23] When, at the end of the opera, Cio-Cio-San realizes that Pinkerton has married an Ameri-

can woman, she bows to the Buddha—for the first time in the opera—takes this knife, and as the curse theme reappears in the music, reads the inscription: "One dies with honor / who cannot serve
life with honor" ("Con onor muore / chi non può serbar vita con
onore"). Some productions, such as the film version directed by
Jean-Pierre Ponnelle, signal this return to her Japanese culture in
the end by having her die with the proper ritual for seppuku—
with bound legs and thighs, for instance. In other words, her death
fuses two Western concepts of suicide: that of personal suicide
(here, out of pain of lost love and shame for the dishonor of a false
marriage, for she has been raised in a traditional code of behavior)
and that of the institutional suicide endorsed by Japanese society—at least in European constructions of it. Perhaps because seppuku would never have been allowed a woman, Japanese audiences
have never found Cio-Cio-San's death very "Japanese" but rather a
purely foreign construction.[24]

But even a modern, Western, doubled understanding of this suicide does not fully explain its power or why this is different from
the other operas on this theme. We have left out one important
detail in our account of this death: the presence of the son of
Pinkerton and Cio-Cio-San. No vision this time, the child is physically present on stage, blindfolded and waving an American flag,
as his mother dies. He is also, however, in a very real sense the
cause of her death. She openly tells him that she is going to die for
him. This is a sacrificial death meant to redeem a life. He will now
go to live in that America she had always longed to see and with
the man she had always wanted to love and to live with. That
Pinkerton is a cad and unworthy of her devotion has been clear, for
the audience, from the start. We have watched her innocence and
loving trust being abused, and we cannot but react to this sacrifice. Some productions play her death as a final revenge against
Pinkerton—having her wait until he enters the room, crying out
her name in anguish, before she kills herself. But the libretto sets

up this final meeting more as a symbol of the impossibility of East and West ever understanding each other. Just as Pinkerton doesn't care about Japanese customs, except insofar as he finds them entertaining, so Cio-Cio-San arguably (and tragically) never understands American ways. This is symbolized by her inadvertent inverting of his initials (from B. F. to F. B. Pinkerton): no American would confuse Benjamin Franklin with Franklin Benjamin.[25] Puccini's use of both the American national anthem and authentic or quasi-authentic Japanese music gives voice to this cultural difference. The audience is treated throughout to both the exotic and the familiar, thereby allowing both distance and identification, perhaps. However, the fact that this love could not transcend culture and merge these differences is symbolized musically: the lovers only sing in the familiar Italian operatic idiom. And Pinkerton is the one in control—at least until the end, when the "gong strikes, its harmonics echo; she is dead now."[26] In these words, Catherine Clément condemns the opera's Orientalist and antifeminist politics; but another way to read this suicide is as a final taking back of power and even autonomy by Cio-Cio-San. Ending her alienation from her own society by her death (and the means of its accomplishment), she ceases to be a culture-crossed (rather than star-crossed) lover. She has restored what *she* sees as her honor and can thus offer her death in ritual sacrifice for her son's life. Agreed, this is not the traditional reading of the opera in our feminist and postcolonial times, but we argue that the power of this suicide on stage comes from a layering of many different Western ideas about the taking of one's own life.

"Appropriate Death" and Social Indictment

The chapter on Wagner's *Ring* cycle introduced Avery Weisman's theory of "appropriate death"—the death one might choose for oneself, if one could do so. Could this concept be extended to explain the audience's strange feeling that some staged suicides are "appropriate" in the sense that they offer satisfying moral or aesthetic closure, no matter how odd that may seem? Cio-Cio-San's suicide feels both validated and tragic at the same time. Similarly, in operas in which people are responsible for some crime, say for the death of another, suicide might be seen as appropriate expiation for moral guilt. Benjamin Britten's *Peter Grimes* (1945) and Alban Berg's *Wozzeck* (1925) provide test cases for this theory. Both are complicated by the fact that they are modern dramas of psychic disintegration played out in the context of social alienation, in part created by society's active abuse.

Peter Grimes, as its title suggests, tells the tale of one man against a society, known here collectively as "the Borough."[27] Although individualized by their human frailties, the members of the Borough unite to oppose the strange and reputedly violent outsider, Grimes. The opera opens with a prologue presenting a Moot Hall inquest into the death of the boy who had been the apprentice to the fisherman Grimes. Only Ellen Orford, the schoolteacher, stands up for Grimes, called "callous, brutal, and coarse" by the Coroner, who refuses to declare Grimes innocent, knowing he'll be judged by the people when the death is announced as caused by "accidental circumstances." With Ellen's support, Peter tries to restore his good name. To do so, he needs another apprentice to help him. Only then can he earn enough money to buy them a home, respect, and "freedom from pain / of grinning at gossip's tales"— since money is all the Borough understands. At the start of the opera, then, Grimes is distressed, violent, ambitious, and determined; he is not psychotic. But he is deeply alienated from the oppressive Borough society, which is symbolically represented by the collectivity of the chorus.

Although the critical writing on this work has always centered on this theme of the individual versus society, there have been many ways of interpreting that antagonism. One line of argument presents Grimes as conflicted within himself as well as against society, desiring security and respectability but at the same time treasuring his isolation and making it inevitable with his impulsive cruelty.[28] Another view—a strong one from the start because articulated by British novelist E. M. Forster and by Grimes's first interpreter, tenor Peter Pears—suggests that Grimes is a misunderstood Byronic hero: imaginative, poetic, idealist, introspective, oversensitive.[29] When Grimes sings his aria "Now the great Bear and Pleiades" in the inn, the Borough takes him for mad, but the critics take him for visionary. Not all critics, however, have been able to resist the text's implications that, as the opera progresses, Grimes becomes more and more dysfunctional as he is more and more socially alienated; this is certainly how tenor Jon Vickers played the role.[30] Still others, led by Philip Brett, have read the opera as an allegory of repression, in which the pacifist and homosexual Britten portrayed a man's internalization of his society's view of him: self-loathing therefore explains his psychic disintegration.[31]

All of these interpretations of the individual–social division in this opera would support our reading of the opera in Durkheimian terms, that is, in terms of the suicide being motivated by social causes. As the Methodist character, Boles, puts it most powerfully: "This lost soul of a fisherman must be / shunned by respectable society." And he is. Grimes is not, of course, presented as totally innocent: his second apprentice bears the bruises of his hard treatment. To convince the audience of Grimes's potential for violence, the opera shows him striking the one person about whom he cares, the one person for whom he works and dreams: Ellen. As if in realization of the enormity of what he has just done and the failure of this important (and his only human) relationship, Grimes echoes the Borough's collective "Amen" from the church and sings "So be it—and God have mercy on me!" As Peter Garvie notes: "The heavy, accented downward phrase, like a judgment falling upon him, is repeated by the orchestra."[32] Has he echoed the "Amen" as a

Jon Vickers as Peter Grimes, Metropolitan Opera, New York.

sign of his accepting the Borough's values—and thus of self-loathing? Or is this where the society has driven him, despite himself? The music of his "and God have mercy on me!" is used as the main theme of the chorus as the Borough works itself up to protest Grimes's violence, singing, "Grimes is at his exercise!"

When the chorus-posse closes in on his hut, looking for evidence of his maltreatment of his apprentices, Grimes, in angry haste and utter desperation (to get out to fish and make more money), is responsible for the death of his second apprentice, who falls as they rush from the hut. The Borough finds it empty and neat. Balstrode, one of the few people sympathetic to Grimes, hopes this will quell gossip. Of course, it cannot, since evidence of the boy's death soon appears. Balstrode and Ellen agree to find and help Grimes in his "unearthly torment." When his boat reappears on shore, the Borough again goes hunting, singing "Who holds himself apart, / lets his pride rise. / Him who despises us / we'll destroy." The interlude before Peter himself comes onstage is short and "rhapsodic," forming a prelude to what can only be called a "mad scene"; the music here "refers to phrases of Peter's earlier songs, only to disintegrate them."[33] The man who enters is indeed not the same as the one we last saw: traumatized, he babbles incoherently about the two boys' deaths, ignoring Ellen's entreaties. His delirium is accompanied only by the foghorn and the sound of the posse in the distance. In the silence that follows, Balstrode speaks—does not sing, but speaks—the lines that bid Grimes to go out and sink his boat and thus kill himself.

The next scene portrays the indifferent Borough folk being told a boat is out at sea sinking, but since it's out of reach, no one reacts; life continues normally. There is no musical evocation, in other words, of Grimes's death, just as there is no textual recognition of it. Ironically, it is Grimes's death that has made this normality possible for the Borough. The peace of the society has been purchased at individual expense by expelling the scapegoated

Grimes. For the audience too, perhaps, moral order has been re-stored: the cause of the boys' deaths has himself died. But some-thing else is going on here: we carry out of the opera house the work's powerful indictment of an alienating and badgering society that we watched drive a man to his death.

Grimes's suicide acts as both an escape from that society—from which he wanted only the simplest of things—and an accusation against it. But audience identification is made problematic here: Grimes is an outsider, yes, but he is also brutal and possibly sadis-tic. Yet the alternative would be to identify with the equally brutal and sadistic Borough, and that is made equally impossible.[34] We are not being asked to identify with Grimes simply because he is an outsider.[35] He is both sinned against and sinning, both victim of social oppression and victimizer of others. It is his suicide that changes the identification possibilities, for it can indeed be seen as a righting of moral wrongs. However, as Durkheim taught us, sui-cide is a social act, as well as an individual one. The audience's re-sponse to the opera's indictment of the Borough can be as power-ful as any sympathy it might feel for its victim: "I think we hate the Chorus in this closing scene," states Patricia Howard. "It is an opera so full of judgments, right and wrong, misguided and willfully malicious, that the audience is compelled to react very strongly to it."[36]

Today's audience is probably as "psychiatrically sophisticated" as any in history, and that background knowledge too may have an impact on its response to Grimes's fate.[37] It would certainly affect the reaction to Berg's *Wozzeck*, where the psychopathology is more evident and more extreme.[38] The opera opens at a moment of psy-chic crisis in the protagonist's life. Wozzeck is described by the Captain as "harassed" ("verhetzt"), but the official says that the man is basically a good fellow ("ein guter Mensch"), even if the fact that he has an illegitimate child proves that he obviously has no sense of morality. Wozzeck articulates strongly in this scene the social dimensions of what will soon clearly be his psychic problems: "We poor folk!" ("Wir arme Leut!"), he protests, could be virtuous if we had money, but we are "unfortunate" ("unselig") in this world and the next. This refrain of "Wir arme Leut!" will be repeated later to remind us of the centrality of poverty in Wozzeck's fate as the victim of a society that will not grant him the basic necessities, but instead will exploit and oppress him, even as he simply attempts to make a bit of extra money for his woman, Marie, and their child. The Captain worries that Wozzeck thinks too much ("denkt zu viel") and that this will prey upon him.

In the next scenes we witness precisely how that preying occurs. Although this opera sets up its protagonist as alienated from an alienating society as much as (if not more than) does *Peter Grimes*,[39] the psychic cost of the lack of social integration is more evident. Both the text and the music underscore Wozzeck's aberrations: in the second scene of Act I, his auditory and visual hallucinations cause him to think the forest cursed ("verflucht"). When his companion asks if he is mad ("Bist du toll?"), the audience can only answer "yes" as it witnesses his paranoia about the Freemasons and his fears that the hollow earth hides some malign force. When he later tells Marie of his visions, she is right to be anxious about his "haunted" ("vergeistert") state of mind. In his paranoia, he is sure he is on the track of many things that will start to make sense ("Ich bin Vielem auf der Spur!"). Wozzeck's consistent quoting of apocalyptic moments in the Bible—the destruction of Sodom and Gomorrah, for instance—and his hallucinatory apocalyptic perceptions (the moon as blood red) give us a sense of the psychic and religious context in which this individual interacts with his society.[40]

We watch Wozzeck victimized by that society in the person of the Doctor, whom he allows to do dietary experiments on him in order to earn more money for Marie and the child. Sadistic in the extreme, the Doctor is overjoyed when Wozzeck tells him about his visions, about hearing fearful voices, about the world being dark and disintegrating like spiders' webs, and about trying to understand why toadstools grow in circles. In short, the Doctor's diagnosis is an "aberratio mentalis partialis"—and Wozzeck is given a raise. It is the Doctor and the Captain—as the symbolically and generically named representatives of society—who taunt Wozzeck with the news of Marie's infidelity with the Drum Major. It is the Captain who asks him if he'll shoot himself in response, given his desperate state ("verzweifelt"). Confronting Marie, Wozzeck moves to strike her in his jealousy, only to have her say that she'd rather have a knife in her body than let him lay a hand on her ("Lieber ein Messer in den Leib, als eine Hand auf mich"). Obsessively repeating "Lieber ein Messer", Wozzeck calls humanity an abyss that makes him dizzy to contemplate.

In the next scene, Wozzeck sits alone by the door of the inn, his physical separation from the others symbolizing his social isolation, as he watches Marie and the Drum Major dance. His alienation from his fellow soldiers is clear in the next scene in the barracks, where he relives the dancing in his mind and is haunted by the image of a knife, while praying not to be led into temptation. We understand the meaning of these details in the scene that follows, in which Wozzeck stabs Marie, goes to the inn, and is seen to be covered in blood. Running back to the scene of the murder, he looks frantically for the knife he used and throws it into the pond. He fears the (apocalyptic) blood-red moon will betray him. Deciding that the knife is in water too shallow to hide it, he wades into the pond. The reflected moon gives him the feeling that he is covered in blood (as Lady Macbeth too felt in her guilt). As the enormity of his crime dawns on him, he drowns himself. The heartless, indifferent Doctor and Captain hear him do so, comment on the death sounds, and leave the stage.

The orchestral interlude that follows is a threnody based on Siegfried's Funeral March in Wagner's *Götterdämmerung* that

Michael Devlin as the Doctor and Falk Struckmann in the title role of *Wozzeck,*
Metropolitan Opera, New York. Photo by Winnie Klotz.

moves stylistically from nineteenth- through to twentieth-century musical conventions.[41] It is as if the music grieves for Wozzeck's suicide in a way that the society never did. Berg himself called this an epilogue that contained a "confession of the author" and an "appeal to humanity through its representatives, the audience."[42] The cruelty of a society that drove Wozzeck to this end is condemned, for now the only sympathetic characters in that society are both dead—by murder and suicide. In light of the apocalyptic imagery, Marie's infidelity is marked as a symbolic act of depravity, as if in Sodom and Gomorrah, and her death becomes, in Wozzeck's tormented mind, a ritual execution.[43] But there is no greater purpose suggested, no higher good that this death or Wozzeck's might justify. There is no transcendence and no redemption in this bleak vision of human fate. In the final scene, children cruelly tease the deceased couple's child. Their horrible deaths are merely the source of taunting. Here, as in *Peter Grimes,* suicide is both an escape from society and an accusation against it. We can easily identify with the isolation of the characters, without identifying with their madness or, in both cases, with the isolating societies. That social order is *not* one we want to see restored at the end, even if we do witness its victory. Yet, to return to the notion of "appropriate death," the audience's sense of ethical closure comes in part from the suicides as restitution, as expiation for the deaths of others, for both men are indeed responsible for others' deaths.

Despite the fact that both source texts—the Crabbe and the Büchner—date from an earlier period, these operas offer very modern portrayals of suicide as psychic disturbance caused by social alienation. There can be little straightforward pleasure in watching a society grind down an individual onstage; yet such bleakness remains a hallmark of much of the modern art that followed World War I. Durkheim's insights into the social context of individual suicide have the effect for audiences today of offering a context for the many other interpretations of suicide that Western culture has offered over time—as criminal, as sinful, as sign of weakness and despair, as rational alternative, as romantic apotheosis, as medical symptom. Watching a suicide on stage is a *contemplatio mortis* of another kind, a more fraught and personal kind, since this is a voluntary death. It inevitably provokes audience members to review their own positions on this, the only "truly serious philosophical problem."

6

The Undead

Yet in death peace will be.
So wird Ruh im Tode sein.
Mozart, *The Magic Flute*

Opera is obviously an art form obsessed with death as the narrative device of choice to conclude either its melodramatic or its tragic tales. As a result, audiences have come to see staged death as emotionally wrenching yet dramatically satisfying. In real life, the former is a more likely response than the latter. Although death is a biological reality for us all, our life stories are rarely plotted like those of opera. Yet what would happen if we tried to imagine living without the threat of final death? Psychological studies in which people were asked to consider precisely that question have shown that close to 70 percent found little positive value in such a situation—either in social or personal terms. Certainly, in a world without death, we would be free from the fear of the end and able to preserve human relationships and expand our personal experiences, but most people felt that these advantages were counterbalanced by a decrease in motivation and meaning in life,

not to mention an increase in suffering due to aging and physical deterioration. What would also be lost, for many, is that sense
of death as an important part of the natural process of life or
of a divine plan.[1] Immortality, in other words, may not make
for a happy life. Literature and philosophy are rich with fer-
vent testimonials to the fact that it is death that gives meaning to life. Its very ephemerality is what gives our existence its
value and poignancy. The appeal of freshly cut flowers that bloom
and die so quickly may perhaps lie in how they remind us of our
fate.

Gothic Living

This chapter will investigate less the philosophical and literary dimensions and more the dramatizations of the relation of life to
death, of immortality to mortality. In earlier centuries, the word
"undead" was used to refer to those (like God) not subject to
death. However, at least since the publication of Bram Stoker's
1898 novel *Dracula,* if not before, most people likely associate the
word with vampires and other creatures known collectively as the
"living dead." What earlier and later uses of the term share, however, is a sense of existing on the uneasy borderline between life
and death. Vampires—literary, staged, and cinematic—have taken
both Europe and North America by storm over the last two centuries in part because they are so disturbingly ambivalent. They both
triumph over death and undo "the safe and secure boundaries between the living and the dead," between the self and the other.
They disrupt the continuity and stability of our human order.
They upset our sense of "wholeness, intactness and survival," argues Elisabeth Bronfen.[2] They are "interstitial" creatures that exist
across multiple categories of being, but conform to none of them.
The undead are living and not living. They have a horrifying glow
of vitality.[3] They are not ghosts; they are the paradoxically living

dead in all their materiality and physicality. Although vampire tales
appear in the folklore of most parts of the world, from India to
China to Europe, their power for Western Christian audiences
may lie to some extent in their nightmare inversion of Christ's
death and resurrection.[4]

From the later eighteenth century onward, Europeans had delighted in what came to be labeled as the "gothic"—developing a
taste for the supernatural, the irrational, the uncanny, and the mysterious, indeed for all that was eerily beyond the visible and the
present. This delight has been linked by historians to a new kind of
fear of death and of the dead, a new terror of personal annihilation.[5] A number of factors already explored in earlier chapters con-
tributed to this change: for instance, the secularization of death
and the erosion of the belief in an afterlife; the social shift to treat-
ing death as a private and personal experience, rather than a communal one; and lastly, the beginnings of the attempt of science and
medicine to make death into a purely physiological phenomenon.[6]
The uncanny interpenetration of life and death that the undead
represent, however, also exposed the limits of human reason—so
prized by the Enlightenment—and made people vulnerable to new
apprehensions. The gothic taste for these borderline beings reflects
the age's "existential disorientation, wrought by the loss of defining
structures" of authority (reason, religion, class, and so on).[7] It was
also one of the ways to exorcize that new kind of fear of death. The
frisson of terror caused by the contemplation of the undead was
perhaps therapeutic for readers and audiences; maybe playing out
the anxiety of death in such an obviously overwrought manner reduced it to the unreal and the fantastic.

There is, however, yet another way to account for the power of
the living dead in the human imagination. Mary Douglas and others have pointed to the general unease created by the borderline
and the liminal; ambiguity upsets those accustomed to clear categories.[8] Life and death, of course, are usually clear categories. But

in the nineteenth century, an anxious fascination arose about the ambiguities created by crossing the borders of precisely these states. The much-discussed terror of premature burial is but one manifestation of this. Typical (and vivid) is John Snart's 1817 *Thesaurus of Horror; or the Charnel House Explored!!* in which he examined, in great prurient and sadomasochistic detail, the liminal state between life and death by imagining just such a premature entombment: "Madness—rage—all!—no power to live! no power to die! no power, alas, to cry for aid! but pent, barricaded, and pressed by accumulated condensation! The brain distracted! the eyes starting from the sockets! the lungs ruptured!"[9] Another nineteenth-century manifestation of the worried fascination with the undead was the widespread interest in mesmeric states (magnetism, trances, hypnotism), frequently linked to visionary moments preceding—and postponing—death, as so powerfully articulated in Edgar Allan Poe's story "The Facts in the Case of M. Valdemar."[10]

Typified by unnerving ambiguity, the gothic in general and the undead in particular straddled the natural and the supernatural, the rational and the irrational, good and evil, life and death.[11] Judging from recent critical debates, today the most common way to interpret the appeal of the undead is simply in terms of sexuality, with psychoanalysis as the methodology of choice.[12] But the history of gothic art forms and their interpretation is much more complex than this critical restriction of focus suggests. Nevertheless, the prominence of psychosexual interpretations is enough to make us wonder if, in fact, these readings do not represent yet another denial of the underlying and continuing terror of death. Western society in the twenty-first century is certainly heir to that earlier sense of mortal anxiety. And anxiety about borderline states has not disappeared, even in our postmodern boundary-crossing world. In other words, contemporary audiences, watching and listening to nineteenth-century operas that explore these liminal states, may find themselves interpreting them in other than psychoanalytic terms. As Ernest Becker argued, and as we suggested in Chapter 1, fear of death, rather than sexuality, may be just as likely a driving force of modern life. In what follows, we examine a series of different operatic investigations of the borderline between mortality and immortality, death and life, in order to answer a series of questions. Can one imagine a life without death? What value would such an existence have? What meaning would death take on in such a world?

Choosing Mortality: The Loves of Water Spirits and Mortals

In the fantasy world of the gothic, a familiar theme that captured the imagination of artists and audiences alike is that of a supernatural being who deliberately chooses to become mortal—because of either love or a desire to give meaning to existence by (paradoxically) acquiring an immortal soul. Early nineteenth-century European culture offers multiple explorations of this theme in ballets, operas, plays, poems, stories, and paintings. Usually the supernatural creature is a female and an elemental (most often water) spirit.[13] Perhaps the best known literary example is Hans Christian Andersen's famous story "The Little Mermaid" (1839), in which a mermaid falls in love with a human prince she saves from drowning. She is not immortal, but she can live for three hundred years; the problem is that she has no soul. As her grandmother explains, "when our life here comes to an end, we become nothing but foam on the water and never even have a grave down among our loved ones. We have no immortal soul; we never have another life. . . . Human beings, however, have a soul which lives for ever, lives after the body has turned to dust."[14] The only way for a water spirit to acquire this immortal soul is to be loved faithfully by a human—something mortal creatures seem to be incapable of doing. Adapted to the operatic stage in Antonín Dvořák's *Rusalka* (1901) (from a libretto by Jaroslav Kvapil), the opera tells the story of a water nymph who seeks to become a mortal being with a soul, a creature full of love, and so persuades a witch to grant her a human body and soul. Her immortal father warns her that she will be a mere mortal and will come back worn out by life. And indeed, when her human lover loses interest in her, she laments, "I am neither a woman nor a nymph, I can neither live nor die" ("nemohu zemřít, nemoku žít"). But, despite losing her youth and beauty, she is in the end reunited with her lover—in death.

We should, however, back up a little, for it was earlier, on the German Romantic opera stage, that this theme proved particularly popular, likely because of the publication in 1811 of the tale of "Undine" by Friedrich de la Motte Fouqué. Seen as the culmination of the Romantic interest in the relationship between humanity and nature,[15] this story of the water spirit named after the waves (*unda* being Latin for "wave") is always said to reflect its creator's interest in elemental spirits. Yet it may also reflect Fouqué's interest in questions of mortality. Willing to trade her long-lived youth to become a loving, suffering woman with a soul, Undine seeks commitment in exchange for accepting human mortality. The appeal of this theme of crossing the boundary between forms of life—and death—was a strong one at the time. In 1816, E. T. A. Hoffmann composed a "Zauberoper" (magical opera) he named *Undine,* based on the Fouqué source text. In it he was careful to differentiate musically between the human world of pain and suffering and the supernatural realm, with its otherworldly sounds.[16] The entire operatic narrative is presented as being under the shadow of death: it opens with the transformed water spirit having been adopted by a fisherman and his wife who are still grieving the loss of their daughter. Although the human lover in this version also proves unfaithful to Undine and must die for his transgression, through her intense love they are reunited "in a pure love-death" ("zum reinen Liebestod"). This early use of the famous (and later, Wagnerian) term "Liebestod" is uttered by the holy man who had originally consecrated their love and noted that death is also a blessing "if love delivers it."[17]

The impact of Hoffmann's opera is clear on both Carl Maria von Weber's *Der Freischütz*—the most famous and influential of Romantic operas—and Richard Wagner's early work *Die Feen.*[18] But Wagner changed the focus of the Undine story in a way that foreshadows a major theme of all this later work. He retains the idea of a long-lived or immortal creature choosing to become mortal out of love, but he discards the idea that the aim is to gain an immortal soul. Instead, here the greatest sign of the power of human love is that an immortal would choose mortality—that is, death. Love and death, Eros and Thanatos, are defined in terms of one another even in this early work, written when he was only in his early twenties. Composed in 1833–1834, *Die Feen* is derived from Carlo Gozzi's story "The Serpent Woman" ("La donna serpente"). Acting as his own librettist, Wagner created a text through which echo obsessively the words "unsterblich" ("immortal") and "sterblich" ("mortal").

The fairy Ada is willing freely to renounce her immortality ("Unsterblichkeit") for the love of the mortal Arindal. When, because of his disobeying of one of the fairy rules, the lovers are separated, Ada complains about her immortal state:

> What was once so sublime, so beautiful—
> what a sad and hard fate
> immortality has become for me!

> *was sonst so hehr, so schön—*
> *zu traurig hartem Lose*
> *wird mir Unsterblichkeit!*

For her love, she is willing to accept mortality and death, if Arindal is strong enough to withstand the test of love with which she is forced to present him:

What is immortality?
A boundless, eternal death!
While every day with him
is a new, eternal life!—

Was ist die Unsterblichkeit?
Ein grenzenloser, ew'ger Tod!
Doch jeder Tag bei ihm
ein neues, ew'ges Leben!—

So great is her love that the fact that it is a life that ends in physical death does not concern her. Immortality can only be a form of death—that is, if life is defined as being with the beloved. Wagner chose not to leave the lovers dead in the end (as he would later in *Tristan und Isolde*), but rather to have them both become "unsterblich," or immortal—surrendering to the conventional form of the happy ending for perhaps the last time in his creative life.

The opera's intricate plot is of less interest here than the fact, as he explained almost twenty years later in "A Communication to My Friends," that in this ending was "the germ of a weighty factor in my whole development."[19] What did Wagner mean? Given that later "development," he could have meant either or both of two things: the theme of redemption through a woman's devotion and the related theme of the transfiguration of mortality and death through love. Later works, most obviously *Der fliegende Holländer* and *Tristan und Isolde,* are built upon precisely these themes. But in *Tannhäuser* as well, the hero chooses to leave the Venusberg, where (as the lover of Venus) he is treated as a god, in order to return to the mortal world of human pain and beauty defined by the inevitablity of death: "there, after death I seek, / to death am I drawn!" ("hin zum Tod den ich suche, / zum Tode drängt es mich!")

In *Der Ring des Nibelungen,* Brünnhilde does not seek mortality, but rather has it thrust upon her, as a punishment for her act

of disobedience to her father, Wotan. At the end of *Die Walküre,*
she is cut off from "the eternal race" ("der Ewigen Stamm") of
Valkyries and gods because she responded to the human love
of Siegmund for Sieglinde; for this, she is herself condemned to
that human love—and death. Her magical steed, Grane, is likewise reduced to being a normal horse. In one of the most powerful
stage metaphors we have ever seen of this transition from immortality to mortality, in Herbert Wernicke's 1991 production of the
Ring in Brussels, Wotan transformed Grane from magical uni-
corn to mere horse by brutally snapping off his single horn. The
audience's collective gasp of horror at this objective correlative
of Brünnhilde's reduction to humanity brought home the enormity of what she called her most horrible disgrace ("grässlichsten
Schmach").

At the end of *Siegfried,* the next opera in the cycle, we see her
reawaking from the sleep into which Wotan had cast her, to both
joy (that Siegfried is the one who found her) and terror. No longer
a Valkyrie, she is just a defenseless woman, vulnerable in the face of
Siegfried's passion for her. With no sense of her identity ("I am no
longer Brünnhilde" ["Brünnhilde bin ich nicht mehr!"]), she fears
she will lose her wisdom with her immortality and waxes nostalgic
about her earlier state—even in the moment of surrender to his
love:

> Eternal was I
> eternal am I
> eternal in sweet
> yearning bliss—
>
> *Ewig war ich*
> *ewig bin ich*
> *ewig in süss*
> *sehnender Wonne—*

Not surprisingly, the lovers' final duet is a song to death, that is, to mortality as the inevitable accompaniment of human love. Eros and Thanatos join once again in the music drama's last words: "luminous love, / laughing death!" ("leuchtended Liebe, / lachender Tod!"). At the end of the next and final work of the cycle, *Götterdämmerung*, Brünnhilde will sacrifice her mortal life on Siegfried's funeral pyre, bringing about (as we saw in Chapter 3) not only her own end but, as the opera's title suggests, the end of the world of the gods as well.

This constant Wagnerian theme of the redeeming and even transfiguring of death through love is first developed in *Die Feen*, as is the equally important and equally persistent notion throughout his work that the inability to die is actually a negative.[20] Later, however, in *Der fliegende Holländer*, this theme is linked not only to ideas of supernatural immortality but also to the concept of the undead. Obviously, as a word, *un*dead seeks, in its very negational form, to leave out any positive connotations of life. In the realm of the gothic, the undead existence is "a physical state unhallowed by any infusion of spirit or soul,"[21] a fate it shares with the life of the long-lived water spirits whose stories we have been exploring. But to understand the Wagnerian undead, we must look first at the particular form of the liminal "living dead" that influenced Wagner's early imagination: the vampire.

Enforced Immortality: Operatic Vampires

Bram Stoker's 1898 novel *Dracula* offers a late but influential version of the vampire in literature. The particular interest it holds for us here is in the death-haunted novel's insistence that the power of the undead comes from the "curse of immortality": "they cannot die, but must go on age after age adding new victims and multiplying the evils of the world; for all that die from the preying of the Un-Dead become themselves Un-Dead, and prey on their kind."[22]

As liminal creatures, vampires are neither living nor dead, human nor inhuman: keeping themselves in their undead state by sucking the blood of humans, "they are simply more alive than they should be."[23] But the particular qualities of their form of vitality were first described in much earlier representations than Stoker's.

Over eighty years before, the English Romantic poet Byron had written a fragment about a vampire that his physician and traveling companion, Dr. John Polidori, had expanded into *The Vampyre,* published in 1819. The seductive, treacherous Lord Ruthven of this version was modeled on Byron himself, it is said. Perhaps that alone accounts for some of the popularity of the tale of virginal sacrifice to vampiric lust, especially in France where a three-act melodrama (by Pierre Carmouche, Achille Jouffrey, and Charles Nodier) became an instant hit in 1820. Changing the story to fit the conventions of the genre (and perhaps the national culture), the playwrights made the vampire into a passionate though deadly womanizer who is carried off at the end to the underworld of nothingness ("le néant")—à la Don Giovanni.[24] Adapted and translated into English by James Robinson Planché in the same year, *The Vampire; or The Bride of the Isles* made its villain a somewhat more sympathetic character, in part because vampirism is presented as a curse upon him for his crimes and in part because this undead creature has qualms about his bloody doings.

Although vampires have mutated throughout the nineteenth and twentieth centuries, their major operatic manifestations date from this same general period of the story's popular success. Both Peter Joseph von Lindpaintner and Heinrich August Marschner composed operas on the theme in 1829; both were initially very popular German Romantic works, although they have fallen into relative obscurity since, perhaps because of the film monopolization of the vampire figure. There have been over 130 film versions of *Dracula* alone, and over 600 vampire movies in the last century—all equally death-obsessed.[25] F. W. Murnau's famous 1922 film *Nosferatu* made the vampire into a carrier of death and disease, indeed into a personification of death. Carl Dreyer's 1931 film *Vampyr* was also permeated with death, but it was Tod Browning's *Dracula* (1931) with Bela Lugosi that brought Eros clearly into the cinematic realm of Thanatos. Women wrote fearful, fascinated love letters to Lugosi, who recalled: "They hoped I was Dracula . . . It was the embrace of Death their subconscious was yearning for. Death, the triumphant final lover."[26] From 1958 to 1972, Hammer Films specialized in the related theme of vampiric sex and violence, but it wasn't until recent years, with the film adaptation of Anne Rice's fiction and movies like Francis Ford Coppola's (1992) *Bram Stoker's Dracula,* that the vampire as sympathetic rebel whose end we feel as tragic begins to right the Eros/Thanatos balance that was so carefully set up in the original tales.

Operas have also continued to be written about vampires,[27] and, not surprisingly, some of them—such as Randolph Peters's *Nosferatu* (1993)[28]—seem to have been influenced by film: by Murnau's (silent) film and, even more obviously, by the 1936 cinematic version of the story in *Dracula's Daughter* in which the titular daughter assists at the ritual cremation of her father's body with the words "Be thou exorcised, O Dracula, and thy body, long undead, find destruction throughout eternity in the name of thy dark, unholy master."[29] In the operatic version, Camilla's persistent dreams of "embracing darkness, longing for eternity" lead her to seek her father Nosferatu who, we learn, sustains his immortality by feeding on the blood of the living. As much a political fable about modern vampiric capitalism as a personal tale of a familial quest, *Nosferatu* is also a meditation on mortality and immortality. Nosferatu claims to "balance life and death, forever," rejecting the "finality of death, the baseness of life." He taunts his daughter:

> Are you afraid to die?
> People die unwillingly.

> In agony bodies wither, they wither . . .
> bones, blood, muscle mutilated by age, disease, bad
>   fortune . . .
> And after death, what happens?
> Decay, rot, stench, disintegration
> You become nothing. Nothing.

To her question "You are dead and alive?" he responds: "Be like me"—"die and live forever. / Taste the blood of an innocent. / . . . Feel its strength!" Her refusal provokes his assertion that "Blood is knowledge . . . Understanding forever." Camilla is tempted: "O, eternity—so real—so close." But in the end she sees that power and knowledge will not bring happiness. "When you live forever," she tells her father, "you have no reason to live!" She then repeats this line again, throwing it in the face of his scorn ("Your sacred finite life! / From beginning to end, you toil, and suffer, only to die!"). To his "I am your pathway to eternity," she offers, as she destroys him, "And I am yours—to humanity!" This theme—that death is what makes life precious—has its converse in the notion that, when we cannot die, everlasting life is but a torment.

Nineteenth-century opera too had offered a number of perspectives on this theme. As we noted, it was Polidori's original story that inspired the libretti of both Lindpaintner and Marschner, and it was specifically the latter's *Der Vampyr* that directly influenced Wagner.[30] Nevertheless, once again, the changes Wagner made in the notion of the undead are as interesting as his borrowings. In Marschner's story the newly created vampire, Lord Ruthven, makes a deal with the Vampire Master to gain another year on earth before facing damnation to hell for eternity. This, then, is an undead creature who does not want to die and cease to exist in the physical world. Already articulated in *Die Feen*, Wagner's new twist on this undead story—that is, the idea that immortality is actually a curse—is most fully developed in *Der fliegende Holländer* some dozen years later. It was on more than a mere whim that Bram Stoker had originally planned for his novel *Dracula* to include a scene in which Jonathan Harker attends this very opera by Wagner before going to meet the count in Transylvania.[31]

Condemned to Life

While writing *Der fliegende Holländer*, Wagner was influenced in terms of both plot and music by Marschner's *Der Vampyr;* this is abundantly clear from his letters and autobiographical writings.[32] But it is equally evident in the libretto that Wagner himself wrote. In it, his heroine Senta sings a folk ballad about a pale, otherworldly man ("der bleiche Mann") that echoes, in its strophic style and even its macabre and demonic content, a song from Marschner's opera known as Emmy's Romanze ("See, Mother, there the pale man" ["Sieh, Mutter, dort den bleichen Mann"]).[33] *Der fliegende Holländer* already contains all the standard Wagnerian themes that later works developed more fully: fathers and daughters, alienated outsiders, the material versus the spiritual, the redemption by a faithful woman. But here all are filtered through the eerie figure of a man cursed to live forever, that is, cursed to endure an undead existence. The Dutchman and his plight brought together two significant strands of nineteenth-century German culture: the folk tradition of supernatural legends and border ballads (and, through those, a means of connecting to the *Volk*'s imaginative power and closeness to nature) and the gothic tradition of experience closed off to rational discourse. As we saw in Chapter 2, the reaction against the Enlightenment by the German Romantics took many forms, among them an interest in the supernatural and the otherworldly, as well as in the darkness of night, death, and unreason so eloquently hailed by Novalis.

Wagner's autobiographical writings show his deep and early attraction to the uncanny and the mysterious, as experienced in the stories of E. T. A. Hoffmann and operas like Weber's *Der Freischütz.*[34] He shared Hoffmann's interest—which, of course, was that of the age—in inexplicable human experiences, ranging from mesmerism to the undead.[35] In short, Wagner's early work reflected the fact that the spirit world, the supernatural, and the demonic were very "in" in the 1820s and 1830s in Germany.[36] The incompatibility of the human and spirit worlds, the tense line between normality and mystery inspired Weber and Marschner—and, through them, Wagner, who wrote: "*Der Freischütz* in particular appealed very strongly to my imagination, mainly on account of its ghostly theme. The emotions of terror and dread of ghosts formed quite an important factor in the development of my mind. From my earliest childhood certain mysterious and uncanny things exercised an enormous influence over me."[37] Weber's opera almost single-handedly created the German Romantic taste for gloomy forests, echoing hunters' horns, supernatural dangers, and young love threatened. Musically, two aspects likely inspired the young Wagner: Weber's use of the diminished seventh—"Romantic music's most graphic embodiment of shock and horror"[38]—and the new desire to have the music actually motivated by the demands of the drama (an idea Wagner would later develop into the concept of the *Gesamtkunstwerk,* or the total work of art).

Together with Marschner's "Schaueroper" (horror opera) *Der Vampyr,* Weber's tale of supernatural forces and human love stands in the background of *Der fliegende Holländer'*s portrayal of the interaction of mortals and immortals. Originally Wagner had planned to have the action of his opera take place in gothic, exotic Scotland, where Marschner's had been set, but changed his mind, no doubt to heighten the autobiographical connection to his own personal experience on a terrifying sea voyage from Riga to London in 1839.[39] His actual source text for the story of the undead Dutchman, however, was Heinrich Heine's *From the Memoirs of Herr von Schnabelewopski (Aus den Memoiren des Herrn von*

Schnabelewopski) (1834). Although the legend of the phantom ship known as the *Flying Dutchman* appears to have grown up in the eighteenth century in the wake of British naval supremacy and earlier sea battles against the Dutch, there were many other nineteenth-century versions of the tale.[40] In this one, however, the narrator sees a play in Amsterdam about "the dread Mynherr," a Dutch sea captain who swears by all the devils in hell that he'll round a certain cape, even if he has to keep sailing until Judgment Day. The Devil takes him at his word—unless he can be redeemed by a faithful woman's love (which the cynical Devil believes to be impossibile). The captain laments that life rejects him and death refuses him, and like an empty barrel tossed by the waves, he is tossed between life and death. Once every seven years, he takes a wife and achieves salvation for a time; but, Heine writes, he is always happy to be saved from matrimony by his current wife's infidelity and to return to his ship and its ghostly crew. When his latest beloved is warned of her doom, were she to link her fate to his, "Frau fliegende Holländer" (as Heine calls her) leaps into the sea to redeem her Dutchman, whose ship is then engulfed by the waves. So far, the basic story sounds close to that of Wagner's opera. But Heine's ironic double moral is that women shouldn't marry flying Dutchmen and that men will always founder through women—and thus should always beware. No Wagnerian sentimentality, no transcendence here.

Wagner ignored the irony, but kept the plot details and steeped them in the preoccupations of his time and place—specifically, those themes of death and love with which he himself was obsessed.[41] As Philippe Ariès has shown, the changing concept of death at this time not only was founded on those new apprehensions but also gradually came to incorporate new ideas of death, specifically as repose and reunion, perhaps as a consolation: "the prevailing mythology liked to think of death as a desirable and a long-awaited refuge."[42] The ambiguities suggested by the undead—in their liminal, in-between, transitional state—were therefore doubly disturbing.[43] But it is this Romantic idea of death that explains to some extent the undead Dutchman's anguished yearning to die. When he first appears on stage, he is utterly worn out by his wandering and his inability to bring his existence to an end. "Die Frist ist um" ("The term is up"), his opening utterance, has been called the first of Wagner's "monologues of exhaustion":[44]

> How often into the sea's deepest abyss
> have I thrown myself, full of yearning:—
> but no! Death, I did not find!
> There, where lies the fearful grave of ships,
> I drove my ship aground on the cliffs:—
> but no! My grave did not close over me!—
> Jeering I threatened pirates,
> in wild battles I hoped for death: . . .
> Nowhere the grave! Never death!
> This is damnation's terrifying decree.—

> *Wie oft in Meeres tiefsten Schlund*
> *stürzt ich voll Sehnsucht mich hinab:—*
> *doch ach! Den Tod, ich fand ihn nicht!*
> *Da, wo der Schiffe furchtbar Grab,*
> *trieb mein Schiff ich zum Klippen grund:—*
> *doch ach! Mein Grab, es schloss sich nicht!—*
> *Verhöhnend droht' ich dem Piraten,*
> *im wilden Kampfe hofft' ich Tod: . . .*
> *Nirgends den Grab! Niemals der Tod!*
> *Dies der Verdammnis Schreckgebot.—*

Sung to a repeated "despairing octave descent," the words "Nirgends den Grab! Niemals der Tod!" underline the Dutchman's horror of his undead existence.[45] All he can hope for, he goes on to

say, is the annihilation he assumes will come with the end of the
world on Judgment Day, a sentiment expressed in a line repeated
(for emphasis) by the unseen ghostly chorus of his men: "Eternal
oblivion, receive me!" ("Ewig Vernichtung, nimm mich auf!").

The opera ends, of course, with a different kind of salvation
through annihilation. The final stage directions tell us that, as
Senta casts herself into the sea: "The Dutchman's ship, with all her
crew, sinks immediately. The sea rises high, and sinks back in a
whirlpool. In the glow of the sunset are clearly seen, over the wreck
of the ship, the forms of Senta and the Dutchman, embracing each
other, rising from the sea, and floating upwards."[46] In order to understand this double death in its nineteenth-century Romantic
context—that is, not as a tragedy but as both a choice and a glori-
ous transfiguration of mortality through love—we have to remind
ourselves once again of this period's very different interpretation of
death and dying. Ariès describes the two elements of "Romantic
death" that are most important here: "The first is the release, the
deliverance, the flight into the immensity of the beyond; the second is the intolerable separation that must be compensated for
by a restoration in the beyond of what has been temporarily removed."[47] So, when a modern theorist like Theodor Adorno casti-
gates Wagner for ending the opera with Senta's redeeming self-sacrifice and the Dutchman's final release into death, he rather misses
the point—at least for Wagner and his nineteenth-century audience. Calling it "dressing up death as salvation," Adorno asserts
that the redemptive double death is "a homecoming without a
home, eternal rest without eternity, the mirage of peace without
the underlying reality of a human being to enjoy it."[48] Perhaps this
is how Wagner's resolution could appear to modern eyes, but that
is not how Wagner or his audience would have seen this acceptance of death as deliverance. They would not have mocked or
mourned these deaths any more than they would have mocked or
mourned those of Tristan and Isolde. Rather, like Nietzsche, they

would have celebrated the lovers' reunion and release into the beyond.

There is yet another important cultural and historical context that helps us understand how death can be presented here as positive. This involves another legendary undead figure. Like Heine in the source text for the opera, Wagner is explicit about comparing his Dutchman not only to figures like Ulysses, wandering far from Ithaca, or Prometheus, defying the gods, but also to the figure from Christian legend known as the Wandering Jew.[49] First appearing in Europe in the thirteenth century, this legend tells the story of the man who was supposed to have taunted Christ on the way to his crucifixion and so was condemned forever to wander the world and never die. The tale seems to have been repeated by Christians throughout the centuries, predictably at times of significant anti-Semitism. But it is also true that the Wandering Jew took on more positive (if still, arguably, anti-Semitic) associations in revolutionary nineteenth-century Europe, associations with those heroic striving figures like Faust, the Ancient Mariner, and Odysseus. In this way, he came to stand for the Promethean revolutionary spirit of the 1840s, and yet, in his suffering, he could still stand as a symbol of the trials and sorrows of humankind.

Which of these various associations did Wagner himself intend to convey? Well, the answer is complex. Once again, it is crucial to use our historical imagination since, for the Romantics and certainly for Wagner (at least in 1842), the Wandering Jew seems to have represented precisely this *positive* figure of the alienated artist, the outcast outsider, and the heroic rebel with whom Wagner himself clearly identified. However, there is no doubt that the composer's anti-Semitism led him to reinterpret the Wandering Jew in more negative terms within the next decade.[50] But at this point, in 1842, this was still a figure that commanded Wagner's respect and engaged his imagination. The Wandering Jew is a defiant, isolated hero to be admired and pitied—because of his yearning for a death he can never attain. In Wagner's words, he was a "wanderer, forever doomed to a long-since outlived life, without an aim, without a joy, there bloomed no earthly ransom; death was the sole remaining goal of all his strivings; his only hope, the laying down of being."[51] Wagner was not alone at the time in his fascination with this undead figure and his sufferings. We need only recall such other manifestations as the twelve wood engravings that Gustave Doré created in 1856 to accompany Pierre Dupont's poem "Le Juif errant"—which, of course, is also the title of the 1852 opera by the French Jewish composer Fromental Halévy, derived from Eugène Sue's famous novel about Ahasuerus, the Wandering Jew.

When Death Abdicates

The Wandering Jew, then, was the figure upon which Wagner consciously modeled his tortured undead Dutchman. In his words, "Like Ahasuerus, he yearns for his sufferings to be ended by Death; the Dutchman, however, may gain this redemption, denied to the undying Jew, at the hands of—*a Woman* who, of very love, shall sacrifice herself for him. The yearning for Death thus spurs him on to seek this Woman."[52] In 1996, Christopher Alden's controversial, bold production of *Der fliegende Holländer* for the Canadian Opera Company confronted both this early legend and the more recent history of the Nazi appropriation of Wagner (and his obvious anti-Semitism). The production dressed the undead Dutchman and his ghostly crew in prisoner costumes, but inevitably (given other stage clues—and despite the different direction of the stripes) these were interpreted as representing concentration camp prisoners. The production managed to convey the idea that the Holocaust context is what would represent to a contemporary audience the most potent image of a situation in which life may not be worth living, when death could mean deliverance and redemption.

Costume sketch for the Dutchman and his crew, designed by Allen Moyer for the Canadian Opera Company, 1996.

Although on the surface the Shoah would not seem a likely operatic framework for an affirmation of the positive value of death, in fact it provided precisely that in *Der Kaiser von Atlantis (The Emperor of Atlantis)*, an opera written by Viktor Ullmann and Petr Kien when the two were in the concentration camp at Theresienstadt in Czechoslovakia in 1943–1944, just before they were sent to their deaths at Auschwitz.[53] Everyone who writes about this opera inevitably feels, as do we, intimidated by this history. Everyone also agrees that its very existence is a testament to the resilience of the human spirit.[54] After all, it is openly an opera about death. But, perhaps surprisingly, it is one in which Death is an actual character who refuses to do his job: in disgust at the mechanization of both human life and human destruction in war, he decides that people will not be allowed to die anymore.

Of the original cast of the camp production (banned by the SS after the dress rehearsal), only Czech bass Karel Berman survived the war. Appropriately and yet ironically, Berman was to sing the role of Death. His description of life in Theresienstadt, the "model camp" with its rich cultural and religious life (which Hitler exploited in his propaganda efforts), puts into perspective the creation, in such a setting, of an opera about death: "Grown-ups and children, in constant expectation of death, lived a full, noble life, between outcries of pain and anxiety . . . in hunger and misery, among the hundreds of corpses of those that died daily, amongst hearses taking the corpses out of town and bringing back bread, under constant physical exertion, they lived a life that was a miracle under the given conditions."[55] Such is the site of both miracle and resistance—psychological and cultural.

Der Kaiser von Atlantis opens with the startling sounds of a trumpet playing a citation of the death motive from Joseph Suk's symphony named *Asrael* (after the Jewish angel who carries away the souls of the dead). Suk, of course, is also remembered today for being Dvořák's student and later his son-in-law. Written between

Costume sketch for Death, designed by Teresa Przybylski for the Canadian Opera Company production of *The Emperor of Atlantis*.

1904 and 1906, following the deaths of Suk's wife and father-in-law, this symphony came to be used by the First Czechoslovak Republic as the official music for occasions of national mourning. Because of this association, the projected Czechoslovak camp audience who would have attended the performance (had it taken place as planned) would have immediately made the connection with death (a connection most of us would have to learn to make today). This music is first heard right at the start but it echoes throughout the opera. So too does another sound that we come to associate with death: the syncopated motive that a character simply known as the Drummer plays and to which the character referred to as the Loudspeaker sings the words "Hallo, hallo." The Loudspeaker's role at this point in the opera is likely inspired by the plays of Bertolt Brecht. His job is to distance us, to stand between us and the action, and to introduce the characters and the allegory of the plot.

The Loudspeaker informs the audience that two characters, Death and Harlequin, find themselves stuck in a kind of limbo—but it is a distinctly negative kind of limbo, a world in which one can neither enjoy life nor embrace death. Harlequin is a stock character from the commedia dell'arte tradition, associated in general terms with love and high spirits; Death as a personified character is straight out of the medieval mystery plays.[56] The secular and the religious, the comic and the tragic mix, then, from the start in this opera. Harlequin tells Death he should do away with him. He cannot bear the boredom of his life any longer. Death disagrees, saying that laughter that knows how to mock itself is immortal. In other words, Harlequin can never be done away with. So, Harlequin responds with nostalgia—both in the music and in the text—wishing he could enjoy life again as he once had. Death ups the ante, recalling his own glory days as he accompanied victorious armies fighting real wars—but he does so to music that suggests the songs played in 1920s German satiric cabarets:

So often have I raced alongside the small
horses of Attila,
with Hannibal's elephants and the tigers
of Genghis Khan that my bones
are too weak to be able to
follow the motorized cohorts.
All I can do now
is limp after the new angels of death,
a small artisan of death.

So oft bin ich mit den kleinen
Pferden Attilas um die Wette
gelaufen, mit den Elefanten
Hannibals und den Tigern
Dschehangirs, dass meine Beine
zu schwach sind, um den
motorisierten Kohorten folgen
zu können. Was bleibt mir übrig,
als hinter den neuen Todesengeln zu
hinken, ein kleiner Handwerker des Sterbens.

Their one-upmanship game of former glory and present misery is
interrupted by the arrival of the Drummer, whose pompous mili-
tary music fits her message well, for she is the (mezzo soprano) an-
nouncer of the will of the megalomaniac Emperor Overall. In the
German text, his name is in English; perhaps, in the camp, to call
him "Überall" would have been too openly provocative. However,
at the point at which she announces that the Emperor has just de-
clared "a great and blessed war of all against all" ("den grossen,
segensreichen Krieg aller gegen alle")—the music pointedly offers
a grotesque distortion of the national anthem "Deutschland über
alles." Death is enraged at the Emperor's taking over of his power
to summon souls, and in anger Death breaks his sword and de-
clares that he will no longer do his job. People will no longer die.

In the next scene we witness the result of Death's action. The Emperor Overall is barricaded in his bunkerlike fortress, protecting himself against both the war raging outside and the assassination attempts on his own life. He is in touch with the world only through the unseen Loudspeaker, from whom he learns that an assassin hanged over an hour before has not yet died. Four times, the Loudspeaker repeats: "Death must arrive at any moment!" ("Der Tod muss jeden Augenblick eintreten!"). But Death will not arrive; Death has abdicated. When the Emperor realizes this, he is distraught. Without Death, he has no power to demand obedience:

> Have I gone crazy?
> Is Death to be wrested from my hands?
> Who will still fear me in the future?
> Does Death refuse to serve?
> Has his old sword been broken to bits?
> Who will obey
> the Emperor of Atlantis anymore?

> *Bin ich wahnsinnig geworden?*
> *Ringt den Tod man aus der Hand mir?*
> *Wer wird in Zukunft mich noch fürchten?*
> *Weigert sich der Tod zu dienen?*
> *Hat sein altes Schwert zerbrochen?*
> *Wer wird dem Imperator von Atlantis*
> *noch gehorchen?*

He learns that there is an epidemic: people "wrestle with life, in order to be able to die" ("ringen mit dem Leben, um sterben zu können") but cannot. Ever the political opportunist, however, the Emperor then decides to make good use of this, and so he bestows on his soldiers the gift of eternal life—so that they will fight all the more fiercely for him and the fatherland. This he sings to appropriately Wagnerian Wotan-like tones:

We, the one and only Overall, bestow
on our loyal soldiers a
secret means to eternal life.
He who possesses it is safe from
death, and no wound and no
sickness can prevent him from
taking up his sword for his lord
and for the fatherland. Death, where is
thy sting? Hell, where is thy victory?

*Wir, Overall, der Einzige, schenken
unseren verdienten Soldaten ein
Geheimmittel zum ewigen Leben.
Wer es besitzt, ist gefeit gegen den
Tod, und keine Wunde und keine
Krankheit kann fortan hemmen, das
Schwert für seinen Herrn und das
Vaterland zu führen. Tod, wo ist
dein Stachel? Hölle, wo ist dein Sieg?*

There is a shift in scene 3 in both the music and the plot direction. A soldier and a girl from the enemy camp meet on the bat-
tlefield and find they are unable to kill each other as they should,
despite the Drummer's offstage reminders of their duty. Their music is sentimental, melodic, rather like that of a 1930s film operetta—moving into what sounds like real happy-ending "movie
music" by the end of the girl's aria. The Drummer tries to lure
the soldier back to the seductions of heroic battle, through music
reminiscent of Schoenberg's cabaret songs as sung in the style of
Marlene Dietrich. The lovers, however, rejoice (lyrically and sentimentally) in the knowledge that Death is dead. In their eyes there
is no longer any need to fight, as they sing of a Tristan-like notion
of the beauty of death when united with love: "Now is in full
bloom that which makes death / beautiful, the flower of love / that

reconciles all to all" ("Nun ist sie erblüht, die den Tod / verschönt, die Blume der Liebe, / die alles, alles versöhnt").

When the curtain falls, however, we enter a very different world. The orchestral intermezzo is a dance, but one referred to as the dance of the "living dead" ("Die lebenden Toten"). This fox-trot-like music is considerably darker in tone color, preparing us for the announcement to the Emperor by the Loudspeaker that "Hospital 34 for the living dead was stormed by rebels; doctors and instructors are defecting en masse" ("Spital 34 für lebende Tote wurde um drei Uhr von den Empörern gestürmt; Ärzte und Instruktoren gingen in Massen über"). The Emperor then removes the cover from a mirror on stage. Reflected in its frame is his literal and figurative mirror-image, Death. In an aria offering a new definition of death, this time in terms of nature, Death sings that now he is the gentle gardener, not Death, the rapacious reaper. Through this domestic and benign natural image of the gardener, he presents to us and to the Emperor a positive evaluation of what death does: death is a release from suffering and pain; death is freedom; death is calm and peace.

> I am Death, the gardener Death,
> and I sow sleep in pain-filled
> furrows.
> I am Death, the gardener Death,
> and I pluck like faded weeds weary creatures.
> I am death, the gardener Death,
> and I reap the corn of suffering
> in the fields.
> I am the one who delivers you from pestilence,
> and not the pestilence itself.
> I am the one who brings you redemption from suffering,
> not the one who lets you suffer.
> I am the comfortable warm nest,
> to which tormented life flies.

I am the greatest celebration of freedom
I am the final lullaby.
Still and peaceful is my welcoming abode!
Come, take rest.

Ich bin der Tod, der Gärtner Tod,
und säe Schlaf in schmerzgepflügte
Spuren.
Ich bin der Tod, der Gärtner Tod,
und jäte welkes Unkraut müder Kreaturen.
Ich bin der Tod, der Gärtner Tod,
und mähe reifes Korn des Leidens auf den
Fluren.
Bin der, der von der Pest befreit,
und nicht die Pest.
Bin, der Erlösung bringt von Leid,
nicht, der euch leiden lässt.
Ich bin das wohlig warme Nest,
wohin das angstgehetzten Leben flieht.
Ich bin das grösste Freiheitsfest.
Ich bin das letzte Schlummerlied.
Still ist und friedevoll mein gastlich Haus!
Kommt, ruhet aus!

Despite the continuities with the Romantic conception of death, it is difficult not to read this aria today as either a form of psychological wish-fulfillment or a very powerful acceptance of (rather than simply resignation to) an unavoidable existential reality, made all the more poignant in this particular context, since the opera's creators and singers were presumably faced daily with the threat of transport to the death camps.

This scene between Death and the Emperor is complex and confusing, however, especially for contemporary audiences, who know the history of the Holocaust and of the creators' fates. Over-

all begins by asking Death to return to them: "We humans cannot live without you" ("Wir Menschen können ohne dich nicht
leben"), he says. Death agrees to do so, but only if the Emperor
will be the first to submit to him. If this were an uncomplicated,
straightforward allegory of Nazi power, with the Emperor as Hitler, there would be little way of explaining what then happens:
Overall says, yes, he *is* strong enough to make this sacrifice, but he
doesn't think humanity deserves it. Nevertheless, he agrees to un-
dergo, as he puts it, "what all those suffering are begging you to bestow" ("worum dich alle Leidenden bitten"). He then sings his
"Abschied," his farewell. Again, confusing any simple allegory, the
music is rich in respectful echoes of other German music—from
its opening reminiscence of a Bach cantata (complete with solo
oboe) through quotations from Brahms's "Vier ernste Gesänge"
("Four Serious Songs") and Mahler's "Das Lied von der Erde"
("The Song of the Earth"). These last two pieces begin in bitter-
ness and end with calm acceptance of fate,[57] perhaps suggesting
that this is to be the Emperor's progression as well, as he follows
Death, now transfigured from an old soldier to a young Hermes.
Overall tells the Drummer not to weep for him, because life goes
on even if you aren't there to experience its joys and sorrows. In
lines that make listeners today inevitably think of the place where
the opera was first meant to be produced, he sings:

> For that which is far away is not worth mourning,
> but rather that which is near,
> that which rests in eternal shadows.

> *Denn es ist das Ferne nicht beklagenswert,*
> *vielmehr das Nahe,*
> *das in ewigem Schatten ruht.*

A curious character, this arrogant bully of an Emperor, who has
ordered total war and has stood for nihilistic evil throughout the

opera, suddenly elicits our sympathy. In an oddly poignant scene, he shows himself willing to sacrifice himself for humanity—and, in the alternate Farewell written by Ullmann, he welcomes the return of death as a natural phenomenon—rather than a humanly created one. One way of reading this ambivalence about the Emperor is to see his death as a fantasy. In other words, would that Hitler had willingly gone to his own death before Ullmann and Kien (and millions of others) had died. But here, the text also says that Death "gently" ("sanft") leads the Emperor through the mirror—like Orpheus in Jean Cocteau's film—into death. There is no triumph, only sadness and resignation—and maybe some forgiveness. Perhaps the lesson is that to desire revenge against the Emperor (as many in the audience might well still feel today) would put us squarely in the moral world of the Emperor, a world of human destruction—and this is precisely what must be resisted in the name of tolerance and acceptance.

The final message of the opera, that death is not completely a negative, but a natural and important part of life, is articulated in a final quartet sung by the girl, Harlequin, the Loudspeaker, and the Drummer. Their finale is a highly original musical adaptation of Luther's famous chorale "Ein feste Burg" (in English, "A Mighty Fortress Is Our God"), a Protestant hymn that had already been quoted by other Jewish composers, such as Mendelssohn in his "Reformation" Symphony and Meyerbeer in his opera *Les Huguenots*.[58] In this version, Death is welcomed as an honored guest who will take from us all the pain and suffering of life. Death will also teach us to respect and honor our fellow humans; and, most of all, we will learn never to take "Death's great name in vain":

> Come, Death, you our honoured guest,
> into our heart's chamber.
> Take from us life's suffering and woe,
> lead us to rest after pain and sorrow.

Teach us to honor life's joys and
sorrows in our brothers.
Teach us the most holy commandment:
Thou shalt not take the great name of Death
in vain.

Komm Tod, du unser werter Gast,
in unsers Herzens Kammer.
Nimm von uns Lebens Leid und Last,
führ uns zur Rast nach Schmerz und Jammer.

Lehr uns Lebens Lust und Not
in unsren Brüdern ehren.
Lehr uns das heiligste Gebot:
Du sollst den grossen Namen Tod
nicht eitel beschwören.

Of course, given that we know the fate of Ullmann and Kien, we cannot help reading that knowledge backwards into the opera's text, but, despite the constant threat of death, *they* didn't really know what their end would be when they wrote the piece. In fact, its composition appears to date from a seven-month period in 1943 when transports to the death camps had ceased. Hope may well have prevailed. Perhaps that explains why the ending is not bitter, why the Emperor is such a strangely sympathetic and sacrificial character at the end.

There are also important insights here into the meaning of death in relation to life that transcend the particulars of history. In the opera, we move from a world in which the natural purpose of death, as part of life, has been hijacked by the Emperor and used to political ends, for total war: death has lost its naturalness, and the character of Death abdicates in disgust. The world that results may allow the love of the soldier and the girl to flourish, but it also leads to a world of the living dead who, suffering, desire fervently to be allowed to die. With the Emperor's self-sacrifice, a utopian vision replaces the dystopian, as death regains its natural role as deliverance from pain, as comfort in suffering and final rest.

Ready to Die

In our final example of an opera about death as a positive and thus about the torments of the undead, the protagonist is not Death as a character but Emilia Marty, a.k.a. Elena Makropulos, a woman over three hundred years old as the opera opens, who chooses in the end to die—when she could go on living another three hundred years. With this longevity theme, Leoš Janáček's *Věc Makropulos* (usually translated as either *The Makropulos Affair* or *The Makropulos Case*) returns us to the questions with which we began this chapter, questions about what it is that gives meaning and value to life. What would life be like if death were not our inevitable end? This 1926 opera remains timely and topical today, as modern medicine (like Elena's physician father over three centuries before) still studies ways to extend the life of human cells. Today the answers are sought not in potions or fountains of youth but in various theories involving exercise, diet, drugs, and genetic intervention. The media, of course, constantly refer to the results of this longevity research as "ways to beat death."

This kind of denial of death is also not new. Stories of the quest for immortality or longevity would appear to be as old as humanity itself. In the Babylonian epic *Gilgamesh* and the Egyptian Book of the Dead, in alchemical research and in legends about the Golem, humans have told tales of this search and its related search for eternal youth.[59] Interestingly, all the variations on this theme either betray overt wish-fulfillment about avoiding death or else offer lessons on the inevitability of death as a natural part of life. Sometimes, even on the operatic stage, both messages are sent simultaneously. In Frederick Delius's *The Magic Fountain* (composed 1893–1895, but not premiered until 1977), a sixteenth-century Spanish imperial agent in newly "discovered" Florida is obsessed with finding both gold and the magic fountain of youth. Based loosely on Ponce de Leon's similar search in 1513, this story tells of a "fountain ready for those prepared to drink it in wisdom and truth." The protagonist sings:

> Once having drunk of its waters divine
> Eternal youth
> Eternal love
> Life everlasting mine.
> What grand possibilities!

Of course, if the drinker is *not* "prepared," Indian legend has it that the fountain's waters bring death, and so they do in the opera.

This theme of eternal life fascinated the aging Janáček during his last decade, his most productive period. In his 1924 opera *Příhody Lišky Bystroušky (The Cunning Little Vixen)*, he "came to terms with human mortality by accepting the notion of the immortality of Nature. Bystrouška [the vixen] is overtaken by the deadly bullet just as the game-keeper is overtaken by old age. But among them are the others—the new little Bystrouška, 'the living image of her mother'—life goes on and Nature continues undisturbed with its eternal song and permanent regeneration."[60] The composer's own daughter had died at the age of twenty-one; a son had died even earlier, at age two. In his letters, however, the clear comfort he derived from the sense of nature's infinite continuity is contrasted with his belief that humans are happy because we know that our life is not long.[61] This paradox helps explain his attraction to Karel Čapek's 1922 play about the more than three-hundred-year-old beauty whose youthful appearance masks "complete satiety, cynicism and deathly spiritual weariness."[62] Spiritually dead, she is left with what Janáček called "only burnt-out feeling! Brr! Cold as ice!"[63] The trick, for the composer, was to make his audience both like and feel for the woman who envies others their short but meaningful lives. In an interview the year he died, Janáček explained what had gripped him: "it is terrible, the emotion of an individual who will never meet her end. A true misery. She does not want anything, does not wait for anything."[64] Elena Makropulos is in fact a scientific perversion of nature, the result of an emperor's greed for life. She was made to test the longevity potion that her father, the emperor's physician, had prepared for him. She lives out her allotted three hundred years, changing identities but retaining her initials: Elian MacGregor, Ekaterina Myshkin, Elsa Müller, Eugenia Montez, Emilia Marty. In the last of these identities, she enters the world of the opera as a famous diva, seeking the parchment upon which is written the charm that will allow her to extend her life once again. Although no one knows this history, each of the men in the story cannot help falling in love with her, despite her coldness to them. As one says, it's as if she'd risen from the grave. Of course, she has no compunction about using them in her quest; her time is almost up.

The complaint of the man with whom she has sex in return for the parchment gives a vivid sense of this world-weary "femme fatale who exudes ennui":[65] "Cold as ice. Like embracing a dead thing" ("Studená jak led. Jak bych držel mrtvou"). She is even unmoved by the suicide of a young man who dies for her and by the recriminations of those who confront her in the final scene. Now aging, she cares even less, but now for a different reason. She had thought she wanted the charm so that she could renew her youth. But, she asks, "Now I am sure that death laid his hand on me. Why was I afraid of it?" ("Cítila jsem, že smrt na mne sahala. Nebylo to tak hrozné?"). She sees the others in the room as mere shadows and dead things, a line echoed for emphasis by the male chorus, as is another important one: "Dying or living—it's all one, it's the same thing!" ("Umřit neb odejít—vše jedno, to je stejné!"). The chorus also repeats the final line of her despairing outburst:

> Ah, It's a mistake to live so long!
> Oh, if you only knew how easy life is
> For you!
> You are so close to life!
> You see in life some meaning!
> Life for you has some value.
> Fools, how happy you all are.

> *Ach, nemá se tak dlouho žít!*
> *Ó kdybyste věděli, jak se vám*
> *lehkožije!*
> *Vy jste tak blízko všcho!*
> *Pro vás má všecko smysl!*
> *Všecko má pro vás cenu.*
> *Hlupci, vy jste tak šťastni.*

The diva explains to her astonished audience that they only believe in mankind, love, virtue, and progress because they are going to die one day—and soon.

Having used "speech melody" throughout, Janáček now lets melody flood the music for great emotional impact as the woman faces the atrophy of her immortal but amoral soul:

> But my life has come to a standstill,
> Jesus Christ! And there's nothing more.
> How dreadful this loneliness!
> In the end, it's the same, Krista,
> Singing and silence.

There's no joy in goodness, there's no joy in evil.
Joyless the earth, joyless the sky!
When you know that, your soul dies with you.

Ale va mně se život zastavil,
Ježíši Kriste! A nemůže dál.
Ta hrozná samota!
Je to, Kristinko, stejně marné,
zpívat či mlčet.
Omrzí být dobrý, omrzí být špatný.
Omrzí země, omrzí nebe.
A pozná, že v něm umřela dušc.

After this revelation of the meaninglessness of life without death, she renounces the charm written on the parchment, but offers it to the young Krista, whose lover's suicide she caused. But Krista burns the parchment. As the flames destroy it, the diva cries out to God in her original Greek tongue—"Pater hemon" (Our Father)—and collapses. The orchestra "howls with agony" and the curtain falls: "Emilia Marty tells us boldly that to live forever kills the soul; Janáček's music, terrible in its anguished splendor, *shows* us what she means. Marty's final aria is, fittingly, a *Liebestod*."[66] It is the brevity of life and the inevitability of death that grant life its meaning and value; it is death that grants the diva her humanity.

This opera could be seen as a mature and courageous resignation to mortality, to the complexities of human existence. Its protagonist's end should not, therefore, be greeted with sadness by audiences, any more than the demise of Senta and the Dutchman. Rather, it is her meaningless life that should evoke sympathy, as the composer suggested. If *Příhody Lišky Bystroušky (The Cunning Little Vixen)* celebrated the infinite renewal of nature, then *Věc Makropulos* perhaps celebrated the aging Janáček's growing realization that only death can bring peace. As an aberration of nature, this Elena Makropulos has violated that natural cycle of life and death so powerfully reasserted at the end of *Der Kaiser von Atlantis,* and so can only destroy others and what remains of her own humanity. Humans may paradoxically attribute value to immortality because of their own mortality, but to choose to accept death is to face life and all its challenges.

Coda

"Be Acquainted with Death Betimes . . ."

Death does not make me tremble . . .
Der Tod macht mich nicht beben . . .

Mozart, *The Magic Flute*

The title for this brief concluding section comes from Henry Montagu's *Contemplatio Mortis et Immortalitatis* published in 1631.[1] The author goes on to inform us that through acquaintance, death will lose its horror and become familiar, even comely. He had preceded this confident assertion with the claim that meditation on death would, in fact, help us die in ease, alleviate pain, expel fears, ease cares, cure sins, and "correct" death itself. Such listing of the effects of this kind of dramatized meditation on death is, in part, what provoked us to try to think beyond the usual explanations given for the pleasure that operas about death and dying afford. Could opera be an "art of dying" in its own right?

Death, like love, is obviously an aspect of the human condition for which there are always many questions and never easy answers. Does this fact, combined with death's inevitability, account for its continuing fascination for audiences? Perhaps, but there seems to

be something else going on, and none of the most obvious explanations—masochism, sadism, voyeurism—seems to us to account
for the bizarre position of the audience when we witness the staging of death in opera. We project our imaginations onto the action
we see and hear in a peculiarly paradoxical manner: we identify
strongly with the staged drama, in large part because of the emo-
tive power of the music, but we are also consciously distanced from
that drama by the conventions of the singing and the simulation of
the acting. Here, there is none of the engrossing realism of film, in
other words. Both the emotional identification and the intellectual
distancing are paradoxically enhanced in opera. Therefore, when
the subject is death and dying, we can experience its power—but
safely—just as Montagu said one could during the *contemplatio
mortis* exercise. Watching these operas, we would argue, is analogous to imaginatively experiencing the emotions associated with
dying and, in a sense, even working through your own death or
that of a loved one.

Many have argued that it is the very *form* of our "working
through"—our story-telling, if you like—that helps us find not
only consolation but also meaning in death and, indeed, in life.
Holocaust survivor and psychotherapist Viktor E. Frankl is among
those who argue that "striving to find a meaning in one's life is the
primary motivational force" in humanity.[2] And stories are one of
our ways of finding—or making—that meaning: "Human beings
understand their experiences in and through the telling and hearing of stories. Narration is the forward movement of description of
actions and events which makes possible the backward action of
self understanding."[3] Our modern narratives of science and technology can only go so far in guiding our understanding of incom-
mensurables like death. And where they stop, the human imagination takes over, proffering order and meaning as needed. As Frank
Kermode has argued in *The Sense of an Ending,* we "make considerable imaginative investments in coherent patterns which, by the

provision of an end, make possible a satisfying consonance with the origins and with the middle."[4] How do art forms like opera fit in? Well, as Kermode says, we have to project ourselves "past the End, so as to see the structure whole, a thing we cannot do from our spot in time in the middle." So we rehearse death in order to give life meaning: we watch Blanche overcoming her fear of dying or Wotan facing up to his mortality. Our aesthetic pleasure in the closure these operas afford is paralleled by a sense of psychological fulfillment and even ethical completion.

We believe this is why, in all the operas we have studied, death is not presented or experienced as conventionally tragic. As noted earlier, we did not consciously set out to find operas that offered positive messages about dying; in a way these operas found us. It was their stubborn persistence in *not* fitting into the tragic mold that made us want to explore them further, using as many tools as were at our disposal from the many different fields in which death has been studied. For, you must admit, these operas are puzzling and even counterintuitive in their positive valuing of our human mortality. Blanche de la Force, at the moment of her death, overcomes the mortal fear that has plagued her young life, and faces her end with courage and integrity. Reversing the normal order of the day (world), Tristan and Isolde can finally be united in love in the night world of death. Wotan comes to face his end with the equanimity that can only come with putting his own life in order, righting the moral wrongs he has committed and which have caused the sacrificial deaths of so many others. His "good death" is hard earned in his world of power. Orpheus, in his many operatic incarnations, lives through the story we all dread having to endure—that of the loss of a loved one. These operas enact both the human pain of bereavement (sometimes pathological) and also the comforting balm of ritual. Even suicide can take on positive meaning when it is presented as a rational choice, as in Seneca's case, or as an escape from unbearable circumstances, as for Cio-Cio-San.

For the audience, the sense of moral justice that comes when a wrong is made right—when someone who has killed someone else then takes his own life (as with Wozzeck or Peter Grimes)—can amplify the sense of aesthetic closure and cushion the negative impact of the deaths onstage. The positive view of death is perhaps most clear in the case of the undead in opera: here death is seen as release, as reunion, as the desired end. Death is, quite simply, what gives meaning to life.

Why, then, do we fear it? To contemplate death, even on the operatic stage, is inevitably to feel, and perhaps to face, our mortal anxieties. But, as Sherwin B. Nuland explains, that is still only half of the story: "To most people, death remains a hidden secret, as eroticized as it is feared. We are irresistibly attracted by the very anxieties we find most terrifying; we are drawn to them by a primitive excitement that arises from flirtation with danger. Moths and flames, mankind and death—there's little difference."[5] This too is part of the appeal of watching operas about death, even those in which the End is presented as a positive, complete with the consolations of closure and ritual. We should also not forget the simple fact that characters dying on stage can generate an intense relationship with spectators, driving home the values and meanings the art work has granted to death. As usual, Shakespeare understood this well, and so, given his musical metaphor, we think he should be given the last word, for in *King Richard II,* he wrote: "O, but they say the tongues of dying men / Enforce attention like deep harmony" (2.1, l. 5).

Notes

Introduction

The translations of the chapter epigraphs from *Die Zauberflöte* are rhymed singing translations from the English version provided in the libretto accompanying the Herbert von Karajan, Berliner Philharmoniker recording by Deutsche Grammophon. Through these citations, we suggest that even operas that are not usually considered death-obsessed, in fact, do dwell on this theme.

1. Technically dying as a process and death as a final state are separate and separable, but here we have chosen to follow the practice of others writing on this topic and conflate them.

2. Philippe Ariès, *Western Attitudes toward Death: From the Middle Ages to the Present*, trans. Patricia M. Ranum (Baltimore: Johns Hopkins University Press, 1986); originally published as *Essai sur l'histoire de la mort en occident* (Paris: Seuil, 1975); and *The Hour of Our Death*, trans. Helen Weaver (New York: Oxford University Press, 1991); originally published as *L'Homme devant la mort* (Paris: Seuil, 1977). The critiques of these books have come from many directions. His periodization and the reliability of his data both come under attack by Laurence Stone in "Death and Its History," *New York Review of Books*, 25 (1978): 29. Pat Jalland, in *Death and the Victorian Family* (New York: Oxford University Press, 1996), and Jonathan Dollimore, in *Death, Desire and Loss in Western Culture* (New York: Routledge, 1998), attack Ariès's tendency to describe rather than analyze and to generalize from too narrow data. His work is clearly open to other critiques: that it is too class-limited, focusing only on middle- and upper-class populations; that its stress on cultural

objects as data is too limiting, given that other representations of death—from life tables to official reports on mortality to death certificates—may tell us more about how societies explain and interpret death.

3. Ariès, *Western Attitudes,* p. 2.

4. Ibid., p. 27.

5. See Stone, "Death and Its History," 29.

6. Ariès, *Western Attitudes,* p. 56.

7. Ariès, *The Hour,* p. 608.

8. Ariès, *Western Attitudes,* p. 58.

9. Respectively, ibid., p. 82, and Ariès, *The Hour,* p. 611.

10. Sherwin B. Nuland, *How We Die: Reflections on Life's Final Chapter* (New York: Knopf, 1994), p. xv.

11. Stone, "Death and Its History," p. 26.

12. Many discussions in newspapers and on the internet suggest that death has become quite the voguish subject. Tony Walter's ideas as expressed in *The Revival of Death* (London: Routledge, 1994) would support this view in a different way.

13. Jean-François Lyotard, *The Postmodern Condition: A Report on Knowledge,* trans. Geoff Bennington and Brian Massumi (Minneapolis: University of Minnesota Press, 1984).

14. Linda Hutcheon and Michael Hutcheon, *Opera: Desire, Disease, Death* (Lincoln: University of Nebraska Press, 1996).

15. Kent Neely, "Death: (Re)Presenting Mortality and Moribundity—PRAXIS: An Editorial Statement," *Journal of Dramatic Theory and Criticism,* 12 (1997): 97.

16. Catherine Clément, *Opera, or The Undoing of Women,* trans. Betsy Wing (Minneapolis: University of Minnesota Press, 1988); originally published as *L'opéra: ou, La défaite des femmes* (Paris: Grasset, 1979).

17. Linda Hutcheon and Michael Hutcheon, *Opera: Desire, Disease, Death* (Lincoln: University of Nebraska Press, 1996).

18. See Michael Cameron Andrews, *This Action of Our Death: The Performance of Death in English Renaissance Drama* (Newark: University of Delaware Press; London: Associated University Presses, 1989), pp. 21–22.

19. See, respectively, Beatrice Corrigan, "'All Happy Endings: Libretti of the Late Seicento," *Forum Italicum,* 7 (1973): 250–267; and Frederick

W. Sternfeld, "Lieto fine," in Stanley Sadie, ed., *The New Grove Dictionary of Opera* (London: Macmillan, 1992), 2:1260.

20. Ariès, *Western Attitudes,* p. 58.

21. Oscar Wilde, "The Critic as Artist Part II [with some remarks on the importance of doing nothing]," *Oscar Wilde,* ed. Isobel Murray (Oxford: Oxford University Press, 1989), p. 274.

22. See Michael Neill, *Issues of Death: Mortality and Identity in English Renaissance Tragedy* (New York: Oxford University Press, 1997). Our thanks to Jill Matus for this reference. Jacques Choron argues the same rehearsal function for philosophy, by citing Plato's *Phaedo* and Montaigne's "That to philosophize is to learn to die" (*Essays* 1:20). See Choron's "Death as a Motive of Philosophical Thought," in Edwin S. Shneidman, ed., *Essays in Self-Destruction* (New York: Science House, 1967), pp. 61–63 especially.

23. In *The Semiotics of Theatre and Drama* (London: Routledge, 1980), Kier Elam defines "horizon of expectations" as the "spectator's cognitive hold on the theatrical frame, his knowledge of texts, textual laws and conventions, together with his general cultural preparation and the influence of critics, friends, and so forth" (p. 94).

24. Paul Bouissac, "The Semiotic Approach to the Performing Arts: Theory and Method," in Roberta Kevelson, ed., *High Fives: A Trip to Semiotics* (New York: Peter Lang, 1998), p. 41.

25. *Bodily Charm: Living Opera* (Lincoln: University of Nebraska Press, 2000).

26. Elam, *The Semiotics,* p. 3.

1. The Contemplation of Death

1. Poulenc's Catholic faith had been renewed in 1936 during a trip to Rocamadour that occurred shortly after the death of his friend and rival, the composer Pierre Octave Ferroud. He then wrote his first religious work, *Litanies à la vierge noire.* In 1941, he wrote a *Salve Regina* for a cappella chorus. But the idea to write an opera based on the play by Georges Bernanos called *Les dialogues des Carmélites* actually came from Guido Valcaranghi at Ricordi, his publisher.

2. Avery Weisman, *On Dying and Denying: A Psychiatric Study of Terminality* (New York: Behavioral Publications, 1972), p. 14. The citation following this is from the same page.

3. . Sigmund Freud, "Thoughts for the Times on War and Death" (1915), in James Strachey et al., ed. and trans., *The Standard Edition of the Complete Psychological Works of Sigmund Freud,* vol. 14 (London: Hogarth Press and the Institute of Psycho-Analysis, 1953–1974), p. 289. On Klein, see A. G. Levin, "The Fiction of the Death Instinct," *Psychoanalytic Quarterly* 25 (1951): 259. See also Gregory Zilboorg, "Fear of Death," *Psychoanalytic Quarterly* 12 (1943): 465–475.

4. *Life against Death,* quoted in Richard Loretto and Donald I. Templer, *Death Anxiety* (Washington, D.C.: Hemisphere, 1986), p. 3.

5. Ernest Becker, *The Denial of Death* (New York: Free Press, 1973), p. 210.

6. Franz Rauhut, "Les Motifs musicaux de l'opéra *Dialogues des Carmélites* de Francis Poulenc," *Etudes Bernanosiennes* 14 (1972): 221.

7. Becker, *Denial,* p. 210.

8. Irving Yalom, *Existential Psychotherapy* (New York: Basic, 1980), p. 146.

9. On gender, see D. I. Templer, C. F. Ruff, and C. M. Franks, "Death Anxiety: Age, Sex, and Parental Resemblance in Diverse Populations," *Developmental Psychology* 4 (1971): 108. Templer developed a Death Anxiety Scale in 1970. The Sarnoff Fear of Death Scale was used by Stephen I. Golding, George E. Atwood, and Richard A. Goodman, "Anxiety and Two Cognitive Forms of Resistance to the Idea of Death," *Psychological Reports* 18 (1966): 359–364. For other examples of scales, especially separating death and dying, see L. Collett and D. Lester, "The Fear of Death and the Fear of Dying," *Journal of Psychology* 72 (1964): 179–181. For the critiques of these scales (their definition of anxiety; their limitation to anxiety rather than including other responses such as rage, sorrow, positive feelings; their sample study population—inevitably college students who are young), see Robert Kastenbaum, *The Psychology of Death,* 2nd ed. (New York: Springer, 1992), pp. 146–150. See also Irving E. Alexander, Randolph S. Colley, and Arthur M. Adlerstein, "Is Death a

Matter of Indifference?" *Journal of Psychology* 43 (1957): 277–283, for an even earlier study using college students as subjects.

10. Douglas Davies, *Death, Ritual and Belief: The Rhetoric of Funerary Rites* (London: Cassell, 1997), p. vii.

11. Cheryl Mattingly, *Healing Dramas and Clinical Plots: The Narrative Structure of Experience* (Cambridge: Cambridge University Press, 1998), p. 1.

12. Herbert Lindenberger, *Opera: The Extravagant Art* (Ithaca: Cornell University Press, 1984), p. 53.

13. See Daphna Ben Chaim, *Distance in the Theatre: The Aesthetics of Audience Response* (Ann Arbor, Mich.: UMI Research Press, 1984), p. 103, for a historical summary of the theorizing of this concept of distance. Edward Bullough's 1912 article has been a modern touchstone for many subsequent theorists: "'Psychical Distance' as a Factor in Art and an Aesthetic Principle," in his *Aesthetics: Lectures and Essays,* ed. Elizabeth M. Wilkison (London: Bowes and Bowes, 1957), pp. 91–130. George Steiner, in *The Death of Tragedy* (London: Faber and Faber, 1961), argues for music and verse as setting up important barriers between tragic action and audience (p. 242). As Susan Bennett sums up the argument in *Opera Audiences: A Theory of Production and Reception* (London: Routledge, 1990), "When distance disappears then art does too" (p. 16).

14. See "Psychopathic Characters on the Stage," *The Complete Psychological Works,* vol. 8, pp. 305–310. See also "Creative Writers and Day-Dreaming," in vol. 9, pp. 143–153, on the "aesthetic" bribe of pleasure, which liberates tensions caused by distressing fantasy. Norman Holland, in *The Dynamics of Literary Response* (New York: Oxford University Press, 1968), expands this notion into one of form as displacement of anxiety-producing fantasy elements, and thus as defense.

15. Elisabeth Bronfen, "Death and Aesthetics," in Michael Kelly, ed., *Encyclopedia of Aesthetics,* vol. 1 (New York: Oxford University Press, 1998), pp. 507 and 510.

16. See Chris Bartley, "Ars Moriendi," in Glennys Howarth and Oliver Leaman, eds., *Encyclopedia of Death and Dying* (London: Routledge, 2001), p. 31.

17. In *Death, Desire and Loss in Western Culture* (London: Routledge, 1998), Jonathan Dollimore discusses this genre (which he calls the "death meditation") as a performative "social practice"—private yet gaining its meaning from an "existing cultural history" (p. 87).

18. Michael Flachmann, "Fitted for Death: *Measure for Measure* and the *Contemplatio Mortis*," *English Literary Renaissance* 22 (1992): 227 and 236 respectively.

19. For these citations, see Richard Schechner, "Ritual and Performance," in Tom Ingold, ed., *Companion Encyclopedia of Anthropology: Humanity, Culture and Social Life* (London: Routledge, 1994), pp. 625, 613, and 632, respectively.

20. For these citations, see Victor W. Turner, "Dewey, Dilthey, and Drama: An Essay in the Anthropology of Experience," in Victor W. Turner and Edward M. Bruner, eds., *The Anthropology of Experience* (Urbana: University of Illinois Press, 1986), pp. 34, 41, and 41 respectively. See also Emile Durkheim, *The Elementary Forms of the Religious Life* (London: George Allen and Unwin, 1915), p. 397, on the social function of funerary rituals.

21. Régine Crespin, "D'une Prieure à l'autre," *L'Avant-Scène Opéra* 52 (1983): 107.

22. Benjamin Ivry, *Francis Poulenc* (London: Phaedon Press, 1996), pp. 192–193.

23. Cori Ellison, "Cafés and Catechisms," *Opera News,* 58 (March 5, 1994): 53.

24. Crespin, "D'une Prieure," p. 107.

25. Wilfrid Mellers, *Francis Poulenc* (Oxford: Oxford University Press, 1993), p. 112.

26. See Hans Aaraas, "Bernanos in 1988," *Renascence* 41 (1989): 19–20; Henri Hell, *Francis Poulenc: Musicien français* (Paris: Fayard, 1978), p. 224; Albert Béguin, *Bernanos par lui-même* (Paris: Seuil, 1958), pp. 31–33, 48–52; Joseph Boly, *Georges Bernanos,* Dialogues des Carmélites: *Etude et analyse* (Paris: Editions de l'école, 1960), pp. 15, 80; S. Meredith Murray, *La genèse de "Dialogues des Carmélites"* (Paris: Seuil, 1963), p. 133.

27. Mellers, *Francis Poulenc,* p. 111.

28. Béguin, *Bernanos,* p. 48.

29. Arguably, audiences who have seen the opera before *do* know. But we would argue that while actually experiencing this scene, spectators are more likely caught up in the narrative and suspend that knowledge to become part of the interpretive here and now of the experience.

30. Jean-Jacques Nattiez, *Music and Discourse: Toward a Semiology of Music,* trans. Carolyn Abbate (Princeton: Princeton University Press, 1990), pp. 75–77, where he discusses this reception process as the "aesthetic" dimension (as opposed to the "poietic," which involves the creator's process).

31. See Henry J. Schmidt, *How Dramas End: Essays on the German Sturm und Drang, Büchner, Hauptmann, and Fleisser* (Ann Arbor: University of Michigan Press, 1992), p. 99, on poeticizing as a way of compensating for the horror of death; Jean Duvignaud on the socialization and transformation, as cited by Schmidt, p. 7.

32. See Anne Ubersfelt, *Reading Theatre,* trans. Frank Collins (Toronto: University of Toronto Press, 1999), p. 30.

33. See, in particular, for more on Freud's view, his "On Psychotherapy," in *The Complete Psychological Works,* vol. 7, p. 260.

34. Freud, *Beyond the Pleasure Principle,* vol. 18 of *The Complete Psychological Works,* p. 17; "Dostoevsky and Parricide," vol. 21, p. 188; "Psychopathic Characters on the Stage," vol. 7, pp. 305–306.

35. See M. Owen Lee, *A Season of Opera: From Orpheus to Ariadne* (Toronto: University of Toronto Press, 1998), p. 177.

36. Father Lee, ibid., p. 177, tells of its current use; William Bush, in *Bernanos' "Dialogues des Carmélites": Fact and Fiction* (Compiègne: Carmel de Compiègne, 1985), p. 21, argues that its historical use makes this a song of foundation, not annihilation. But perhaps the doubled association is equally appropriate.

37. Lee, *A Season of Opera,* p. 177.

38. Francis Poulenc, *Entretiens avec Claude Rostand* (Paris: René Julliard, 1954), pp. 213–214.

39. Mellers, *Francis Poulenc,* p. 104.

40. On this theory of catharsis, see the summary of arguments by Krishna Gopal Srivastava, *Aristotle's Doctrine of Tragic Katharsis: A Critical Study* (Allahabad: Kitab Mahal, 1982), p. 122.

41. Martin Esslin, *The Field of Drama: How the Signs of Drama Create Meaning on Stage and Screen* (London: Methuen, 1987), p. 174.

42. Schmidt, *How Dramas End,* p. 7.

43. Frank Kermode, *The Sense of an Ending: Studies in the Theory of Fiction* (New York: Oxford University Press, 1967), respectively pp. 7, 8, 58.

44. Peter Brooks, *Reading for the Plot: Design and Intention in Narrative* (New York: Knopf, 1984), p. 95.

45. For more on this process, see June Schleuter, *Dramatic Closure: Reading the End* (Madison, N.J.: Fairleigh Dickinson University Press; London: Associated University Presses, 1995), pp. 24 and 47.

46. See Barbara Herrnstein Smith, *Poetic Closure: A Study of How Poems End* (Chicago: University of Chicago Press, 1968), for an argument about poetry and closure along these lines.

47. George Steiner, *The Death of Tragedy* (London: Faber and Faber, 1961), p. 284.

48. Kermode, *Sense,* p. 82.

49. For this theory see James L. Smith, *Melodrama* (London: Methuen, 1973), p. 15. He further argues that melodrama "dramatizes the fears and threats which oppress us, and reduces them to a comforting emotional pattern. It gives us the courage and confidence to go on living" (pp. 54–55).

50. Music clearly ups the ante on the already "high-voltage emotionalism" of melodrama. See Frank Rahill, *The World of Melodrama* (University Park: Pennsylvania State University Press, 1967), p. xv. But in Aristotle's *Politics* (in response to Plato), music is in fact presented as the producer of purging catharsis, not of emotions themselves.

2. Eros and Thanatos

1. The letter dates from 16 December 1854, as cited in John Luke Rose, "A Landmark in Musical History," in *Tristan and Isolde,* ENO Opera Guide (London: John Calder, 1981, 1983), p. 12. On the impact of Schopenhauer, see Richard Wagner, *My Life,* trans. Lord Harewood (London: Constable, 1994), p. 615; Bryan Magee, "Schopenhauer and Wag-

ner," *Opera Quarterly* 1 (Autumn 1983): 148; Thomas Mann, *Pro and Contra Wagner,* trans. Allan Blunden (London: Faber and Faber, 1985); Edouard Sans, *Richard Wagner et la pensée schopenhauerienne* (Paris: Klincksieck, 1969), p. 263. For more detail on the debate about when Schopenhauer's influence is visible/audible in Wagner's work, see Thomas S. Grey, *Wagner's Musical Prose: Texts and Contexts* (Cambridge: Cambridge University Press, 1994), p. 4.

2. Arthur Schopenhauer, *The World as Will and Representation,* vol. 2, trans. E. F. J. Payne (New York: Dover, 1966), p. 492.

3. On Wagner's anticipating Freud, see Peter Wapnewski, *Tristan der Held Richard Wagners* (Berlin: Severin und Siedler, 1981), p. 29; for Freudian readings of *Tristan und Isolde,* see Françoise Ferlan, "Le Roi Marke," *L'Avant-Scène Opéra* 34–35 (1981): 177–181; Denis de Rougemont, *Love in the Western World,* trans. Montgomery Belgion, rev. ed. (New York: Harper and Row, 1956, p. 243); Françoise Barteau, *Les romans de Tristan et Yseut: Introduction à une lecture plurielle* (Paris: Larousse, 1972), p. 188; Lawrence Kramer, *Music as Cultural Practice 1800–1900* (Berkeley: University of California Press, 1990), pp. 136–137.

4. Slavoj Žižek, in his book with Mladen Dolar, *Opera's Second Death* (New York: Routledge, 2002), offers a Lacanian reading of this opera, buttressed by Heidegger, Hegel, and Kierkegaard rather than Freud and Schopenhauer, because he interprets the work in the light of Jean-Pierre Ponnelle's Bayreuth staging, arguing that Lacan is the "ultimate and last Wagnerite" (p. 187). He reads the Freudian death drive as *"the very opposite of dying"* and death as the moment of liberation from the death drive itself (pp. 106–107, emphasis his).

5. See Iago Galdston, "Eros and Thanatos: A Critique and Elaboration of Freud's Death Wish," *American Journal of Psychoanalysis* 15 (1955): 124.

6. Sigmund Freud, *Beyond the Pleasure Principle* (1920), in James Strachey et al., ed. and trans., *The Standard Edition of the Complete Psychological Works of Sigmund Freud,* vol. 18 (London: Hogarth Press and the Institute of Psycho-Analysis, 1953–1974), pp. 49–50.

7. See, for example, A. J. Levin, "The Fiction of the Death Instinct," *Psychoanalytic Quarterly* 25 (1951): 257–281.

8. Freud, *Beyond the Pleasure Principle,* p. 35.

9. See Cathy Caruth, "Preface" to her edition of *Trauma: Explorations in Memory* (Baltimore: Johns Hopkins University Press, 1995), p. vii; Caruth, "Introduction: Trauma and Experience," ibid., p. 4; and Bessel A. van der Kolk and Onno van der Hart, "The Intrusive Past: The Flexibility of Memory and the Engraving of Trauma," ibid., p. 167. Caruth herself, in *Unclaimed Experience: Trauma, Narrative, and History* (Baltimore: Johns Hopkins University Press, 1996), defines a "double telling" that we will see to be relevant to Isolde: "the oscillation between a *crisis of death* and the correlative *crisis of life:* between the story of the unbearable nature of an event and the story of the unbearable nature of its survival" (p. 7).

10. See discussions of this in Richard Boothby, *Death and Desire: Psychoanalytic Theory in Lacan's Return to Freud* (New York: Routledge, 1991), p. 13; and Ellie Ragland, "Lacan's Concept of the Death Drive," in *Essays on the Pleasures of Death* (New York: Routledge, 1995), p. 89.

11. In *Death, Desire, and Loss in Western Culture* (New York: Routledge, 1998), Jonathan Dollimore argues that, for humans, "death inhabits sexuality: perversely, lethally, ecstatically" (p. xi). Therefore, in Western culture, death, desire, and their connection, mutability, are central.

12. See Art Groos, "Wagner's 'Tristan und Isolde': In Defence of the Libretto," *Music and Letters* 69 (1988): 465–481; Leo Spitzer, *A Method of Interpreting Literature* (Northampton, Mass.: Smith College, 1949), p. 49; Ulrich Weisstein, "The Little Word *und: Tristan und Isolde* as Verbal Construct," in Leroy R. Shaw et al., eds., *Wagner in Retrospect: A Centennial Reappraisal* (Amsterdam: Rodopi, 1987), pp. 70–90. It is Theodor Adorno, *In Search of Wagner,* trans. Rodney Livingstone (New York: Verso, 1991), p. 103, who most famously claimed that the music simply repeats what the words say—an overdetermination that works to the detriment of the music, in his view.

13. See Grey, *Wagner's Musical Prose,* p. 319: "Wagner himself, as we know, did not speak of *Leitmotiven,* but employed a variety of other terms and circumlocutions to describe the thing we know by that name: *melodische Momenten, Themen, Melodien, Grundthemen, Hauptthemen, Grundmotiven, plastische Natur-Motiven, musikalische Motiven,* or simply

Motiven." We will continue, however, to use the term "motive" as most Wagner criticism in fact does.

14. Adorno, *In Search,* pp. 37 and 60 respectively.

15. See Robert Bailey, *Richard Wagner, Prelude and Transfiguration from* Tristan and Isolde (New York: Norton, 1985), pp. 113–146, on the importance of repetition in the score.

16. Many of the interpreters of the Tristan chord have made this point. See, for example, Günter Hartmann, "Schon wieder: der (?) Tristan-Akkord," *Musikforschung* 42 (1989): 40; William J. Mitchell, "The *Tristan* Prelude: Techniques and Structure," *The Music Forum* 1 (1967): 163–203; Carl Dahlhaus, *Richard Wagner's Music Dramas,* trans. Mary Whittall (Cambridge: Cambridge University Press, 1979), p. 62 (where it is also noted that Marke's motive is the inversion of Tristan's). In his famous 1933 essay on Wagner, Thomas Mann saw the yearning motive specifically as the representation of Schopenhauer's will in the form of love's desire (*Pro and Contra,* p. 127). For summaries and analyses of the debates, see Erika Reiman, "The 'Tristan Chord' as Music-Historical Metaphor," *University of Toronto Quarterly* 67 (1998): 768–773.

17. Reprinted in Bailey, *Richard Wagner,* p. 47.

18. Cited by Dahlhaus, *Richard Wagner's Music Dramas,* p. 57. The letter dates from 29 October 1859.

19. Dalhaus, ibid., p. 51: "[T]he drink is a love potion only insofar as it is believed to be a death potion . . . [I]f it is a yearning for death which is turned into love by the drink, it was from love that the yearning for death previously grew." See also Alain Gueullette, "La mer profonde," *L'Avant-Scène Opéra* 34–35 (1981): 165.

20. See Anthony Negus, "A Musical Commentary," *Tristan and Isolde,* ENO Opera Guide, p. 20.

21. See Vladimir Jankélévitch, "La Nocturne," *Cahiers du Sud* (1937): 75–83. Earlier cultures—such as Greek—also saw light as life and darkness (witness Hades) as associated with death. See Christiane Sourvinou-Inwood, "To Die and Enter the House of Hades: Homer, Before and After," in Joachim Whaley, ed., *Mirrors of Mortality: Studies in the Social History of Death* (London: Europa, 1981), p. 21. Martin Jay, in *Downcast Eyes: The Denigration of Vision in Twentieth-Century French Thought*

(Berkeley: University of California Press, 1993), p. 107, argues that dark began being positively valued in late eighteenth-century philosophy as part of a waning of Enlightenment trust in sight.

22. See Hartmut Reinhardt, "Wagner and Schopenhauer," trans. Erika and Martin Swales, in Ulrich Müller and Peter Wapnewski, eds., *Wagner Handbook,* trans. and ed. John Deathridge (Cambridge: Harvard University Press, 1992), p. 291; Arthur Prüfer, "Novalis *Hymnen an die Nacht* und ihren Beziehungen zu Wagners *Tristan und Isolde*," *Richard Wagner Jahrbuch* (1906): 293; Siegfried Krebs, *Phillip Otto Runges Entwicklung unter dem Einflusse Ludwig Tiecks* (Heidelberg: Carl Winters Universitätsbuchhandlung, 1909), pp. 137–138; Dieter Borchmeyer, *Das Theater Richard Wagners: Idee-Dichtung-Wirkung* (Stuttgart: Reclam, 1982), p. 261. See also Cosima Wagner's later diary entry for 19 April 1879: "and then he read aloud something from and about Novalis in Carlyle" ("und dann liest er einiges von und über Novalis in Carlyle vor") (*Die Tagebücher,* vol. 2, ed. Martin Gregor-Dellin and Dietrich Mack [Munich: R. Piper, 1977], p. 333). That Wagner had likely read Novalis himself long before this is suggested by the echoes of the latter's *Hymnen* in *Tristan's* libretto. See Jill Scott, "Night and Light in Wagner's *Tristan und Isolde* and Novalis's *Hymnen an die Nacht:* Inversion and Transfiguration," *University of Toronto Quarterly* 67 (1998): 774–780. For an overview of German Romanticism's "Thoughts of the Night," see the section by that name in Hermann Glaser, ed., *The German Mind of the Nineteenth Century: A Literary and Historical Anthology* (New York: Continuum, 1981), pp. 11–35.

23. Schopenhauer, *World,* vol. 2, pp. 533–534.

24. Bryan Magee, "Wagner and Schopenhauer, Part 1," *Opera Quarterly* 1 (1983): 159.

25. Schopenhauer, *World,* vol. 2, p. 532.

26. See Barry Millington, *Wagner* (New York: Vintage, 1984), p. 230; Reinhardt, "Wagner and Schopenhauer," p. 291.

27. Barry Millington, "Tristan und Isolde," in Sadie, ed., *New Grove Dictionary,* 4: 818–819. The citation following is on p. 819. See also Marc A. Weiner, *Richard Wagner and the Anti-Semitic Imagination* (Lincoln: University of Nebraska Press, 1995), pp. 24–25, on the explicit mimetic sexuality of the music here.

28. Others have offered different readings of Tristan as Orphic. When

Jean-Jacques Nattiez, in *Wagner Androgyne: A Study in Interpretation,* trans. Stewart Spencer (Princeton: Princeton University Press, 1993), p. 153, calls Tristan a "latter-day Orpheus," he does so to stress the reflexive, self-conscious identity of Tristan as a singer from another world. So too does Carolyn Abbate, in "Wagner, 'On Modulation,' and *Tristan,*" *Cambridge Opera Journal* 1 (1989): 48–49, drawing from the fact that, in the Gottfried poem, Tristan is a musician and composer. In fact, there are many Orphic analogies in that version: for instance, Tristan's singing and harp-playing are said to bewitch those who find him in his small boat off the shores of Ireland. See Joseph Campbell, *The Masks of God,* vol. 4, *Creative Mythology* (New York: Viking Press, 1968), p. 227.

29. See Novalis in Simon Reynolds, ed., *Novalis and the Poets of Pessimism, with an English Translation by James Thomson of* Hymns to Night (Whitby, U.K.: James Russell, 1995), pp. 30, 34, 48, 52; for commentary, see Eric A. Blackwell, *The Novels of the German Romantics* (Ithaca: Cornell University Press, 1983), p. 216; Maurice Blanchot, *The Space of Literature,* trans. Ann Smock (Lincoln: University of Nebraska Press, 1982), p. 111. For Novalis's diary entry about the apparition of his beloved, see Reynolds, *Novalis,* p. 17. It should be noted that Thomas Mann felt that both Novalis's poems and Wagner's music drama grew out of the more "lascivious" domains of Romanticism (*Pro and Contra,* p. 68, in a letter from 1920).

30. Erwin Koppen, *Dekadenter Wagnerismus: Studien zur europäischen Literatur des Fin de Siècle* (Berlin: Walter de Gruyter, 1973), p. 172. See also Gerhard Schulz, "Liebestod: The Literary Background of Wagner's *Tristan und Isolde,*" in Peter Dennison, ed., *Miscellanea Musicologica* 14, *The Richard Wagner Centenary in Australia* (Adelaide: University of Adelaide, 1985), pp. 121–128; Siegfried Krebs, *Phillip Otto Runges,* pp. 130–131; Paul Kluckholm, *Die Auffassung der Liebe in der Literatur des 18. Jahrhunderts und in der deutschen Romantik* (1922; reprint Tübingen: Max Niemeyer, 1966), pp. 390–395. See also the dissertation on the topic by Maria Christina Bijvoet, "Liebestod: The Meaning and Function of the Double Love-Death in Major Interpretations of Four Western Legends," Ph.D. diss., University of Illinois at Urbana-Champaign, 1985. Death-ridge, in "Post-mortem on Isolde," *New German Critique* 69 (Fall 1996): 108, appears isolated in his claim that the word was rare at this time. He

uses this assertion to claim that E. T. A. Hoffmann's *Undine* (1816) is Wagner's major source.

31. Spitzer, *A Method*, p. 48; the link to Baudelaire's famous poem, "Correspondances," has been made by many. See, for example, Martial Petitjean, "L'extase tristanienne: une initiation métaphysique," *L'Avant-Scène Opéra* 34–35 (1981): 162. A recent work by Sven Friedrich, *Das auratische Kunstwerk: zur Äesthetik von Richard Wagners Musiktheaterutopie* (Tübingen: Max Niemeyer, 1996), argues Wagner's theory of a synesthetic "aural artwork."

32. See the excellent analyses of this by Groos, "Wagner's 'Tristan und Isolde,'" and Weisstein, "The Little Word."

33. See Schopenhauer, *World*, vol. 2, p. 495. Kramer, in *Musical as Cultural Practice*, sees *gender* differentiation as what is lost here, but the important difference is simply in terms of individuals, whatever their sex. We also argue that Deathridge's gender-allegorical reading ("Post-mortem," pp. 107–111) of the triumph of absolute music renders Isolde much too passive.

34. Schopenhauer, *World*, vol. 2, p. 507.

35. We would obviously disagree, then, with both Deathridge's assertion of the "exalted saintliness of Isolde's renunciation of earthly desire in her death scene" ("Post-mortem," p. 116) and Father M. Owen Lee's view that "the lovers reject the sensuality and abandon of physical love for something we may quite rightly call meta-physical" (*A Season of Opera: From Orpheus to Ariadne* [Toronto: University of Toronto Press, 1998], p. 132).

36. Millington, "Tristan und Isolde," p. 819.

37. Wagner's "Program Notes" for the prelude, in Bailey, *Richard Wagner*, p. 48.

38. "Yet what Fate divided in life now springs into transfigured life in death: the gates of union are thrown open. Over Tristan's body the dying Isolde receives the blessed fulfilment of ardent longing, eternal union in measureless space, without barriers, without fetters, inseparable," wrote Wagner in his "Program Notes" to the Verklärung, in Bailey, *Richard Wagner*, p. 48. See Russell Kilbourn, "Redemption Revalued in *Tristan und Isolde*: Schopenhauer, Wagner, Nietzsche," *University of Toronto*

Quarterly 67 (1998): 781–788, for more on transfiguration and redemption.

39. See Gwyneth Jones interviewed by Monique Barichella, "Un message spirituel," *L'Avant-Scène Opéra* 34–35 (1981): 191.

40. Groos, "Wagner's 'Tristan und Isolde,'" pp. 467–468. On the re-definition, see Kramer, *Music as Cultural Practice,* pp. 161–166 especially, and Reiman, "The 'Tristan Chord.'"

41. For an extended discussion of this tension, see Jean Laplanche, *Life and Death in Psychoanalysis,* trans. Jeffrey Mehlman (Baltimore: Johns Hopkins University Press, 1976).

42. Friedrich Nietzsche, *The Birth of Tragedy* and *The Case of Wagner,* trans. Walter Kaufmann (New York: Vintage, 1967), p. 126. Many have noted the link here to Faust's last words, but Goethe's actual phrasing there is, in fact, "great happiness" ("hohen Glück,") not "most supreme bliss" ("höchste Lust").

43. *Schopenhauer: Essays and Aphorisms,* trans. R. J. Hollingdale (Harmondsworth, U.K.: Penguin, 1970), p. 164.

44. "The metaphysical joy in the tragic is a translation of the instinctive unconscious Dionysian wisdom into the language of images: the hero, the highest manifestation of the will, is negated for our pleasure, because he is only phenomenon, and because the eternal life of the will is not affected by his annihilation" (Nietzsche, *The Birth,* p. 104). The previous citation is from pp. 103–104.

45. Ibid., p. 141.

46. Cited in Dietrich Fischer-Dieskau, *Wagner and Nietzsche,* trans. Joachim Neugroschel (New York: Seabury Press, 1976), p. 90.

47. Nietzsche, *The Birth,* pp. 126–128.

48. Schopenhauer, *World,* vol. 2, p. 448.

49. Gerhard J. Winkler, "Der 'Schleier der Maja,'" in Thomas Steiert, ed., *'Der Fall Wagner'* (Laaber: Laaber-Verlag, 1991), pp. 248–249.

3. "All That Is, Ends"

1. Since it is likely true that, as many have pointed out, in a very real sense the *Ring* is about everything, a long note of introduction may be

useful, since it probably is not only (to use George Bernard Shaw's terms) the "coyer subtleties of the score" that give this work its "Beethovenian inexhaustibility and toughness of wear" (*The Perfect Wagnerite: A Commentary on the Nibelung's Ring* [1899; reprint New York: Dover, 1964], p. 106). For Shaw, writing in the late nineteenth century, the *Ring*, "with all its gods and giants and dwarfs, its water-maidens and Valkyries, its wishing-cap, magic ring, enchanted sword, and miraculous treasure, is a drama of today, and not of a remote and fabulous antiquity" (p. 1). He found its obsession with power, love, and death "frightfully real, frightfully present, frightfully modern" (p. 11). For other related allegorical readings, see Warren Darcy, "'Everything That Is, Ends!' The Genesis and Meaning of the Erda Episode in *Das Rheingold*," *Musical Times* 129 (September 1988): 443–447. For Herbert Lindenberger, the *Ring* is a "long chronicle of deceit, betrayals, and murders resulting from a lust for power" (*Opera: The Extravagant Art* [Ithaca: Cornell University Press, 1984], p. 275). Deryck Cooke (in *I Saw the World End* [Oxford: Oxford University Press, 1979] p. 86), Barry Millington (*Wagner* [New York: Vintage, 1984] p. 227), and a host of others also see some combination of the themes of power, love, suffering, and death as what gives the *Ring* its undeniable power. German novelist Thomas Mann, torn between his suspicion of and his admiration for Wagner, called the *Ring* the "German contribution to nineteenth-century art in the monumental tradition" (*Pro and Contra Wagner,* trans. Allan Blunden [London: Faber and Faber, 1985], p. 192) and admitted that, as a young artist, he had fallen under the influence of the techniques of Wagner's great narrative passages, rather than those of the dramatic action (p. 46): "The recurrent motif, the self-quotation, the symbolic phrase, the verbal and thematic reminiscence across long stretches of text—these were narrative devices after my own heart," he wrote, explaining how they influenced his writing of *Buddenbrooks*. Mann felt the "monumental tradition" in other nations took the form of the "great social novel," but, while sharing the urge for "moralizing grandeur," the German version was "uninterested in the social and the political" and moved to timeless, nonhistorical poetic and musical forms. This ("What I want is the folk tale") was at the root, he felt, of the rise of National Socialist power: "Except that in the realm of politics fairy tales become lies" (p. 193). L. J. Rather also feels Wagner fed into nineteenth-century Europe's nostalgia for its northern past (*The Dream of Self-Destruction: Wagner's 'Ring' and the Modern World* [Baton Rouge: Louisiana State University Press, 1979], p. 4). Lindenberger, however, feels that Wagner renewed the possibilities of the traditional epic with its important relation to communities and fused that with "the national Germanic themes and the linguistic forms of early medieval heroic tales, the religious and communal experience of the Aeschylean tragic trilogy [*Oresteia*], and the grandeur and solemnity of the Beethoven symphony" ("Wagner's *Ring* as Nineteenth-Century Artifact," *Comparative Drama* 28 [1994]: 299). For other critics—and for many audiences—the *Ring* is as much a spiritual or psychological drama as a music drama. For Father Owen Lee, "the human soul is the real landscape on which the four dramas of the *Ring* are enacted" (*Wagner's Ring: Turning the Sky Around* [New York: Summit, 1990], p. 71), while Jean-Jacques Nattiez sees it as telling "the story of sexual awakening, a story of life and death" (*Wagner Androgyne: A Study in Interpretation,* trans. Stewart Spencer [Princeton: Princeton University Press, 1993], p. 281).

2. See Carolyn Abbate, *Unsung Voices: Opera and Musical Narrative in the Nineteenth Century* (Princeton: Princeton University Press, 1991), p. 211, especially.

3. Wagner drafted the text of *Siegfrieds Tod* in 1848 and began sketching the music in 1850. He then added a prelimary drama, *Der junge Siegfried* (1851), and then *Die Walküre* and *Das Rheingold* (1851–1852). But these additions meant that the original *Siegfrieds Tod* required rethinking, since the changes had made Wotan, not Siegfried, the central character. Wagner did not begin to write the music to what became *Götterdämmerung* until 1860 (completing it in 1872). The full score was completed in 1874. One of the reasons for this protracted composition time is that he had broken off the composition of *Siegfried* before Act 3 to write both *Tristan und Isolde* and *Die Meistersinger.*

4. Elisabeth Kübler-Ross, *On Death and Dying* (New York: Macmillan, 1969). See Tony Walter, *The Revival of Death* (London: Routledge, 1994), pp. 70–85, for a detailed summary of the different studies that have disagreed with her findings. Some have found it a political/religious tract for the secular: see D. Klass, "Elisabeth Kübler-Ross and the Tradition of the Private Sphere," *Omega* 12 (1981): 241–265; D. Klass

and R. Hutch, "Elisabeth Kübler-Ross as a Religious Leader," *Omega* 16 (1985): 89–109. A. Kellehaer, in *Dying of Cancer: The Final Years of Life* (Chicago: Harwood Academic, 1990), pp. 19–22, argues that it is the shock of the news of death and not the death idea itself that is significant. Both V. W. Marshall, "A Sociological Perspective on Aging and Dying," in V. W. Marshall, ed., *Later Life: The Social Psychology of Aging* (Beverly Hills: Sage, 1986), pp. 139–143, and R. Blythe, in *The View in Winter: Reflections on Old Age* (Harmondsworth: Penguin, 1980), argue that the elderly do not even go through these stages and, in fact, accept death more easily. The many different dangers of too-easy categorization into stages are outlined by J. Retsinas in "A Theoretical Reassessment of the Applicability of Kübler-Ross's Stages of Dying," *Death Studies* 12 (1988): 207–216, and by R. Schulz and D. Aderman, "Clinical Research and the Stages of Dying," *Omega* 5 (1972): 137–143. For some, the stages are not universal at all: see the pointed critique of C. Corr, "A Task-Based Approach to Coping with Dying," *Omega* 24 (1991): 81–94. For some, the stages are a response to "incarceration in a total institution," such as a hospital: see V. W. Marshall, *Last Chapters: A Sociology of Aging and Dying* (Monterey: Brooks/Cole, 1980), pp. 64–70. Robert J. Kastenbaum claims, in *Death, Society, and Human Experience,* 5th ed. (Boston: Allyn and Bacon, 1995), that the stages have not been empirically validated (pp. 104–109) and disputes their ordering (p. 106). Avery Weisman challenges the sequencing as well (*On Dying and Denying: A Psychiatric Study of Terminality* [New York: Behavioral Publications, 1972], p. 109), and he takes on the ease of naming stages versus the difficulty of the reality (in *The Ritualization of Death* [New York: Jason Aronson, 1974], p. 87).

5. Weisman, *On Dying and Denying,* p. 13. Further page references will be in parentheses following citations.

6. Slavoj Žižek, in *Opera's Death* (New York: Routledge, 2002), uses the Lacanian notion of the second death to discuss Wotan: "the fact that the subject died in peace, with his accounts settled and with no symbolic debt haunting his or her memory" (p. 110). But this argument demands that he downplay the "immediate biological life cycle" (p. 111) of actual death, which, as we shall argue, is very much at the core of the entire libretto text.

7. Cooke, *I Saw the World End*, p. 11.

8. Freud claims that we know death is "natural, undeniable, and un-avoidable," but "we behave as if it were otherwise" because "in the unconscious every one of us is convinced of his own immortality" ("Thoughts for the Times on War and Death," in James Strachey et al., ed. and trans., *The Standard Edition of the Complete Psychological Works of Sigmund Freud,* vol. 14 [London: Hogarth Press and the Institute of Psycho-Analysis, 1953–1974], p. 289).

9. Directed and designed by the late Herbert Wernicke, produced by Gérard Mortier, this production opened at the Théâtre de la Monnaie in the fall of 1991 and was repeated in Frankfurt in the spring of 1995.

10. Freud, "Thoughts," p. 291, ellipses ours.

11. Jesse L. Weston, *Legends of the Wagner Drama: Studies in Mythology and Romance* (New York: Scribner's, 1900), p. 83; Bryan Magee, *Aspects of Wagner* (1968; rev. ed. Oxford: Oxford University Press, 1988), p. 15.

12. Our thanks to Old Norse expert Roberta Frank for teaching us that the usual translation of this term as the "twilight" of the gods is in fact incorrect; the correct translation of the root is "judgment."

13. Without the apples the gods will "schwinden," or vanish, Loge says. Cooke notes that the apples were not part of the first draft of the story (*I Saw the World End,* p. 189). Neither, of course, was the earth goddess Erda herself, since it was the "Schicksalsfrauen" who gave the forecast of the ending; there was no second meeting of Wotan and Erda, no Norn narrative, no gloomy reports from Waltraute about Valhalla (see Abbate, *Unsung,* p. 158). In this version, the story ended with no final apocalyptic destruction of the world, but with Brünnhilde and Siegfried rising from the funeral pyre in glory on their way to Valhalla. With the entry of Erda and the increasing focus on Wotan and death (and the final destruction of the world), the need to point to the gods' mortality (or, rather, their lack of immortality) might have been felt more strongly—and hence the addition of the necessary apples of youth.

14. Freud, "Thoughts," p. 289.

15. Ernest Becker, *The Denial of Death* (New York: Free Press, 1973), p. 84. The citation that follows is from p. 90.

16. In both cases, too, something must be sacrificed: Wotan loses an

eye, and Alberich renounces love. And, as Father Lee has pointed out, Wotan, like Alberich, has been a source of evil in the world (*Wagner's Ring,* p. 57).

17. Quoted in Cooke, *I Saw the World End,* p. 132.

18. Although the figure of Erda is derived from the Volva figure who lives in the land of the dead in the *Poetic Edda,* she is very much Wagner's own creation. See Cooke, *I Saw the World End,* pp. 226–229. In the "Voluspo" or the "Wise-Woman's Prophesy" in the *Poetic Edda,* the chief of the gods, Othin, aware of impending disaster and eager for information, bids the wise woman to rise from the grave. The stress on death is especially strong in the source text since Othin is called "Valfather," or Father of the Slain; Valhall is the Hall of the Slain; and the Valkyries are etymologically (as well as narratively) the Choosers of the Slain.

19. See Darcy, "Everything," p. 443.

20. Quoted in James A. Massey, "Introduction," in Ludwig Feuerbach, *Thoughts on Death and Immortality,* trans. James A. Massey (Berkeley: University of California Press, 1980), p. xl. Feuerbach had a major impact on Wagner's thinking before his discovery of the very different philosophy of Arthur Schopenhauer. Feuerbach's influence can best be seen in Wagner's *Das Kunstwerk der Zukunft (The Art-work of the Future),* which he addressed to Feuerbach. For the influence of the other, see Chapter 2.

21. Once again, we are aware of the critiques—from those of Wagner himself to those of Carl Dahlhaus (in "The Music," in Ulrich Müller and Peter Wapnewski, eds., *Wagner Handbook,* trans. and ed. John Deathridge [Cambridge: Harvard University Press, 1992], pp. 309–310)—of the labeling of motives in superficial and rigid ways, but this example is a good one of the aptness as well as of the complexity of associations accrued by the end of the dramas.

22. Quoted in Shaw, *The Perfect Wagnerite,* p. 81n.

23. Our thanks to Ian Lancashire for this reminder.

24. Freud, "Thoughts," p. 290.

25. This is the thesis of Marc Weiner, *Wagner and the Anti-Semitic Imagination* (Lincoln: University of Nebraska Press, 1994).

26. This can only be called a monologue because the Valkyrie is specifically referred to as the embodiment of Wotan's "will," and so speaking to her is like speaking only to himself.

27. Cooke, *I Saw the World End,* p. 68.

28. Abbate, *Unsung Voices,* p. 173.

29. See Barry Millington, "The Music," in Millington, ed., *Wagner Compendium,* p. 295.

30. Weisman, *On Dying,* pp. 62 and 114, respectively.

31. Hartmut Reinhart, "Wagner and Schopenhauer," trans. Erika and Martin Swales, in Müller and Wapnewski, eds., *Wagner Handbook,* p. 293.

32. Quoted in Daniel Coren, "The Texts of Wagner's *Der junge Siegfried* and *Siegfried," Nineteenth Century Music* 6 (1982): 30.

33. Many critics of *Siegfried* indeed confidently assert this. For example: "Fate is to be overcome; and so Wotan's final knowledge is a great and final step forward on Erda's," and so she can be dismissed (Cooke, *I Saw the World End,* p. 213).

34. Coren, "The Texts," p. 28.

35. Michael Mulkay, "Social Death in Britain," in David Clark, ed., *The Sociology of Death* (Oxford: Blackwell/Sociological Review, 1993), pp. 32–33.

36. If the reader will pardon a long note—on a related and important topic: Wotan's planned meeting of Siegfried and Brünnhilde must come about somehow, however, for that meeting is central to the death focus of the *Ring*. Wotan, therefore, must yield to Siegfried. The man who did not know the meaning of fear (Siegfried) must learn that love, like death, is fearful, for it involves the annihilation of the self, while seeming to promise immortality. By August 1849, Wagner had read Feuerbach's *Thoughts on Death and Immortality (Gedanken über Tod und Unsterblichkeit)* (1830) wherein the oneness of love is likened to the oneness of death, for both enable one to transcend the individual ego. Wagner had broken off his writing of *Siegfried* a little before this scene to write *Tristan und Isolde,* and that work's romantic obsession with death and love certainly spills over into this strangest of love duets, as Wotan's planned pair meet. Brünnhilde, now human and no longer a Valkyrie, can for the first time experience love, but this new experience comes only to her as a mortal who will die. Thus she sings of "laughing death" ("lachender Tod"). In other words, death defines and gives meaning to life, just as love is what gives light to darkness ("leuchtende Liebe"). Without the *Ring's* obsession with death, it would perhaps seem quite odd to have the heroine sing

"wildly and joyfully" to her beloved: "laughing let us perish— / laughing go to our doom!" ("lachend lass' uns verderben— / lachend zu Grunde geh'n!"). Nevertheless, they do not laugh at the end, of course. Nor has the move to even this position of seeming acceptance of mortality been a simple one for either lover. Both love and death—perhaps only love and death—have the power to generate such extremes of fear and anxiety. It is no accident that Siegfried's description of Brünnhilde's impact on him echoes exactly Wotan's depiction of the impact of Erda's prediction of his end: she binds him in "fetters of anxious fear" ("Mit banger Furcht / fesselst du mich"). But only love and death can restore rightful order in the end, so that initial fear must, at all cost, be overcome. When it is, Brünnhilde, as mortal, can herself bid farewell to the world of the gods. More importantly, however, she can also will that race and world to end ("End' in Wonne, / du ewig Geschlecht!").

37. See Carl Dahlhaus, "Wagner's Place in the History of Music," in Müller and Wapnewski, eds., *Wagner Handbook,* p. 114.

38. Abbate, *Unsung Voices,* p. 234.

39. Darcy, "Everything," p. 447.

40. For more on this idea of the "good" death, see not only Weisman, *On Dying,* p. 40, but John Hinton, "The Dying and the Doctor," in Arnold Toynbee, ed., *Man's Concern with Death* (London: Hodder and Stoughton, 1968), p. 44; Allan Kellehear, "Good Death," in Glennys Howarth and Oliver Leaman, eds., *Encyclopedia of Death and Dying* (London: Routledge, 2001), pp. 209–210; and, in the same volume, Clare Gittings, "Good Death, Historical Perspectives," pp. 210—211.

41. Wagner did not, in the end, put to music certain Schopenhauerian lines that made explicit what Brünnhilde learned from her experience— "I saw the world end" ("enden sah ich die Welt"). Although Wagner was ostensibly taking the advice of his wife, Cosima (Cooke, *I Saw the World End,* p. 22), perhaps Wagner trusted the music and the subsequent dramatic action to convey Brünnhilde's realization—and Wotan's—that the world as they knew it must end, as Erda foresaw. On the various versions of the text and music of the ending, see Robert Bailey, "Wagner's Musical Sketches for *Siegfrieds Tod,*" in Harold Powers, ed., *Studies in Music History: Essays for Oliver Strunk* (Princeton: Princeton University Press, 1969), pp. 459–494, and his "The Structure of the *Ring* and Its Evolu-

tion," *Nineteenth Century Music* 1 (1997): 48–61. It is generally accepted that Wagner's first version was influenced by Feuerbach and the final one by Schopenhauer. His decision not to set Brünnhilde's very Schopenhauerian speech to music, however, suggests that Wagner may well have been as willfully independent in his response to his mentor here as he was in *Tristan und Isolde.*

42. Friedrich Nietzsche, in *The Case of Wagner,* argues that "There is nothing about which Wagner has thought more deeply than redemption: his opera is the opera of redemption" (*The Birth of Tragedy* and *The Case of Wagner,* trans. Walter Kaufman [New York: Vintage, 1967], p. 160), but argues that the rewritten Schopenhauerian *Ring* is "a story of redemption: only this time it is Wagner who is redeemed" (p. 163).

43. Christopher Wintle points this out in "The Numinous in *Götterdämmerung,*" in Arthur Groos and Roger Parker, eds., *Reading Opera* (Princeton: Princeton University Press, 1988), p. 211. On Wagner's identification with Wotan, see the letter of 23 August 1856 to Röckel on the shift from an interest in Siegfried to one in Wotan, as cited in Nattiez, *Wagner Androgyne,* p. 277. On the "dying Wotan," see Rather, *The Dream,* p. 60. On Wotan as artist-figure, see Rudolph Sabor, *The Real Wagner* (London: Sphere, 1989), p. 172.

44. Quoted in Nattiez, *Wagner Androgyne,* p. 277. Nattiez discusses at length Wagner's obsession with death: see pp. 182 and 192 especially.

45. Richard Wagner, *The Art-Work of the Future,* trans. William Ashton Ellis (Lincoln: University of Nebraska Press, 1993), p. 199, his emphasis.

46. Mann, *Pro and Contra,* p. 192.

47. Freud, "Psychopathic Characters on the Stage," *The Standard Edition,* vol. 7, p. 306. The next citation is from the same page.

48. See Lindenberger, "Wagner's *Ring,*" p. 300.

4. Orphic Rituals of Bereavement

1. Rather than list all these operas here, we will refer the reader to the many works of Frederick W. Sternfeld for an account of all the operas on this Orpheus theme. See his overview on "Orpheus" in Stanley Sadie, ed.,

The New Grove Dictionary of Opera (London: Macmillan, 1992), 3: 776–
778. That the theme was tied to opera's origins is evident in the fact that,
while Peri's opera played in Florence, the first opera on a Roman stage
was Stefano Landi's *La morte d'Orfeo* (1619). It has further been argued
that the first opera to play in France was Luigi Rossi's *Orfeo* (1647). See
Philippe Beaussant, "Orphée et la naissance de l'opéra," in *Les métamorphoses d'Orphée* (Toucoing: Musée des beaux arts; Strasbourg: Musées
de la Ville de Strasbourg; Bruxelles: Musée communal d'Ixelles: Snoeck-
Ducaju et Zoon, 1995), p. 94. For more on the general history of the Orpheus myth and its fate in literary culture, see Walter Strauss, *Descent and
Return: The Orphic Theme in Modern Literature* (Cambridge: Harvard
University Press, 1971), and Charles Segal, *Orpheus: The Myth of the Poet*
(Baltimore: Johns Hopkins University Press, 1989).

2. For typical views of Orpheus as the prototypical operatic hero be-
cause he is a composer/singer, see Silke Leopold, *Monteverdi: Music in
Transition,* trans. Anne Smith (Oxford: Clarendon Press, 1991), pp. 84–85;
Edward Cone, *Music: A View from Delft* (Chicago: University of Chicago
Press, 1988), p. 135; Peter Conrad, *A Song of Love and Death: The Meaning
of Opera* (New York: Poseidon Press, 1987), p. 19; Eve Barsham, "The Orpheus Myth in Operatic History," in Patricia Howard, ed., *C. W. von
Gluck:* Orfeo (Cambridge: Cambridge University Press, 1981), pp. 2–3.
Even Mladen Dolar's Lacanian reading of the Monteverdi opera is, in the
end, traditional: *"Music is what moves the deity to yield, music can defy
death itself"* (Slavoj Žižek and Mladen Dolar, *Opera's Second Death* [New
York and London: Routledge, 2002], p. 8, his italics). For an opposing
view, see Carolyn Abbate, *Unsung Voices: Opera and Musical Narrative
in the Nineteenth Century* (Princeton: Princeton University Press, 1991),
p. 122.

3. The citation is from Jahan Ramazani, *Poetry of Mourning: The
Modern Elegy from Hardy to Heaney* (Chicago: University of Chicago
Press, 1994), p. 18.

4. On mourning rituals, see Clare Gittings, "Bereavement, Historical
Perspectives," in Glennys Howarth and Oliver Leaman, eds., *Encyclopedia
of Death and Dying* (London: Routledge, 2001), p. 53. See also Marian
Osterweis, Frederic Solomon, and Morris Green, eds., *Bereavement: Re-*

actions, Consequences, and Care (Washington, D.C.: National Academy Press, 1986), pp. 4, 208; Christiane Sourvinou-Inwood, "To Die and Enter the House of Hades: Homer, Before and After," in Joachim Whaley, ed., *Mirrors of Mortality: Studies in the Social History of Death* (London: Europa, 1981), p. 27.

5. Budden, "Orpheus," p. 624. For a detailed musical and verbal comparison of the laments in a series of Orpheus versions, see F. W. Sternfeld, *The Birth of Opera* (Oxford: Clarendon Press, 1993), Chapter 6 on "The Lament," pp. 140–196.

6. In the chapter "Orpheus: One Last Performance," in *In Search of Opera* (Princeton: Princeton University Press, 2001), Carolyn Abbate argues that smart composers didn't try: "Suppressing Orpheus's primal song seems to distinguish great Orpheus opera from silly ones. Lesser composers put Orpheus directly in front of Pluto and are diminished by their hubris" (p. 27).

7. Susan McClary, in *Feminine Endings: Music, Gender, and Sexuality* (Minneapolis: University of Minnesota Press, 1991), interprets Monteverdi's Orfeo as being made vulnerable and thus feminized by this change in the mourning voice: "The audience itself has auditory mastery over him, as it is permitted to 'eavesdrop' on his private grief" (p. 46).

8. Frederick W. Sternfeld, "Orpheus, Ovid and Opera," *Journal of the Royal Musical Association,* 113 (1988): 179. The medieval Christianizing allegorical reading of Orpheus as the precursor of Christ in harrowing hell is responsible for this particular and very partial reading of the story.

9. Henry Staten, *Eros in Mourning: Homer to Lacan* (Baltimore: Johns Hopkins University Press, 1995), p. xii. Plato himself condemned the poetry of mourning not only because it proved the poet's lack of transcendence (and therefore of perspective on human mortal reality), but also because it could stimulate this "unwise" response in audiences. See ibid., pp. 3–5.

10. Arnold van Gennep, *The Rites of Passage,* trans. Monika B. Vizedom and Gabrielle L. Caffee (1908; reprint Chicago: University of Chicago Press, 1960), p. 147.

11. The classic article on the stages of grief is E. Lindemann, "Symptomatology and Management of Acute Grief," *American Journal of Psychi-*

atry 101 (1944): 141–148. For a review of this and other theories, see Richard Schulz, *The Psychology of Death, Dying, and Bereavement* (Reading, Mass.: Addison Wesley, 1978), pp. 142–148. Another model is that of Savine Gross Weizman and Phyllis Kamm in *About Mourning: Support and Guidance for the Bereaved* (New York: Human Sciences Press, 1985), p. 39.

12. For the "power of music" tradition in the myth's interpretation, see Celine Richard, "La légende d'Orphée et d'Eurydice au XVIe siècle," in *Les métamorphoses d'Orphée,* p. 46. But there is also a long tradition in opera of Orpheus's aesthetic failure, likely influenced in part by Plato's decision in the *Symposium* that Orpheus was a coward who misused his talents because he wasn't brave enough to die for/with his Euridyce, and so is given merely the phantom of her, not the real thing, as Richard explains (p. 43). This is the antiheroic Orpheus of the (1672) Sartorio/Aureli *Orfeo*—no brave man and no musical power. Other early musical works about Orpheus's final death also concentrate much less on the power of music: Stefano Landi's *La morte d'Orfeo* (1619) and Gabriele Chiabrera's *Il pianto d'Orfeo* (1608).

13. Ross Chambers has articulated this argument in print, but for us most forcefully in his graduate course, "Death at the Door: Witnessing as a Cultural Practice," given when he was the Northrop Frye Professor of Literary Theory at the University of Toronto in 1998. For this course, and for the stimulation of the course in general and many conversations about mortality, our warm thanks.

14. For a comparison of the Peri/Rinuccini and the Monteverdi/Striggio texts and music, see Ellen Rosand, "The Orpheus Legend and Opera," in her edition of *L'Orfeo* by Aurelio Aureli and Antonio Sartioro (Milan: Ricordi, 1983), pp. x–xii; Leopold, *Monteverdi,* pp. 86–88 (with a chart); Gary Tomlinson, "Madrigal, Monody, and Monteverdi's 'via naturale alla immitatione,'" *Journal of the American Musicological Society* 34 (1981): 60–108.

15. Wilfrid Mellers, *The Masks of Orpheus: Seven Stages in the Story of European Music* (Manchester: University of Manchester Press, 1987), p. 41.

16. For example, Tomlinson, in "Madrigal," points out the tendency to "declaim the opening syllable of a verse on a long note, then rush headlong through the following words on eighth notes" (p. 67) and, here, the unusual melodic descent in the bass line at the end of "Tu se' morta" (it spans an octave and a fourth) (p. 76); the plunging bass line under his final words has more power because of what precedes it (p. 77). Walther Dürer, in "Sprachliche und musikalische Determinanten in der Monodie: Beobachtungen an Monteverdis 'Orfeo,'" *Claudio Monteverdi: Festschrift Reinhold Hammerstein zum 70. Geburtstag* (Laaber: Laaber, 1986), p. 155, points out the "madrigalisms" in the words painted in music: the descending lines on "death" ("morte") or "abysses" ("abissi") and the highest note on "stars" ("stelle"). Leopold, in *Monteverdi,* has written at length about the conventions of the seventeenth-century lament and Monteverdi's use of them (pp. 123–140), and Beaussant, in "Orphée," pp. 91–92, has stressed how Monteverdi developed in this opera a new musical language out of the madrigal form.

17. Leopold, *Monteverdi,* p. 128.

18. See Budden, "Orpheus," p. 624.

19. Mellers, *The Masks,* p. 44.

20. See ibid.; Leopold, *Monteverdi,* p. 94; Budden, "Orpheus," p. 624.

21. See the related reading of Joseph Kerman in *Opera as Drama* (1956; rev. ed. Berkeley: University of California Press, 1988), p. 24.

22. Striggio had written another ending and published it, but no music seems to have been written for it. In this version, Orpheus is torn apart by the Bacchantes. See Jon Solomon, "The Neoplatonic Apotheosis in Monteverdi's *Orfeo,*" *Studi Musicali* 24 (1995): 43–47.

23. Barsham, "The Orpheus Myth," p. 8.

24. Sternfeld, "Orpheus, Ovid and Opera," p. 189.

25. See Rosand, "The Orpheus Legend," p. xvi, on *La lira d'Orfeo* (Draghi/Minato) in Vienna in 1683; *Die sterbende Eurydice oder Orpheus* (Kaiser/Bressand) in Hamburg, 1702; *Orfeo ed Euridice* (Fux/Pariati) in Vienna, 1715; *L'Orfeo* (Graun/Villati) in Berlin, 1702. On the contemporary *Singspiel* versions, see Sternfeld, "Orpheus."

26. See Alfred Einstein, *Gluck,* The Master Musicians Series, trans.

Eric Blom (1936; rev. ed. London: Dent, 1964), p. 71: "This funeral ceremony in *Orfeo* is the most impressive and unforgettable in the whole history of opera, because it is the simplest and richest."

27. Budden, "Orpheus," p. 625.

28. See Mellers, *The Masks,* p. 104; Kerman, *Opera,* p. 30.

29. Tom Sutcliffe, *Believing in Opera* (Princeton: Princeton University Press, 1996), pp. 66–67.

30. Mellers, *The Masks,* p. 108.

31. See Patricia Howard, *Gluck: An Eighteenth-Century Portrait in Letters and Documents* (Oxford: Clarendon Press, 1995), citing a review of an early performance from the *Wienerisches Diarium* 82, suppl., 13 October 1762: "The tragic outcome of the myth is thus turned into a joyful one. All the audience, who would otherwise have returned home burdened with compassion, are most grateful to him for this happy alteration" (p. 60).

32. See Claire Barbillon, "Quelques occurrences d'Orphée dans les arts de la deuxième moitié du XIXe siècle," in *Les métamorphoses d'Orphée,* pp. 69–77, on Salon art in Paris in the 1860s especially. The suffering Orpheus was attractive as a topic because it was read as the allegory of artistic creation, which (since the Romantics) had been associated with "une mélancolie diffuse" (p. 70). Orpheus as the civilizing poet triumphing over resistance was often used in decorating public buildings associated with the arts—opera houses, concert halls (pp. 71–77).

33. See G. Gorer, *Death, Grief, and Mourning* (London: Cresset Press, 1963), for the classic, much-cited version of this argument.

34. See Catherine Camboulives, "L'âme et le sang du poète," in *Les métamorphoses d'Orphée,* pp. 53–67, for a survey of 440 works from the fifteenth to the twentieth century. Only 9 percent are on the subject of Orpheus's death, and almost all are in the twentieth century (p. 55).

35. Darius Milhaud and Armand Lunel's 1926 *Les malheurs d'Orphée,* while domesticating Orpheus and Eurydice as, respectively, a Camargue peasant and a gypsy, has no descent to hell plot, but Orpheus is killed (by Eurydice's sisters, who blame him for her death).

36. See Joseph Jacobs' 1899 "The Dying of Death," *Fortnightly Review* 66 (1899): 264–269.

37. See Ramazani's excellent discussion of the modern elegy and its roots in *Poetry of Mourning,* pp. 11–17, especially.

38. Ibid., pp. ix and x respectively. The citation following is from p. 17.

39. As Maurice Blanchot put it in *The Space of Literature,* trans. Ann Smock (Lincoln: University of Nebraska Press, 1982), he wants her "in her nocturnal obscurity, in her distance, with her closed body and sealed face—wants to see her not when she is visible, but when she is invisible, and not as the intimacy of a familiar life, but as the foreignness of what excludes all intimacy, and wants, not to make her live, but to have living in her the plenitude of her death" (p. 172).

40. Kokoschka claimed to have had hallucinations in which he conversed with Alma Mahler's phantom presence, and out of these came the play. Her famous husband, Gustav Mahler, had been dead for some years at this point, but (like Orpheus in relation to Hades in the play), Kokoschka was extremely jealous of her past love.

41. Henry F. Schvey, *Oskar Kokoschka: The Painter as Playwright* (Detroit: Wayne State University Press, 1982), p. 95. Unlike other modern Orphic figures (as described by Strauss, *Descent and Return,* pp. 12–13), this one is not regenerated by the voyage downward at all.

42. See Freud's theory in his famous essay "Mourning and Melancholia," in James Strachey et al., ed. and trans., *The Standard Edition of the Complete Psychological Works of Sigmund Freud,* vol. 14 (London: Hogarth Press and the Institute for Psycho-Analysis, 1953–1974), pp. 243–258.

43. Not all modern operas have been this negative, of course. Geoffrey Burgon and Peter Porter's chamber opera *Orpheus* makes the link between the pre-Christian myth and the Christian present by stressing continuities among themes of music, love, and death. The medieval allegorical association of Orpheus descending into Hades and Christ harrowing Hell is recalled in this work, but death is from the start presented as a constant part of nature ("ripening and rot") and human life. This ritual of mourning could not be more different from that of Krenek and Kokoschka: its Christianized acceptance of human mortality—that even Christ suffered for humanity's sake—leaves art in the position of memorializing in much the same way that Monteverdi / Striggio's opera did in its Neoplatonic context. But this opera's consolatory message is the exception in the twen-

tieth-century Orpheus repertoire. The others are considerably more conflicted in their response to mourning and death, and to the relation of
both to aesthetic creation.

Harrison Birtwistle and Peter Zinoviev's 1986 *The Masks of Orpheus* is a
complex retelling of various versions of the events of the Orpheus myth,
using singers, mimes, and puppets. But its main focus is on many different rites of passage, and in this it shares the appeal of Orpheus operas that
have considerably simpler plot structures. It too is obsessed with death:
Orpheus and Eurydice both die numerous times on stage and in different
ways. It too is about the process of moving from unwillingness to accept
powerlessness in the face of mortality to an acceptance of human fate.

44. For physiological symptoms of acute grief, see the discussion of
Lindemann, "Symptomatology," in Osterweis, Solomon, and Green,
eds., *Bereavement,* pp. 47–49, and the table of Adult Grief Responses,
p. 148. On adverse health outcomes, see Schulz, *The Psychology of Death,*
on the "Broken Heart Syndrome," p. 52, and Osterweis, Solomon, and
Green, eds., *Bereavement*, on increased suicide, pp. 25–27, and increased
mortality, pp. 32–39. For an overview of psychoanalytic approaches
to mourning and pathological grief states, see Lorraine D. Siggins,
"Mourning: A Critical Survey of the Literature," *International Journal of
Psycho-Analysis* 47 (1966): 14–25.

45. Robbert van der Lek, *Diegetic Music in Opera and Film* (Amsterdam: Rodopi, 1991), p. 72.

46. Jessica Duchen, *Erich Wolfgang Korngold* (London: Phaedon Press,
1996), p. 75.

5. "'Tis a Consummation Devoutly to Be Wish'd"

1. Georges Minois, *History of Suicide: Voluntary Death in Western
Culture,* trans. Lydia G. Cochrane (Baltimore: Johns Hopkins University
Press, 1999), p. 110.

2. In *The Savage God: A Study of Suicide* (London: Penguin, 1971),
p. 81, A. Alvarez offers a list of these ancient examples: "Socrates, Codrus,
Charondas, Lycurgus, Cleombrotus, Cato, Zeno, Cleanthes, Seneca,
Paulina, Isocrates, Demosthenes, Lucretius, Lucan, Labienus, Terence,

Aristarchus, Petronius Arbiter, Hannibal, Boadicea, Brutus, Cassius, Mark Antony, Cleopatra, Cocceius Nerva, Statius, Nero, Otho, King Ptolemy of Cyprus, King Sardanapalus of Persia, Mithridates," and the list could go on and on.

3. Albert Camus, *The Myth of Sisyphus and Other Essays,* trans. Justin O'Brien (New York: Vintage, 1955), p. 3.

4. Maurice Blanchot, *The Space of Literature,* trans. Ann Smock (Lincoln: University of Nebraska Press, 1982), p. 97.

5. See Emile Durkheim, *Suicide: A Study in Sociology,* trans. John A. Spaulding and George Simpson, ed. George Simpson (1951; New York: Free Press, 1959); on the racial and ethnic differences in suicide rates, see Denys deCatanzaro, *Suicide and Self-Damaging Behavior: A Sociobiological Perspective* (New York: Academic Press, 1981), pp. 37–38.

6. J. M. Rist, *Stoic Philosophy* (Cambridge: Cambridge University Press, 1969), p. 237.

7. Seneca, *De Ira,* III.xv 3–4.

8. Durkheim, *Suicide,* p. 222. He would call this "obligatory altruistic suicide" (p. 221); Norman L. Farberow, in "Cultural History of Suicide," in Norman L. Farberow, ed., *Suicide in Different Cultures* (Baltimore: University Park Press, 1975), would call it "institutional suicide" (pp. 1–2).

9. See Helen Silving, "Suicide and Law," in Edwin S. Shneidman and Norman L. Farberow, eds., *Clues to Suicide* (New York: McGraw-Hill, 1957), pp. 79–95, on the history of the legal situation; Louis I. Dublin, *Suicide: A Sociological and Statistical Study* (New York: Ronald Press, 1963), p. 139, on the Christian anathema on suicide. Until the nineteenth century, such things as deprival of burial rights or burial at crossroads only, driving a stake through the body, or hanging it, were widespread across Europe.

10. See Martin Hengel, *The Zealots: Investigations into the Jewish Freedom Movement in the Period from Herod I until 70 AD,* trans. David Smith (Edinburgh: T. and T. Clark, 1989), pp. 262–264, on Masada; on the Donatists and others, see W. H. C. Frend, *The Donatist Church: A Movement of Protest in Roman North Africa* (1952; London: Oxford, Clarendon Press, 1971), p. 175.

11. See, for this entire discussion, Augustine, *The City of God,* trans.

Henry Bettenson (Harmondsworth: Pelican Classics, 1972), Chapter 20 (especially 31) and Chapter 22 (especially 33); Thomas Aquinas, *Summa Theologica,* vol. 2, trans. Fathers of the English Dominican Province (New York: Benziger Brothers, 1925): "Whether It Is Lawful to Kill Oneself," part 2, question 64, p. A5.

12. There are many fine histories of suicide, which rehearse these debates for various countries in Europe. See Minois, *History;* Robert Favre, *La Mort dans la littérature et la pensée françaises au siècle des lumières* (Lyons: Presses Universitaires de Lyon, 1978); Robert Campbell and Diane Collinson, *Ending Lives* (New York: The Open University/Blackwell, 1988); Silving, "Suicide and Law"; George Rosen, "History," in Seymour Perlin, ed., *A Handbook for the Study of Suicide* (New York: Oxford University Press, 1975), pp. 3–29; Ron Melrose Brown, "Suicide," in Glennys Howarth and Oliver Leaman, eds., *Encyclopedia of Death and Dying* (London: Routledge, 2001), pp. 438–442; S. E. Sprott, *The English Debate on Suicide from Donne to Hume* (La Salle, Ill.: Open Court, 1961).

13. Minois, *Suicide,* p. 181.

14. Robert Burton, *The Anatomy of Melancholy,* ed. Thomas C. Falukner, Nicholas K. Kiessling, and Rhonda L. Blair (1628; reprint Oxford: Clarendon Press, 1989).

15. See Glanville Williams, *The Sanctity of Life and the Criminal Law* (London: Faber and Faber, 1958), p. 236.

16. M. Merian, "Sur la crainte de la mort," "Sur le mépris de la mort," and "Sur le suicide," *Histoire de l'Académie Royale des Sciences et Belles Lettres* (1763) (Berlin: Haude et Spener, 1770), pp. 355–406.

17. Alvarez, *The Savage God,* p. 156.

18. Richard Friedenthal, *Goethe: His Life and Times* (1963; London: Wiedenfeld and Nicholson, 1965), p. 128. The reality of the multiple suicides after the novel's publication has been contested by Stuart Pratt Atkins, *The Testament of Werther in Poetry and Drama* (Cambridge: Harvard University Press, 1949), p. 210, who argues: "Although there were cases of suicide committed by individuals who read *Werther,* they were exceptions memorable only because of the notoriety of the novel." Nevertheless, recent studies offer further evidence of the "Werther effect": see A. Schmidtke and H. Hafner, "The Werther Effect after Television Films:

New Evidence for an Old Hypothesis," *Psychological Medicine* 18 (1988): 665–676; K. Jonas, "Modelling and Suicide: A Test of the Werther Effect," *British Journal of Social Psychology* 31 (1992): 295–306.

19. Other operas include Dejaure's one-act *Werther et Charlotte* (1792); Charles Grelinger's four-act lyric drama published in 1919 and first performed in 1928; Arturo Franchi's *L'Ombra di Werther,* which premiered in 1899.

20. See George Howe Colt, *The Enigma of Suicide* (New York: Summit, 1991), pp. 183–184. Important works of this time include Jean Etienne Dominique Esquirol's *Des maladies mentales considérées sous les rapports medical, hygiénique, et médicolégal* (Paris: J.-B. Baillières, 1838), and Dr. Forbes Winslow's *Anatomy of Suicide* (London: Henry Renshaw, 1840).

21. Alec Roy, "Suicide," in Benjamin J. Sadock and Virginia A. Sadock eds., *Kaplan and Sadock's Comprehensive Textbook of Psychiatry,* 7th ed. (Philadelphia: Lippincott, Williams and Wilkin, 2000), p. 2032.

22. On the Hindu attitude to suicide, see deCatanzaro, *Suicide,* p. 27: "The Brahmins . . . viewed suicide quite favorably, suggesting that it provided a passport to heaven." On the mystic unity with the deity in death, see Marilyn J. Harran, "Suicide," in Mircea Eliade, ed., *Encyclopedia of Religion,* vol. 14 (New York: Macmillan, 1987), pp. 34–35.

23. See Tasuku Harada, "Suicide (Japanese)," in James Hastings, ed., *Encyclopedia of Religion and Ethics,* vol. 12 (Edinburgh: T. and T. Clark, 1958), pp. 36–37, for details on seppuku.

24. See Arthur Groos, "Return of the Native: Japan in *Madama Butterfly / Madama Butterfly* in Japan," *Cambridge Opera Journal* 1 (1987): 167–194, for more detail on this response and the reasons for it.

25. We assume this inversion to be deliberate, since it is repeated in the Italian text in the original Ricordi score and in most Italian libretti, even if sometimes (hyper?) corrected in the translations.

26. Catherine Clément, *Opera, or the Undoing of Women,* trans. Betsy Wing (London: Virago, 1989), p. 47.

27. In so doing, it reverses the emphasis of the source text, George Crabbe's 1810 poem *The Borough,* which stressed the group.

28. Arnold Whittall, *The Music of Britten and Tippett: Studies in*

Themes and Techniques, 2nd ed. (Cambridge: Cambridge University Press, 1990), p. 102.

29. See E. M. Forster, "Two Essays on Crabbe," in Philip Brett, ed., *Benjamin Britten: Peter Grimes* (Cambridge: Cambridge University Press, 1983), p. 20; Pears's reading is in Humphrey Carpenter, *Benjamin Britten: A Biography* (London: Faber and Faber, 1992), pp. 199–212.

30. See Michael Wilcox, *Benjamin Britten's Operas* (Bath: Absolute Press, 1997), pp. 26–27. Vickers's interpretation is in Max Loppert, "Jon Vickers on *Peter Grimes,*" *Opera* 35 (August 1984): 835–843.

31. See Philip Brett, "Britten and Grimes," *The Musical Times* 118 (December 1977): 995–1000; Brett, "Britten's Dream," in Ruth A. Solie, ed., *Musicology and Difference: Gender and Sexuality in Music Scholarship* (Berkeley: University of California Press, 1993), pp. 259–280; Brett, "Musicality, Essentialism, and the Closet," in Philip Brett, Elizabeth Wood, and Gary C. Thomas, eds., *Queering the Pitch: The New Gay and Lesbian Musicology* (New York: Routledge, 1994), pp. 9–26, and, in the same volume, Brett, "Eros and Orientalism in Britten's Operas," pp. 235–256. See also John Simon, "Defiant One," *Opera News* 59 (24 Dec. 1994): 9, and Clifford Hindley, "Homosexual Self-Affirmation and Self-Oppression in Two Britten Operas," *Musical Quarterly* 76 (Summer 1992): 143–168.

32. Peter Garvie, "Plausible Darkness: *Peter Grimes* after a Quarter of a Century," *Tempo* 100 (Spring 1972): 12.

33. Irwin Stein, "*Peter Grimes:* Opera and *Peter Grimes,*" in Donald Mitchell and Hans Keller, eds., *Benjamin Britten: A Commentary on His Work from a Group of Specialists* (London: Rockliff, 1952), p. 128.

34. See Brett, "Britten's Dream," p. 263.

35. Desmond Shawe-Taylor, in "*Peter Grimes:* A Review of the First Performance" in Brett, ed., *Benjamin Britten,* p. 155, finds it shocking that the opera attempts to win our sympathies for Peter simply because he's an outlaw from this society: "in the theatre we may well be lulled into acquiescence; but at home, shall we not begin to wonder?"

36. Patricia Howard, *The Operas of Benjamin Britten* (London: Barrie and Rockliff/Cresset Press, 1969), p. 23.

37. See Muriel Hebert Wolf and Stuart L. Keill, "Opera as a Forum for

the Insanity Defense," *Opera Quarterly* 3 (1985): 17. The audience is seen as a jury receiving impressions and evaluating perceptions, making judgments "regarding the culpability or criminality" of characters on stage (16).

38. The opera was based on Georg Büchner's unfinished play *Woyzeck* (1835–1837); the evil doctor figure in the play was based on an actual practitioner the author knew in Giessen.

39. And the criticism on the work reflects this: see John Ardoin, "Apropos *Wozzeck*," *Opera Quarterly* 3 (1985): 68–69; Patrick Smith, "Order from Disorder," *Opera News* (6 Jan. 1990): 15 and 45.

40. See Leo Treitler, "*Wozzeck* and the Apocalypse: An Essay in Historical Criticism," *Critical Inquiry* 3 (1976): 251–270, for more on the imagery and the echoes here.

41. See Patrick Smith, "Order from Disorder," p. 15.

42. In Douglas Jarman, *Alban Berg:* Wozzeck (Cambridge: Cambridge University Press, 1989), p. 169.

43. Again, for more detail, see Treitler, *"Wozzeck."*

6. The Undead

1. For more details of these studies, see Robert Kastenbaum, *Psychology of Death,* 2nd ed. (New York: Springer, 1992), pp. 50–57.

2. Citations are from Elisabeth Bronfen, "The Vampire: Sexualizing or Pathologizing Death," in Rudolf Kaser and Vera Pohland, eds., *Disease and Medicine in Modern German Culture* (Ithaca: Cornell Studies in International Affairs, 1990), pp. 72, 75, and 72 respectively.

3. Ken Hurley, *The Gothic Body: Sexuality, Materialism, and Degeneration at the Fin de Siècle* (Cambridge: Cambridge University Press, 1996), p. 24.

4. Just as their blood-drinking is a satanic inversion of the eucharistic blood of Christ. See Roxana Stuart, *Stage Blood: Vampires of the Nineteenth-Century Stage* (Bowling Green, Ohio: Bowling Green State University Press, 1994), pp. 14–18.

5. See Glen St. John Barclay, *Anatomy of Horror: The Masters of Occult Fiction* (New York: St. Martin's Press, 1978), p. 9.

6. See Philippe Ariès, *The Hour of Our Death,* trans. Helen Weaver (1981; New York: Oxford University Press, 1991), p. 354; see also Gerald Kennedy, *The Haunted Dusk: American Supernatural Fiction* (Athens: University of Georgia Press, 1983), p. 42.

7. Kennedy, *The Haunted Dusk,* pp. 40–41.

8. Mary Douglas, *Purity and Danger: An Analysis of the Concepts of Pollution and Taboo* (London: Ark/Routledge and Kegan Paul, 1966), p. 35.

9. John Snart, *Thesaurus of Horror; or the Charnel House Explored!!* (London, 1817), pp. 95–96.

10. See Maria Tatar, *Spellbound: Studies on Mesmerism and Literature* (Princeton: Princeton University Press, 1978), p. 123; Robert C. Fuller, *Mesmerism and the American Cure of Souls* (Philadelphia: University of Pennsylvania Press, 1982), p. xi.

11. Stuart, *Stage Blood,* p. 27; see also Glennis Byron, Introduction to *Dracula* by Bram Stoker (New York: St. Martin's Press, 1999), p. 2.

12. See, for only a few examples, the essays in Joan Gordon and Veronica Hollinger, eds., *Blood Read: The Vampire as Metaphor in Contemporary Culture* (Philadelphia: University of Pennsylvania Press, 1997); Bronfen, "The Vampire," on the sexualizing and pathologizing process in Stoker's novel and Murnau's 1922 film *Nosferatu;* see also Byron, Introduction, and Margaret L. Carter, Introduction to *Dracula: The Vampire and the Critics,* ed. Margaret L. Carter (Ann Arbor: UMI Research Press, 1988), pp. 1–10, on a historical overview of critical discourses on *Dracula.* See also Nina Auerbach, *Our Vampires, Ourselves* (Chicago: University of Chicago Press, 1995), pp. 39–47; Stuart, *Stage Blood,* pp. 21–22; and Christopher Croft, "'Kiss Me with Those Red Lips': Gender and Inversion in Bram Stoker's *Dracula,*" *Representations* 8 (Fall 1984): 107–133.

13. Marschner's opera *Hans Heiling* (1833) is an exception. Here a male immortal becomes mortal out of love, but the difference in the plots is that, unlike his female counterparts, as we shall see, Hans feels he has gained nothing from this experience.

14. Hans Christian Andersen, "The Little Mermaid," in *Andersen's Fairy Tales* (London: J. M. Dent, 1958), pp. 21–22.

15. See Mildred Tanner Andrews, "The Water Symbol in German Ro-

manticism Culminating in Fouqué's *Undine*," Ph.D. diss., University of Washington, 1969.

16. See Aubrey S. Garlington, Jr., "Notes on Dramatic Motives in Opera: Hoffman's *Undine*," *Music Review* 32 (1971): 141–144, for a detailed analysis of the musical differences.

17. Albert Lortzing's later (1845) "romantische Zauberoper" *Undine* ends in a somewhat less Christian way, with Undine begging forgiveness for her faithless lover in the underwater palace that had been her home. Again, in this opera mortality is not the issue; love and faithfulness are.

18. See Garlington, "Notes," pp. 142–145; Linda Siegel, "Wagner and the Romanticism of E. T. A. Hoffmann," *Musical Quarterly* 51 (1965): 597–613; R. Murray Schafer, *E. T. A. Hoffmann and Music* (Toronto: University of Toronto Press, 1975), pp. 184–185; Eckhard Roch, "Das Undine-Motiv in Richard Wagners Dramenkonzeption," *Die Musikforschung* 51 (1998): 302–315. Wagner himself talks of the impact of Romantic opera on the work in "A Communication to My Friends" (1851), in *Richard Wagner's Prose Works*, vol. 1, trans. William Ashton Ellis (1892; reprint New York: Broude Bros, 1966), p. 293.

19. See "A Communication," p. 294. See also David Hamilton, "At the Start," *Opera News* 46 (Feb. 27, 1989): 16, on how this prefigures later works like *Tristan und Isolde*.

20. See Jeffrey Peter Bauer, *Women and the Changing Concept of Salvation in the Operas of Richard Wagner* (Salzburg: Verlag Ursula Müller-Speiser, 1994), p. 17: "Ada cannot die, and thus paradoxically cannot enjoy eternal fulfilment" through love.

21. Anne Williams, *Art of Darkness: A Poetics of Gothic* (Chicago: University of Chicago Press, 1995), p. 130.

22. Bram Stoker, *Dracula* (New York: Penguin, 1993), p. 275. Death pervades the novel: Jonathan Harker constantly fears death; Mina (when undead) asks for the Burial of the Dead service to be read to her as she prepares for her death; there are constant references to the angel of death, and cemeteries and coffins abound.

23. Auerbach, *Our Vampires*, p. 6.

24. See Ronald E. McFarland, "The Vampire on Stage: A Study in Adaptations," *Comparative Drama* 21 (1987): 32.

25. See Stuart, *Stage Blood,* pp. 212–217.

26. Lugosi cited in Stuart, *Stage Blood,* p. 238.

27. One example is Claude Lassonde and Claude Gauvreau's *Le vampire et la nymphomane* (composed between 1988 and 1996), in which two immortal creatures renounce their immortality for a triumphant moment of love, even though it means death in suicide.

28. Libretto on a story by Thom Sokoloski by Marily Gronsdal Powell, premiered at the Canadian Opera Company in 1993.

29. Cited in Stuart, *Stage Blood,* p. 225.

30. Lindpaintner's librettist was Cäsar Max Heigel; Marschner's was Wilhelm August Wohlbrück.

31. See David Huckvale, "Wagner and Vampires," *Wagner* 18 (1997): 138.

32. Wagner had conducted *Der Vampyr* in Würzburg and even wrote 142 bars to add to the tenor aria. See too Pamela C. White, "Two Vampirs of 1828," *Opera Quarterly* 5 (1987): 37–41, on the thematic and musical connections between the two works.

33. On the parallels see Robert W. Gutman, *Richard Wagner: The Man, His Mind, and His Music* (1968; reprint, New York: Harcourt Brace Jovanovich, 1990), p. 73; Thomas Grey, "Musical Background and Influences," in Barry Millington, ed., *The Wagner Compendium: A Guide to Wagner's Life and Music* (New York: Schirmer, 1992), p. 75. Grey also links the ballad to Raimbaud's Ballad in Act 1 of Meyerbeer's *Robert le diable* and argues for the influence of French grand opera. However, as Millington suggests in "The Music: *Der fliegende Holländer,*" in his *Wagner Compendium,* p. 278: the "strophic structure of Senta's Ballad sets it firmly in the early 19th-century tradition of interpolated narrative songs." Critics have seen in this vampiric imagery a metaphor of racial otherness and have traced its continuing power into other later operas. See Huckvale, "Wagner and Vampires," p. 127, on *Parsifal* in particular and the vampiric link to blood through Wagner's desire to "maintain the purity of Germanic blood." He also points out that Werner Herzog, in his 1979 remake of the Murnau film, used music from Wagner. Marc Weiner, in *Wagner and the Anti-Semitic Imagination* (Lincoln: University of Nebraska Press, 1995), p. 250, uses the adjective "vampiric" to describe characters like

Mime in the Ring cycle who are associated with Jews and threaten "the life blood of the Volk." But in this early work, it seems to have a less complicated function, although still one connected to issues of race, this time, as we shall see shortly, through the image of another undead creature of legend, the Wandering Jew.

34. For detailed comparisons of Hoffmann and Wagner, see Siegel, "Wagner." See also Hans von Wolzogen's 1906 study *E. T. A. Hoffmann und Richard Wagner: Harmonien und Parallelen,* which L. J. Rather uses to summarize parallels in *Reading Wagner: A Study in the History of Ideas* (Baton Rouge: Louisiana State University Press, 1990), pp. 18–19: "Wagner's own powerful audiovisual imagination was responsible for some near-hallucinatory, Hoffmannesque episodes in his boyhood and youth, and they are described moreover with a truly Hoffmannesque flair in his autobiography."

35. See Siegel, "Wagner," p. 598. In "An Introduction to 'The Flying Dutchman,'" in Richard Wagner, *Der fliegende Holländer / The Flying Dutchman* (London: John Calder, 1982), p. 21, John Deathridge argues that the stage directions for the duet between Erik and Senta suggest that Wagner knew the work of Mesmer and Puységur, two early pioneers in the discovery of the unconscious. Wagner has Senta sink into a "magnetic sleep" and appear to dream the dream Erik is narrating, as if mesmerized by his vision.

36. John Warrack, "Behind 'The Flying Dutchman,'" in Wagner, *Der fliegende Holländer,* p. 8.

37. Richard Wagner, *My Life* (1911; reprint London: Constable, 1994), p. 14. Wagner also linked the appeal of theatre in general to this "childish terror": "the fascinating pleasure of finding myself in an entirely different atmosphere, in a world that was purely fantastic and often gruesomely attractive" was a way to lift him "from the dull reality of daily routine to that delightful region of spirits" (p. 14).

38. Arnold Whittall, "Musical Language," in Millington, ed., *Wagner Compendium,* pp. 253–254. See ibid., pp. 253–255, for a detailed technical description of how Wagner's overture to *Der fliegende Holländer* is related to Weber's Wolf's Glen scene through its use of the diminished seventh.

39. In making himself the center of the narrative, Wagner was rein-

forcing the image of himself as the Romantic genius, moved by inspiration not rules and regulations. Many have commented upon Wagner's creative memory shifts in his many retellings of the story of this sea voyage. See, for example, Barry Millington, "Myths and Legends," in his *Wagner Compendium*, p. 136, and "Richard Wagner," in Stanley Sadie, ed., *The New Grove Dictionary of Opera* (London: Macmillan, 1992), p. 1055; Stewart Spencer, "Sources: Autobiographical Writings," in Millington, ed., *Wagner Compendium*, p. 185.

40. There was a poem by Thomas Moore that alluded to sailors' superstition about a ghost ship called the *Flying Dutchman;* Walter Scott's pirate poem *Rokeby* (1813) mentions a sighting of it near the Cape of Good Hope. Other German manifestations include H. Schmidt's *Der ewige Segler* (1812), Joseph Christian Freiherr von Zedlitz's *Das Geisterschiff,* and tales by Wilhelm Hauff (such as the one of the phantom ship in *Die Karawane,* which bears many similarities to Heine's). Captain Marryatt wrote a novel called *The Phantom Ship,* and Edward Fitzball wrote a "farcical tragedy" (Ernest Newman, *Wagner Nights* [1949; London: Bodley Head, 1988], p. 10). Heine's version can be found in Chapter 7 of *Aus den Memoiren des Herrn von Schabelewopski* in *Heinrich Heine: Werke und Briefe in zehn Bänden,* vol. 4 (Berlin: Aufbau Verlag, 1961), pp. 79–83. Heine himself drew upon a Scottish source, "Vanderdecken's Message Home; or The Tenacity of Natural Affection," in *Blackwood's Magazine* (May 1821): 127–131. In short, this was a well-known legend. See Newman, *Wagner Nights,* pp. 18–19.

41. See, for example, William Vaughan, "Loneliness, Love and Death," in Wagner, *Der fliegende Holländer,* p. 27; Michael Wheeler, *Heaven, Hell and the Victorians* (Cambridge: Cambridge University Press, 1994), p. 28.

42. Ariès, *The Hour,* p. 409.

43. Wheeler, *Heaven,* p. 68, states that the emotions connected to burials and other rituals surrounding death were linked at this time to the fear of in-between states: "These transitional phases were difficult, painful, and in terms of language and symbolism often profoundly ambiguous."

44. Michael Tanner, *Wagner* (London: HarperCollins, 1996), p. 68. The others are Tannhäuser's Rome narration in Act 3, Tristan's account of

his "travels" in the noumenal realm in Act 3; Parsifal's of his in the final act of that opera, and Amfortas's cries of pain in both Acts 1 and 3; and Wotan's narration to Brünnhilde in Act 2 of *Die Walküre.*

45. Tanner, *Wagner,* p. 68.

46. Richard Wagner, *The Flying Dutchman,* trans. Thomas J. Troutbeck and Theo. Baker (n.p.: Shirmer, 1897), p. 247.

47. Ariès, *The Hour,* p. 436.

48. Theodor Adorno, *In Search of Wagner,* trans. Rodney Livingstone (London: Verso, 1981), p. 149.

49. See Heine, *Aus dem Memoiren,* p. 80: "den Ewigem Juden des Ozeans" ("the eternal Jew of the oceans"). Wagner, in his "Autobiographical Sketch" (1843), trans. William Ashton Ellis, in *Richard Wagner's Prose Works,* vol. 1 (1892; reprint New York: Broude Brothers, 1966), p. 16, writes of the Heine story's attraction to him because of the "redemption of this Ahasuerus of the sea." See Newman, *Wagner Nights,* p. 20. Much later, in his last work, *Parsifal,* Wagner would return to this theme in the character of Kundry who lives under the curse of having laughed at Christ. The link to the Wandering Jew is clear in this detail, as it is in her eternal wandering and her desire for the peace of death she cannot achieve: "O eternal sleep, / my only salvation, / how . . . how to win you?" ("O ewiger Schlaf, / einziges Heil, / wie . . . wie dich gewinnen?"). She too lives "between life and death" ("durch Tod und Leben") like the Dutchman, in a state of "yearning for death" ("Todesschmachten").

50. See Paul Lawrence Rose's discussion, in summary, in *Wagner: Race and Revolution* (New Haven: Yale University Press, 1992), pp. 38–50.

51. "A Communication," p. 307.

52. Ibid., pp. 307–308.

53. For a longer study of this opera, see our "'Death, Where Is Thy Sting?' *The Emperor of Atlantis,*" *Opera Quarterly* 16 (2000): 224–239. For information about the lives of the librettist and composer, see H. G. Adler, *Theresienstadt 1941–1945: Das Antlitz einer Zwangsgemeinschaft: Geschichte, Soziologie, Psychologie* (Tübingen: Mohr, 1955); Max Bloch, "Viktor Ullmann: A Brief Biography and Appreciation," *Journal of the Arnold Schoenberg Institute* 3 (October 1979): 150–177; Zdenek Lederer, *Ghetto Theresienstadt* (New York: Howard Fertig, 1983); Ingo Schultz,

"Viktor Ullmann," in *Flensburger Hefte: Anthroposophen in der Zeit des deutschen Faschismus: zur Verschwörungsthese* (Flensburger: Flensburger Hefte Verlag, 1991), pp. 5–26.

We have chosen to use the German word (rather than the Czech, Terezin) for the camp to signal just whose concentration camp this was. For more on Theresienstadt in general and especially cultural life in it, see Adler's *Theresienstadt 1941–1945,* Chapter 19; George E. Berkeley, *Hitler's Gift: The Story of Theresienstadt* (Boston: Branden, 1993); Joza Karas, *Music in Terezin 1941–1945* (New York: Beaufort Books, 1985); Lederer's *Ghetto Theresienstadt;* Schultz's "Viktor Ullmann" and "Viktor Ullmann und seine Musikkritiken: über einen kritischen Begleiter des Theresienstädter Musiklebens," in Ingo Schultz, ed., *Viktor Ullmann: 26 Kritiken über musikalische Veranstaltungen in Theresienstadt* (Hamburg: von Bockel Verlag, 1993), pp. 9–32; the book of collected testimonials called *Terezin* (Prague: Council of Jewish Communities in the Czech Lands, 1965).

54. See, for example, Harold Rosenthal's review of a BBC 2 showing of a filmed production in 1979, in *Opera* 30 (May 1979): 501–502. Vladimir Karbusicky, in "Der Traum von der menschlichen Ohnmacht des Diktators: zum Stoff des 'Kaiser von Atlantis' Viktor Ullmanns," *Musica* 47 (September–October 1993): 272, argues that the opera deserves to be remembered for more than its conditions of composition. For a dissenting view—that the opera would not have survived on musical grounds alone without that context to validate it—see Dana Mack, "Art behind Barbed Wire," *New Criterion* 8 (September 1989): 57.

55. Berman, "Memories," *Terezin,* p. 237. See also Lederer, *Ghetto Theresienstadt,* p. 143, where another inmate's diary is cited as commenting on life in the camp as "Colourful, horrible, full of contradictions. . . . A cabaret on one side and on the other, old people dying . . . a richly coloured mosaic of life and death."

56. Kastenbaum, *Psychology of Death,* pp. 168–171, studied 240 adult responses to the question of how death was personified and noted four types: the macabre, the gentle comforter, the gay deceiver, and the automaton. By the end, Death here, as we shall see, is certainly the "gentle comforter."

57. See Paula Kennedy, "Viktor Ullmann," insert notes for London recording *Der Kaiser von Atlantis,* p. 10.

58. See Kennedy, "Viktor Ullmann," pp. 9–10; Bloch, "Viktor Ullmann," p. 169; Vladimir Karbusicky, "Sen o Lidské Bezmoci Diktátora," *Mudební Věda* 30 (1993): 108; William Lloyd, review of Mecklenburgh Opera's production, *Musical Times* 134 (December 1992): 722.

59. See Gerald J. Gruman, *A History of Ideas about the Prolongation of Life* (Philadelphia: Arno, 1966). The Greek legend of Eos who asked Zeus to give her mortal lover Tithonus eternal life—but forgot to ask for eternal youth—finds its echoes through the years in Oscar Wilde's Dorian Gray and Jonathan Swift's Struldbruggs.

60. J. Vogel, *Leoš Janáček: His Life and Works* (London: Paul Hamlyn, 1962), p. 321.

61. Cited in John Tyrell, *Janáček's Operas: A Documentary Account* (London: Faber and Faber, 1992), p. 304.

62. Vogel, *Leoš Janáček,* p. 322.

63. Cited in Tyrell, *Janáček's Operas,* p. 309.

64. Quoted by Paul Thomason in Paul Thomason and Robert Hilferty, "The Case for—and against—Makropulos," *Opera News,* 62 (11 April 1998): 21.

65. Thomason, in Thomason and Hilferty, "The Case," p. 21.

66. Terry Teachout, "An Affair to Remember," *Opera News* 60 (20 Jan. 1996): 11.

Coda

1. Henry Montagu, *Contemplatio Mortis et Immortalitatis* (1631; New York: Da Capo Press, 1971), p. 98. The setting up of this assertion comes on p. 96.

2. Viktor E. Frankl, *Man's Search for Meaning* (1959; 1962; reprint New York: Washington Square Press, 1984), p. 121.

3. L. R. Churchill and S. W. Churchill, "Storytelling in Medical Arenas: The Art of Self-Determination," *Literature and Medicine* 1 (1982): 73.

4. Frank Kermode, *The Sense of an Ending: Studies in the Theory of Fiction* (New York: Oxford University Press, 1967), p. 17; the following citation is from p. 8.

5. Sherwin B. Nuland, *How We Die: Reflections on Life's Final Chapter* (New York: Knopf, 1994), p. xv.

Acknowledgments

A book this long in the making is indebted to many people. First, we want to thank the various research assistants who worked with us on a series of topics related to this project: as graduate students (all now graduated), Michael Doherty, Sarah Henstra, Russell Kilbourn, Scott Rayter, Helmut Reichenbächer, Erika Reiman, Jill Scott, and as undergraduates, Ellen Park and Colleen Elep. We gratefully acknowledge their inspired suggestions en route, as well as their spirited leg-work. For generously and critically reading the entire manuscript in its final stages, we thank Ann-Barbara Graff, Sarah Henstra, Russell Kilbourn, and especially Scott Rayter and the press's two readers. While any errors or infelicities in this book are ours alone, many people read and commented upon (and therefore helped us improve) individual chapters. Our gratitude, therefore, goes to Mary Hunter, Stephen Burns, David Levin, Kathleen Hansell, Herbert Lindenberger, Caryl Clark, Ross Chambers, the W.I.P.E. group, and any others we may have embarrassingly forgotten. To the late Edward Said goes our gratitude for his support and encouragement. A special thanks is due to the Social Sciences and Humanities Research Council of Canada for funding the research: its commitment to collaborative and interdisciplinary work has been most welcome.

Many of these chapters were first conceived and presented as talks for particular audiences—medical, operatic, or literary. To all those who, on these occasions, responded with critical and constructive comments, our warmest thanks for keeping us thinking and rethinking. A much longer and differently focused version of Chapter 2 appeared as "Death Drive: Eros and Thanatos in Wagner's *Tristan und Isolde*" in *Cambridge Opera Journal* 11 (1999): 267–294. Chapter 3 is a revision of an article that appeared as "'Alles was ist, endet': Living with the Knowledge of Death in Richard Wagner's *Der Ring des Nibelungen*," *University of Toronto Quarterly* 67 (1998): 789–811. A much longer version of the discussion of *Der Kaiser von Atlantis* in Chapter 6 appeared as "'Death, where is thy sting?' *The Emperor of Atlantis*," in *Opera Quarterly* 16 (2000): 224–239.

Index

Other books in the *Convergences* series:

Timothy Brennan, *At Home in the World: Cosmopolitanism Now*

Jean Franco, *The Decline and Fall of the Lettered City: Latin America in the Cold War*

Ranajit Guha, *Dominance without Hegemony: History and Power in Colonial India*

Jeffrey Kallberg, *Chopin at the Boundaries: Sex, History, and Musical Genre*

Amy Kaplan, *The Anarchy of Empire in the Making of U.S. Culture*

Tarif Khalidi, *The Muslim Jesus: Sayings and Stories in Islamic Literature*

Declan Kiberd, *Inventing Ireland*

Jane Miller, *Seductions: Studies in Reading and Culture*

Masao Miyoshi, *Off Center: Power and Culture Relations between Japan and the United States*

Tom Paulin, *Minotaur: Poetry and the Nation State*

Richard Poirier, *Poetry and Pragmatism*

Jacqueline Rose, *The Haunting of Sylvia Plath*

Edward W. Said, *Reflections on Exile and Other Essays*

Tony Tanner, *Venice Desired*

Tzvetan Todorov, *On Human Diversity: Nationalism, Racism, and Exoticism in French Thought*